IDA LUPINO

IDA LUPINO

A Biography

William Donati

 UNIVERSITY PRESS OF KENTUCKY

Editorial and Sales Offices: The University Press of Kentucky
663 South Limestone Street, Lexington, Kentucky 40508-4008
www.kentuckypress.com

All images are credited to the author's collection.

The Library of Congress has cataloged the hardcover edition as follows:
Donati, William
    Ida Lupino : a biography/ William Donati
        p.   cm.
    Includes bibliographical references and index
    ISBN-10: 0-8131-1895-6 (cloth : alk. paper)
    ISBN-10: 0-8131-0982-5 (pbk. : alk. paper)
    I. Lupino, Ida, 1918-1995. 2. Actors—United States—
Biography. 3. Motion picture producers and
directors—United States—Biography. I. Title.
PN2287.L84D66 1995
791.43'082'092-dc20
[B]   95-35549

ISBN 978-0-8131-9648-0 (pbk. : alk. paper)
ISBN 978-0-8131-9686-2 (epub)
ISBN 978-0-8131-9687-9 (pdf)

Member of the Association
of University Presses

TO HARRY
YOU KNEW HER BEST

Contents

Photographs appear after page 160.

PREFACE TO THE NEW EDITION

The twenty-seventh anniversary of the publication of *Ida Lupino: A Biography* calls for a celebration. I worked very hard to document the life of an extraordinary talent, and Ken Cherry, former director of the University Press of Kentucky, guided my book to publication. I am still grateful for Ken's professional expertise in deciding to publish a manuscript that brings the career and life of Ida Lupino to readers. To prepare for this new version with fresh photographs, I listened to Ida's bewitching voice in my taped interviews and was again captivated by her charm. Interviewing Ida was truly a thrilling experience. I never intended to write a biography, but fate intervened.

The week after I met Ida, she asked me to write a book with her. *Ida Lupino: Her Films and Memoirs* would be the title, and it would be filled with photographs and her comments about her distinguished career. I had already been working on the project for three months when we signed a contract in January 1984. I was surprised that Ida had very little memorabilia and only thirty photographs. I conducted research and bought dozens of photographs that I brought to her home to help stir memories of her famous films. In one interview, she made an interesting revelation about actors.

I asked if anyone could become an actor. Ida replied, "When it comes to teaching somebody to act, no, definitely not; if it is within them, certainly they can be helped a great deal by method or by not overplaying. I think it is a born talent within people and can only be polished and made better. I went to the Royal Academy of Dramatic Arts in England, as Vivien Leigh did, a beautiful performer, but I think it is within one, and the strange thing is to be real, to be that person. I can only say I left it up to the audiences as to whether I reached them as that person I was playing."

Ida praised those who were masters of screen magic. "There are so many perfectly brilliant performers that never come across as actors acting. A man like Spencer Tracy, he was always a real person, and Katharine Hepburn, nobody could copy her. She was original–completely wonderful!"

Sadly, our book project was not to be. Though sharp during my interviews, Ida showed signs of mental confusion that alarmed those trying to assist her, and a conservatorship was thereby established. I had met Ida in her senior years, but what was the younger Ida like? I was curious. Well, read on to meet an extraordinary talent and a complex woman. And yes, Ida, just like Spence and Kate, you were always a real person and magnificently captivating on-screen.

William Donati

CREDITS

I am indebted to the following for their assistance in making this book possible: the British Film Institute; the Library of the Academy of Motion Picture Arts and Sciences; the UCLA Film Archives; the Warner Archives at the University of Southern California; the Warner Bros. Legal Department for permission to quote material in the Warner Archives.

Special thanks to Lupino's great friend, the late Harry Mines, a veritable anthology of Hollywood history. Mines, with his phenomenal memory, recalled with amazing clarity myriad events and contemporaries. The late John Franco was of immense assistance. Diane Meredith Volz, professor of journalism, took precious time from her busy schedule for interviews. Rena Lundigan and Paula Stone were also most helpful.

Special thanks also to Malvin Wald for allowing me to examine his voluminous Filmakers file. Wald took time from his teaching and writing to provide extensive information. Sol Saks was invaluable for his advice and interviews. Liz Heasman did a wonderful job of gathering research in England. Most of all I am especially grateful to Ida Lupino. By the end of my research, I was truly convinced she was one of the most accomplished individuals ever to act and direct in films and television.

Many assisted the writing of this book, but I am especially indebted to the following, many of whom have passed away: Lew Ayres, William Bakewell, Jim Barnett, Lawrence Dobkin, Robert Douglas, Robert Eggenweiler, Geraldine Fitzgerald, Sally Forrest, Nadia Gardiner, John Gassman, Michael Gordon, Jerry Hausner, Peter Lind Hayes, Joy Hodges, Joe Hoenig, Nat Holt, Harry Horner, Paul Jarrico, Michael Karg, Andrea King, Richard Kinon, Harry Stanley Lupino, Connie Miles, Hugh O'Brian, Lionel Newman, James Nicholson, David Niven, Jr., Marvin Paige, Diane Paul, Ted Post, John Qualen, Irving Rapper, Ronnie Rondell, Hayden Rorke, Barbara Scharres, Vincent Sherman, Howard Shoup, George Shrader, Stanford Tischler, Audrey Totter, Catherine Turney, Maurice Vaccarino, Richard Wheeler, Cornel Wilde, Buster Wiles, and Toby Wing.

PROLOGUE

One evening in April my telephone rang. "Mr. Donati, I received your letter."

I recognized the vibrant, low voice with the exquisite enunciation even before she said, "This is Ida Lupino." She apologized for disturbing me at dinner, then launched into an attack on a controversial book about Errol Flynn. At the outset, her tone was soft and poised, but as she continued speaking, sparks ignited.

"I can assure you," she said, "that he was never a Nazi. We both hated Nazis! As for Errol being a homosexual—well, I have nothing against those gentlemen, but nothing is farther from the truth."

Eventually the anger subsided and before long Lupino was discussing politics. She expressed displeasure with the Republican administration led by her former Warner Bros. colleague. Though she acknowledged President Reagan's personal qualities, she made it clear she was a Democrat. She spoke of her film career, proclaiming proudly that she usually played dirty rats, hookers or killers. And loved playing those roles, she laughed. She soon had me laughing along with her.

In my first conversation with this remarkable woman, prominent aspects of her personality became clear. The impassioned comments made it apparent that Lupino was a tiger. Yet, as the steam dissipated, a delightful charmer emerged. The enchanting yet ominous voice, which had entranced audiences for decades, cast its spell on me. This was the first of many lively telephone conversations.

When I later came face to face with Lupino, she was in high spirits. She sat regally in her den, lounging on a blue sofa, surrounded by pink pillows. The expressive blue eyes sparkled. Her bright red lips puffed at a Carlton, as she readily discussed her life and career.

"Oh, I'm having a wonderful time," she exclaimed. When I asked her what it was like having her life scrutinized for over fifty years by a curious press and public, she grew serious. "It is fascinating to me that a person's real private life, they never really know about it," she said. "What they don't know, they make up. But what can they say about me when I have gone? They won't have anything left. They've made up so many lies about me when I'm alive."

She recounted a tabloid story that had erroneously given her age as eighty-seven and had claimed that she had climbed a roof and fired off a gun. "I hope I live to be eighty-seven," she laughed, "and can climb a roof, but if they live nearby I'm going to fire, not in the air, but right at them!"

Lupino has an expression for enemies. Smilers with knives. "That's what I call people who smile and are really knifing another badly. I think I'll throw all the smilers with knives into my empty pool and cement it over!"

Capturing the essence of Ida Lupino is a formidable task. Her screen image is that of a magnificent actress who portrayed mad and bad dames; she is known as an accomplished director and is also widely admired for her courage in daring to stand behind the camera and take charge.

The private Lupino is somewhat harder to bring into focus. Her lively personality resembles a pendulum, constantly swinging in an arc between points of wild hilarity and high fury. Between these two extremes lies a brooding intensity and a magical charm. At times she seems to be two distinct women: Lupi, the eccentric, and Ida, the brilliant charmer. When the two halves blend, a unique woman emerges. This is Ida Lupino.

By the time I spoke with Lupino in 1981 she was retired. Ida enjoyed discussing the past, and I eagerly listened to her stories. She was a hypnotic speaker. I soon grasped an essential fact: Lupino took great pleasure in being singled out as different. I found her to be one of the most intriguing women I have ever met.

What lay behind the penetrating blue eyes? I was curious. She craved solitude and attention simultaneously, just as her entrancing eyes harbored both fire and ice, love and hate, brilliance and wildness. The rays of emotion she emitted were intense, like those of a revolving prism, unique and exceedingly bright. I wanted to learn more. This is her story.

1

Drama in Her Veins

You are truly the Royal Family of Greasepaint.
> —KING EDWARD VII

In the last days of January 1918, German aircraft swooped across the Kent and Essex coasts. Their target was the heart of the British Empire. The formidable zeppelins that had once terrorized England had been replaced by Gothas, large three seater biplanes that swept over London dropping deadly explosives with devastating fury. For two consecutive nights, the Gothas penetrated the city's defenses, and death and destruction rained down on the British Lion. The attacks left 68 Londoners dead and 183 injured. The official coroner's report rendered a verdict of "death by misadventure due to the dropping of bombs."

After the nerve-shattering aerial terror, the city was enshrouded by dense fog. London vanished in an eerie, thick grayness. From Charing Cross, the official center of the metropolis, for miles in every direction, the city came to an alarming standstill as buses, trams and trains ceased to run. Anxious pedestrians groped their way through the heavy fog, barely able to see the pavement beneath their feet.

In the midst of the tension gripping war-torn Londoners, another drama was unfolding at 33 Ardbeg Road. On the evening of February 3, Stanley Lupino nervously paced the floor of his home and anxiously awaited the birth of his first child. His wife, Connie, was in labor, but there were unexpected complications. Nurses quietly entered and exited the bedroom where she lay. A thunderstorm raged as the forlorn husband waited helplessly. He had started the evening with high hopes of imminent fatherhood; now he expected the worst.

At age twenty-four, Stanley Lupino was a top name in the realm of musical comedy. For months he had been making audiences laugh in the operetta *Arlette*. On this rainy night, Stanley had called for his understudy to take his place after the third act. He took a taxi home, where he was met by a solemn nurse who informed him that "they didn't expect to save either."

Stanley cherished life and laughter, and the news was bitter. He badly wanted an heir. As a member of the centuries-old Lupino theatrical dynasty, he knew that his mission in life was to entertain. He had suffered poverty and hardship in his youth but had carved his place on the stage as a successful comedian, singer and dancer. Laughter was the essence of his life. His wife was also from a theatrical family, though nothing to match the renowned Lupinos.

Stanley wanted a son. On this dreary night, everything he had hoped for seemed to be slipping away. He wandered aimlessly through the house. He stepped into the downpour and stood in his garden in a state of bewilderment as the mist swirled around him. Through the rest of the terrible night, he sat huddled over a brazier filled with glowing coals, a night-watchman his companion.

When the morning of February 4 arrived, a beaming nurse brought word that both mother and *daughter* were fine. So, on the 185th day of the Great War, Ida Lupino made a dramatic entrance onto the stage of life. When Stanley cuddled his tiny daughter, he had a feeling that she would be the most famous Lupino of them all.

Ida's parents would always be the most important people in her life. Stanley's and Connie's dazzling images inspired her to entertain. Though small in height, only five feet, six inches tall, Stanley radiated immense charm with his warm smile and witty personality. He was a handsome man with a kind face, huge eyes, half-moon eyebrows, high forehead and jet-black hair. Actress Elsie Janis found him to be a comic genius whose luminous eyes "could make you cry right in the middle of a comedy scene if they chose to."

By age twenty-one, Stanley was a headliner in musicals; at thirty-six he was England's best known comedian; at forty he published his memoirs *From the Stocks to the Stars*. Connie knew her husband's true love: "He never stopped thinking day and night, night and day, about the theater. It was in his blood, and it was his whole life."

Nobody could touch Ida's heart like her father. Stanley's wild humor brought smiles and laughter to his daughter. His comedy dancing was a sight she always treasured. They shared a special bond. Stanley made a prediction she never forgot: "My father once said to me, 'Ida, you're a strange, interesting girl. Your mother and I, to be honest with you, prayed when she was pregnant we would have a son. I think you're going to end up doing what my son would have done. You will write, direct and produce.'" Years of constant work enabled the Lupinos to acquire a mansion at 152 Leigham Court Road in Streatham. The ancient, red-brick Tudor dwelling was situated on a vast estate with colorful gardens and rolling lawns. The center of family life was the home's enormous living room, which was as spacious as a hotel lobby. In the evening, the family would gather around the piano for singing. Connie, once billed as "the fastest tap dancer alive," would perform a routine, or Stanley would rehearse his jokes. Each night, Ida was tucked in bed by Gertie, her nanny, and she would always plead for one more story.

As a child, Ida would explore her father's study with curiosity. The private sanctum held cherished treasures, each relic associated with the theater. On display were the last cigar given to Stanley by his great friend Arthur Collins, manager of the Drury Lane Theatre, and an antique bust of Shakespeare. Tucked away in a box was the half crown another of Stanley's idols, comedian Dan Leno, had tossed to a shivering Stanley outside a theater on a cold winter night.

Amid the ancient playbills, paintings and photographs, Ida listened attentively as her father conjured up an unbroken line of troupers. The pride in his voice made it clear that to be a Lupino meant to pursue a career as an entertainer. Ida learned that the hot blood that flowed through her veins was of Italian origin and could be traced to Giorgio Luppino, a nobleman born in Bologna in 1612. Giorgio had fled Italy as a political outcast and made a living as a puppeteer. Altering his name to Georgius, he roamed England as a strolling player, a precarious position since actors were often viewed as rogues and vagabonds. The family never forgot that his son, Charles, had been arrested for reciting in public without a license and had been forced to stand in the stocks as punishment. Stanley's wondrous storytelling ability brought a long line of dancers, comedians, actors, designers and even tightrope walkers. The Lupinos considered themselves the Masters of Comedy; their hereditary symbol was a red-hot poker, indicating their skill at firing up an audience.

Ida's great-grandfather was George Hook Lupino, an actor who had achieved prominence in the Victorian era. His conversations with Charles Dickens formed the portrait of the theatrical family in *Nicholas Nickleby*. He was the father of sixteen children, among them, George Junior, Ida's grandfather, who had been born in a theater. By the time she knew him, though a semi-invalid, her grandfather was still revered in the clan, and he became a major influence in Ida's life. Confined to a wheelchair after a stroke, "Old George" was a handsome man with snow-white hair and an unlined face. As young men, George and his brothers, Arthur and Harry, had formed a triumvirate of talent. George had led his own troupe, traveling constantly in England and Europe.

At sixteen he had been a ballet master, and his expertise had helped him win red-haired Florence Ann Webster, a famous ballerina at Drury Lane. George had been a renowned dancer and had established a world record by turning 210 pirouettes on a pocket handkerchief.

Arthur and Harry were famous for their act, "The Fiddler and His Dog." Arthur played the cello while Harry, costumed as a French poodle, howled each time a sour note was struck. Playwright J.M. Barrie insisted that Arthur be the dog Nana in the first production of *Peter Pan*. His performance was a sensation and provided a model for future performers. The famous "animal impersonator" was in a play, barking onstage, when a blood vessel burst in his head leading to his early death at the age of forty-three. George later became famous for his exciting acting, heightened by the use of traps, a visual thrill for Victorian audiences. From graves, castles and other scenery, actors were sprung through trapdoors and ten to fifteen feet in the air; these were dangerous stunts since the mechanism could misfire and smash the unfortunate into the stage floor or scenery. King Edward VII, an admirer, once accompanied George beneath the stage to observe the sliding doors, springs, ropes and weights. Using a parody of Shakespeare's "Uneasy lies the head that wears a crown," the king quipped: "Uneasy lies the man who plays the clown." After a stirring performance at Drury Lane, George received a compliment he valued more than gold. Said Edward VII: "You are truly the Royal Family of Greasepaint."

The eleventh generation remained true to tradition and became entertainers. George's sons, Barry, Mark and Stanley, and Harry's sons, Wallace and Lupino Lane, were top-billed, but it was Stanley Lupino who towered above them all. He had been brought up in poverty during the family's cycle of failure, which made his later triumph especially sweet. His mother, Florence, had been shopping in Petticoat Lane when her son was born in a hansom cab. She survived only five years longer, and died at the age of thirty-nine, the same day the family home in Kennington Road, a working-class district, was repossessed. Young Stanley joined his father's troupe. At age six he made his debut as a monkey in *King Klondyke.*

For the next twelve years, his life was sheer struggle; he had no formal education nor a permanent home. Often, work and food were scarce. Hired for the tour of *Go to Jericho,* he brooded in a dirty rehearsal hall. Though only twenty years old, he had been cast as an older character. Before long he was in a quarrel with his leading lady, a petite, blue-eyed girl who burst into tears at his rudeness. Stanley shouted that he was quitting the show, then stormed out. When he and the actress later found themselves in the same restaurant for afternoon tea, he apologized for the argument, explaining his professional predicament, and his personal one. His life was no more than a trunk of clothes in a cheap room he shared with a black cat. Connie O'Shea understood his unhappiness. She poured out her own troubles, telling him that she was momentarily the only support of her large thespian family. If Stanley quit the show, the tour would collapse. Since childhood she had performed as one of the Sisters Emerald. Raised in Liverpool, she had already traveled the world and was acclaimed for her dancing. As they exchanged stories of their sad adventures, a bond of sympathy formed between the unhappy couple. Before midnight, they were engaged. The evening of their marriage, a stage manager stopped Connie from

6

joining her new husband backstage. Heated words led to a fight, and Stanley was barred from the theater for several months. The Lupinos could be as ferocious as their surname indicates; derived from the Latin *lupus*, in Italian it means "little wolf."

After their marriage, Stanley and Connie's luck improved. Stanley was soon hailed as one of London's finest comedians. At Christmas he starred in pantomimes, lavish children's musicals filled with singing and dancing. Fifteen-year-old Connie Miles, a dancer, was in awe of his talent. "He was the big star of *Puss in Boots*, rather young, too. He absolutely gave himself to whatever he was doing and, being a Lupino, he could do anything. I asked for his autograph as he came tearing off the stage."

During the war, Stanley was rejected for service because of knee injuries he had suffered in stage falls. Eventually he was forced to wear a leg brace, but after an operation by a prominent surgeon, Sir Alfred Fripp, he was able to dance again.

For Stanley and Connie, the brightest moment of the war years was the birth of their daughter. They had almost named her Aida, after the princess of the Verdi opera, an appropriate suggestion of theatrical royalty. Ida's sister, Rita, was born in 1921. Both children soon learned that emotions were for display; laugh, cry, speak boldly and beautifully. Emotional restraint was not for the Lupinos.

Though jovial and pleasant, Stanley could be a grim taskmaster in his professional life. Once, when Connie was late for a rehearsal, the director was furious. "I should have a little slave to help me with all the work at home," she pleaded. But her husband still berated her before the entire company for her tardiness. "You're a Lupino," had been his withering reply.

Ida never had a normal childhood because of her parents' touring and late hours. She was often cared for by Old George and Granny O'Shea. Her grandmother devised a way to keep the child

7

occupied. A mirror was draped with plush red curtains on the sides and top. Arrayed in her mother's costumes, greasepaint and tap shoes, Ida would gaze at her reflection for hours. Her parents would come home to find their daughter asleep on the floor as she had fallen, out of sheer exhaustion from the weight of her mother's dresses.

She delighted in accompanying her parents to rehearsals. Life was reduced to *scenes*, and the thin line separating fantasy from reality often vanished.

Grandfather George spent many hours with Ida. He taught her how to sing, to compose music and to draw. He had a gruff personality and still wielded the scepter as family patriarch, proudly boasting that no wife, son or daughter had ever deserted the family profession. Ida liked her grandfather's strange canvases of flowing trees, green women and odd-shaped horses. He gave her instructions in oil painting and, as she later recalled, "If he didn't like the way I was doing it, he'd reach over with his cane and smack me." Though he was somewhat irascible because of ill health, Ida revered her grandfather as did all the Lupinos.

George Lupino's last performance had been at his birthplace, the Theatre Royal in Birmingham. He had appeared as a comedian in a harlequinade with his eldest son, Barry. Stanley watched from the audience as George took his final bow, holding aloft the family symbol, the red-hot poker, once used to procure laughs; yet, at that moment it represented the passing of a scepter to a new generation. With tears in his eyes, he handed the poker to Barry; unexpectedly, he faltered in the hushed theater. A policeman helped him from the stage and he collapsed, the victim of a stroke.

George Lupino was a sad figure, confined to a wheelchair, paintbrush in hand. One of his best-known paintings was a scene of a dressing room. A naked light bulb illuminated a dingy dressing table with harsh shadows and stark realism . . . a small mirror, a sink, a shirt collar, powder puffs and tubes of makeup. The painting was entitled "Our Home."

Even at an early age, Ida had a compulsion to dramatize. By seven she had developed "an awful phobia." She ripped up the oldest clothes she could find and, wearing the tatters, went from house to house begging, pitifully crying that she had been "starved and beaten at home." She later admitted: "I believed my own lies completely, so that others believed me." Ida was developing a pattern that would become more pronounced in later years. For her, life had to be filled with drama. If she failed to capture attention, then she was no better than the spectators, ordinary and boring. Stanley and Connie indulged her whims, and Ida became daring, throwing herself into everything she did with intensity. From her father she inherited the art of making a good story better. Ida learned to spin yarns that left listeners wide-eyed, such as her tale of an encounter with "the little people." In a forest, she and Stanley had met a gnome who was working with a tiny hammer. The dwarfish creature was angry at the intrusion, but the gnome, like everyone else, yielded to Stanley's charm. At the end of her tale, with a mischievous glint in her eye, she would present a small gold anvil that the gnome had given to Stanley.

The enormous Lupino residence with its high ceilings, stained-glass windows and dark crannies fired Ida's inventive mind. The Lupinos believed the home was haunted. Spiritualism was widely practiced within the Lupino clan. Stanley claimed he had seen the ghost of Dan Leno in a dressing room at Drury Lane. One night as he was applying makeup, he glimpsed another face in the mirror. "It was looking at me with a smile. There was a line across the forehead where a wig had been removed. There was no mistaking that face."

Ida's imagination was powerfully reinforced by talk of spirit visitations. She came to understand that those who tapped into this mysterious plane held sway over those who did not. Ida reveled in the magic of Napoleon's hand. Stanley was taken with the life of the Little Corporal and he kept a cast of the emperor's hand on a pillow in the den. Stanley felt he could communicate with the spirit of the long-dead Bonaparte by touching the cast. Ida conducted her own intrigues with the strange object. In the darkness of night, she would awaken Rita. "I saw her," Ida would whisper.

She would rouse her sister from bed in search of the ghost of an old woman who haunted the house. In the den, Ida would take Napoleon's hand, and the girls would stalk the corridors. Ida would force her sister ahead, frightening her with the warning: "If the old lady touches the hand, it's going to reach out and grab you!"

Flashing her wide, crystal-blue eyes and puckish smile, Ida was a charmer. Conscious of her ability to command, she led her cousins in daring games. Tonie and Barry Junior were forced to play pirates. Ida insisted on realism. While "walking the plank," Tonie fell and broke her arm. Ida dragged her inside a clump of bushes and unsuccessfully tried to straighten the dangling limb. In Stanley's absence, Uncle Barry often had the task of disciplining his niece. Ida was spanked for dyeing her hair blonde and for refusing to wear long dresses. Secretly, Uncle Barry admired her plucky personality, which made her the center of attention.

Ida also directed the Lupino cousins in amateur movies. On one occasion, the script called for her to pry open the window of a neighbor's house. "Suddenly, there in the back of me was a cop!" She coolly explained to the policeman that she was trying to rob the house. Her cockiness was soon deflated as he escorted her to the police station, despite her protests that "we are just making movies!" At the precinct house, Stanley came to her rescue. They learned that the home had been robbed three weeks earlier.

Other creative efforts can be traced to a year when Ida was on her own. In March 1925, Stanley opened in *Better Days* at the

Hippodrome. He made famous the song "Could Lloyd George Do It?" But his voice soon gave out. A throat specialist recommended a long rest, a sea cruise, but such a vacation was unthinkable to Stanley. He always combined business with pleasure. Stanley sent a telegram to the famous Shubert Brothers, and he and Connie were hired for the Broadway operetta *Naughty Riquette.* Stanley Lupino's inability to enjoy a brief rest was symptomatic of a childhood scarred by poverty. He could never forget the many times he had gone hungry; any slight setback to his career kindled bitter memories, and he would sadly moan, "We're going to the poorhouse." Ida never forgot that frightening utterance.

On a warm August morning, the Lupinos motored to West Brighton. They turned onto Norman Road and pulled to a stop in front of Clarence House, an elite boarding school for girls. The curriculum prepared pupils for careers in music and elocution. Eight-year-old Ida and her little sister stood before the school that would become their home. "But you will come back, promise!" Ida pleaded, not wishing to be left behind. Stanley Lupino was aware of the love and protection he seemed to be denying his children. But family tradition came first. The Lupinos had a mission to entertain. As the car drove off, Connie sobbed. They would be gone for two years.

A steady stream of correspondence kept the girls informed about their parents' adventure in the States. Passing through customs, Stanley was nearly arrested for entering Prohibition America with a half-empty bottle of scotch. At the Cosmopolitan Theater, Lee Shubert stared at the small entertainer as if he "were a piece of cheese." Discovering that his name wasn't even on the marquee, Stanley fumed and vowed to show the yanks what he could do. He sang his hit "Could Lloyd George Do It?" with three encores but his hot Lupino blood boiled and, just to make certain that the management got the point, he took his time returning to the stage for bows.

The following day the *New York Times* verified his success: "Mr. Lupino keeps his pantomime brisk and rich . . . fleeing the pugnacious pugilist, Lupino runs against a door jam, and in pantomime indicates that he has knocked out his teeth . . . the audience is truly convulsed." After the successful premiere, Lee Shubert featured Stanley as "the famous London comic." The Lupinos taught their children that show business was a struggle to stay on top, never give in without a fight.

After success on Broadway Stanley and Connie returned home, pleasantly surprised to discover Ida's blossoming talent. She had written a play, *Mademoiselle,* for her school and starred in the lead role of the French maid. Her fierce desire to create and to excel would last for over half a century.

On their next trip to Broadway, in 1927, Stanley and Connie witnessed an astounding invention in their first talkie, *The Jazz Singer* starring Al Jolson. Though Stanley's realm had been the theater, Wallace Lupino and his brother Lupino Lane were familiar faces in silent movies. Nell O'Shea, Connie's sister, was a pioneer film artist and had established her own studio in Brighton, where she produced, wrote and performed in her own comedies. Ida recognized her aunt's achievement. Stanley excitedly agreed to give the new sensation a try in *Bill's Night Out,* an early sound picture, but his eagerness soon faded. He missed improvisation and spontaneity; he was frustrated by the technical side as the huge and heavy microphone, which Stanley called "a devilish contraption," unexpectedly dropped into scenes, often knocking an actor unconscious. He easily grasped the key to film work: don't act; be natural and sincere. This valuable lesson he would teach his daughter.

Despite their success on Broadway, Stanley and Connie decided to return to England, for their children were growing up.

Though only ten, Ida displayed sophistication far beyond her years. She very much wanted to join the family profession.

Ida arranged a welcome home party and invited the Lupinos and the O'Sheas. After dinner, Ida stood before the gathering and announced: "And now, ladies and gentlemen, we will be proud to entertain you." Ida began directing, placing the guests in rows. Then she and her cousins gave a show. It was her own skit, *Savoy Faire*, that electrified the spectators. The clever scene revolved around characters entering the Savoy after opening night at the theater. The leading lady made a flamboyant entrance, rushing about "my dearing" everyone. Ida played a first-nighter who belittles the players, unaware that her companion is the star's husband. Next came "the has-been," who sits alone and unnoticed, remembered only by the oldest waiter, who listens impatiently as she recalls her past triumphs, finally asking for a handkerchief to dab her tears.

Stanley was stunned by his daughter's innate skill. Genuinely touched by his welcome home present, he asked his daughters what they would like for Christmas. The girls told him that they wanted a theater, similar to a doll's house. Ida said it wouldn't be a plaything but a stage, on which to learn how to face an audience. Stanley built the Tom Thumb Theatre, which could seat fifty. In a blaze of creativity, Stanley wrote a revue for the youngsters. He kept adding material until there were thirty-two scenes and ten musical numbers. The entire Lupino clan pitched in. Stanley was the theater manager. He even prepared contracts for his players to sign. He rehearsed his "Little Company" of youngsters, who ranged in age from five to thirteen. Thirty-six guests were invited, but by opening night there were more than eighty spectators in addition to reporters, photographers and curious theatrical agents. Among the prominent were actress Tallulah Bankhead, author Sidney Howard, Grandfather George, distinguished critics, wealthy physicians and aristocratic friends.

After the audience sang "God Save The King," the lights dimmed. The haunting theme from Leoncavallo's *Pagliacci* filled the theater, then a single spotlight lit the stage. Ida should have been there, but the stage was empty. Stanley bolted off in search of his daughter.

Ida had become so frightened that, when she heard her entrance cue, she hid. Stanley routed her from her hiding place. "No more scathing denunciation has ever been given a murderer," she later revealed. She would never forget his voice, sharp and disbelieving: "Ida, if you ever let your fellow actors down, dry up in a scene or fail to be a good trouper, deliberately or otherwise, I shall disown you." Her stage fright vanished. She stepped into the bright circle of light as a hush swept through the restless crowd. Ida appeared as a clown with a painted face and colored nose. She wore ruffles around her neck and a skullcap with flowing plumes of feathers. her costume was adorned with rectangular black and white squares, reminiscent of harlequin. She recited the history of toy stages, then spoke of her father's wonderful theater, "the dream of all actors' children come true." From her first to her last appearance, Ida captivated the audience.

The three-hour program was filled with song, dance, comedy and dramatic scenes. Cousin Laurie Lane impressed everyone with his depiction of a Roman soldier in battle, defending the gate with his last breath. Barry performed a comic sketch. Rita's scene depicted a little girl who mistakes a burglar for Santa Claus. But Ida stole the show with a scene from *Romeo and Juliet*.

At intermission, the awed spectators congregated at a portable bar and exchanged words of praise. Rather than children, they had seen true thespians guided by Stanley's excellent direction. When the bell sounded, all rushed back to their seats for an equally impressive second half. For the finale, the entire cast, dressed in baggy white clown outfits, did an acrobatic dance called "Sleepy Land." Thundering ovations acknowledged the revue's astounding achievement.

Thereafter, the theater was used to teach Ida and Rita the actor's craft. For the next three years, Ida was coached by her father. He carefully eliminated any type of training that produced childish overacting. Ida was handed mature roles, such as the courtesan in Alexandre Dumas's *Camille*. Mornings were occupied with music lessons; afternoons were for Shakespeare; evenings brought rehearsals.

By age twelve, Ida could transform herself into many characters. She watched people and understood the complex situations of life. She also learned of death. From his emaciated figure and chronic hoarseness, she was aware of her uncle Mark's ill health. He had once been the funniest of the Lupino brothers. His rapier wit had endeared him to all. When a producer told Mark that he couldn't sleep nights, he had replied: "Try counting Lupinos."

But wartime service in the trenches of France had taken its toll on Mark. Gas had blistered his lungs, and his health had deteriorated. Stanley generously provided financial support for his brother. On Mark's last Christmas, he arrived at Leigham Court Road pale and weak. As the gramophone played "I Can't Give You Anything But Love, Baby," Mark Lupino could only clutch his wife's hand and weep.

The Lupinos always remembered the night in Manchester when Stanley strutted onstage singing his popular novelty song "I Lift Up My Finger and Say Tweet! Tweet!" while the packed house roared with laughter. In his pocket was his brother's obituary. As always, Stanley behaved as a member of the Royal Family of Greasepaint and made sure the show went on. He later fulfilled Mark's last wish and had him buried next to their idol, the great clown Dan Leno. Before the ceremony, Stanley had a plaster cast made of his brother's hand, which he planned to use to contact Mark's spirit.

Two years later, the curtain came down for George Lupino. His death at the age of seventy-two was another family tragedy. But true to Lupino tradition, Ida would carry on the family name and make it more famous than ever before.

2

LIKE A LITTLE QUEEN

*Her self-confidence is utterly sumptuous. . . . She left me
a little breathless, this deliciously arrogant child.*

—REPORTER ALMA WHITAKER

At a party celebrating her thirteenth birthday, Ida appeared dressed
in her mother's clothes and high heels. Rather tall for her age, Ida
added sophistication by wearing her hair up; she made a spectacular entrance, and the guests were pleasantly surprised, especially
Lupino Lane. He was directing Stanley in the zany *Love Race*, and he
enthusiastically insisted that Ida appear onscreen.

"Nipper" Lane had been the first family member to achieve
international screen stardom. In 1915, as a child, he was featured
in a series of one-reel comedies produced by Billy Merson and
Company. His great aunt, actress and theater impresario Sara Lane,
agreed to leave the boy everything if he would change his name to
Lane. As an adult, he had a successful run with the Ziegfeld Follies
as a top comedian and later settled with his family at 1812 North
Wilton in Los Angeles. He was joined by his brother Wallace, and
the two appeared in dozens of American films. In *Only Me* in 1929
he played twenty-seven parts, an intricate task that amazed audiences
the world over. Director Ernst Lubitsch hired him as an assistant

and became his mentor. A promising career as a director was likely until the stock market crash and the subsequent Depression ended his high hopes for a career as a director, and Lupino Lane returned to England.

Emboldened by such strong support, Ida pleaded with her father to allow her to go before the camera. But her parents hesitated. She was still young, and they wanted her to receive an education. Ida was determined. She wanted to be an extra in Stanley's picture just to study her father at work.

Her self-confidence had flourished in response to her parents' warm encouragement. Despite her youth, Ida's persistence won out. Not only did Ida make her debut, but she brought along Chuggles, the family sheepdog.

A turning point in her life had been reached. Her screen debut was only a brief moment in a crowd scene, but the effect on her was profound. Charged with excitement and determination, she told her father she was finished with school. Stanley urged her to return to her classes but eventually relented. He knew his daughter could be stubborn, so he made an offer: if she could find work, she could act; if not, she must return to school.

Ida accepted the challenge with aplomb and refused to trade on the family name. Instead, she adopted a pseudonym, Ida Ray, obtained an agent and immediately landed a part. A German director who had seen her on the set of *Love Race* hired the girl with luminous blue eyes and milk-white skin. Ironically, she was dropped from her only scene for fear her attractiveness would overshadow the lead actress. After this happened several times, Ida became known as "the girl who was too good-looking."

Ida was unfazed by her bad luck; she knew she could act. Her cousin Barry Junior learned how convincing an actress she could be. One evening they adventurously tried to enter a shady dance hall but were stopped for being underage. Ida rushed home and donned her mother's clothes and makeup. She was such a convincing older woman that they were admitted.

Ida had another idea to further her career. She decided to attend the Royal Academy of Dramatic Arts. Stanley knew it was her destiny to be an actress, and he gave his approval, though he must have smiled inwardly at the thought of his daughter, or any Lupino for that matter, attending an acting school. In January 1932, Ida officially enrolled in the Royal Academy.

The school emphasized stage deportment and acting technique, accentuating roles from classical plays. To give her a taste of the actor's life, Stanley found Ida a cheap flat over a butcher shop; it was a small room with a tiny fire grate, a bed with mildewed legs and a lumpy mattress. She took her new life seriously, often remaining awake throughout the night to memorize scripts. By March, she had been cast as Agathe in *Les Folies Amoureuses* by Regnard. The play was directed by Alice Gachet, the school's most famous instructor, who liked to coach her pupils in productions from French classical drama. Among her more celebrated students were Charles Laughton and Vivien Leigh. The student plays provided an opportunity for promising thespians to be seen by producers, directors and casting agents. Ida played a variety of roles: a maid in *The Man with a Load of Mischief*, Popilius Lena in *Julius Caesar*, a servant in *The Last of Mrs. Cheney*, Jeanne in *L'Heure du Berger*.

Teachers were impressed by Ida's skills and eagerly passed along words of praise to industry professionals. Often she accompanied Stanley to Elstree Studio, where for hours she studied her father's smooth expertise before the camera. Just be natural, he would advise.

Student life was crowded with activity and admirers flocked around. Before long, Ida had her first boyfriend, a fellow student named Johnny, who nicknamed her "Loops." They spent their free hours together chatting before the fire in Ida's room. Soon their

passion flamed, and they spoke of marrying once they had both succeeded.

At the close of Ida's second term, the Royal Academy announced plans to stage *Heartbreak House* by George Bernard Shaw.
None other than the great man himself would cast the lead roles.
Shaw, then seventy-five years old, was regarded as the greatest living
playwright of the English language and was also a noted critic, wit,
socialist and staunch vegetarian. Shaw was something of an eccentric and prided himself on being such. When an admirer sent him
a dollar for his autograph, he responded: "Dear Mr. Haines, My
autograph is not for sale, but as I should be imprisoned if I sent
your dollar back you must be content with this picture of me.
G. Bernard Shaw."

On a warm afternoon aspiring actresses lined up to meet
the formidable author. Ida fidgeted in a sweltering room with
other hopefuls. The minutes passed with agonizing slowness. She
searched her purse and found a handkerchief to wipe her moist
brow. Finally, she was the only actress left in the room. She dug
through her bag for her comb and ran it through her hair; she took
a deep breath, then opened the door behind which the world's most
famous playwright waited. Shaw looked the nervous girl up and
down without uttering a word. He eyed the information card he
held before him.

The heat and excitement had wilted Ida, and she felt her
reading was poor. Her spirits sagged as she waited for the bearded
deity to finish studying the notecards before him. "Lupino," he
mumbled, "obviously an eccentric." Shaw looked squarely at her.
"Well, if you want to go to all that trouble to attract attention, I
suppose it's all right. . . . I think it's silly myself, but I suppose an
exhibitionist like you would be good in the part. You can have it."

Ida was puzzled by Shaw's comments, until she glanced at
herself in the mirror. Her hair and face were streaked with bright

red; the cap had come off the lipstick in her purse and melted onto her comb and handkerchief. She realized what Shaw had thought: that she had painted herself to win his attention. He later said: "She is the only girl in the world as mad as I am."

Heartbreak House would be Ida's last play at the Royal Academy. She had given fine performances during her two terms; her agent envisioned her as the next Janet Gaynor of England. She would play sweet young girls with hearts of gold. Ida made screen tests at several studios and read dozens of casting calls, without success. During family tea one afternoon, her agent telephoned. He reported that she was wanted for a role in *Her First Affaire*. Ida laughed when she heard the news. She had already tested with several directors and had been rejected for being "too young and innocent." Nevertheless, her agent convinced her to try again.

Ida went to the office of Alan Dwan. He was one of Hollywood's most prolific directors, responsible for such silent classics as *Robin Hood* starring Douglas Fairbanks in 1922. He had already tested dozens of girls for *Her First Affaire* before he came to the Royal Academy and saw her as Ellie in *Heartbreak House*.

Dwan handed Ida a screenplay. "Read this," he ordered. Ida laughed when she saw the title. She repeated the comments she often heard, that she was too young for the role. But Dwan insisted she read it anyway. She returned the script. "Read it? I know it by heart."

Dwan felt she was perfect and arranged a screen test. Ida was enthusiastic until she arrived at the studio. Other girls were also being tested. Ida did her scene, then Dwan chose her. Ida was amazed.

She was given a contract to sign. She would earn forty pounds a week for playing Ann, a young girl madly in love with the married author of romance novels. A blonde Ida was superb as the flirt determined to have a forbidden romance.

The film was so well received in England that in December 1932 it was released in America. Ida was elated by the unexpected success. She had a schoolgirl crush on Dwan and was grateful for his help in launching her career.

"I'll make a level bet," said Dwan, "she will not remain in this country a year."

For Ida, the sensational role marked a turning point in both her personal life and her career. Just as Dwan had foreseen, offers poured in from American studios with promises of long-term contracts and high salaries. But Ida hesitated. She told her father that she wasn't quite ready to leave England, that she wanted more experience before deciding about America. In the fall of 1932, Ida was cast in *Money for Speed*, an action film about motorcycle racing. Authentic speedway sequences, filmed on location at Wembley, involved dangerous stunts with automobiles and motorcycles tearing around a cinder track. In the slim story, Cyril McLaglen and John Loder played rival champions vying for Lupino's affection. It was a role she adored: "I was a very bad little girl." But in one scene she exuded pretend sweetness.

Ida's career nearly ended when she was struck by an automobile. She was hurled high in the air. Her delicate face fell onto a gravel walk. In an article she wrote about her daughter, Connie stated, "Those were pitifully anxious months, waiting for the bandages to be removed." Ida was optimistic. She had read of a similar accident befalling Carole Lombard. But Lombard had returned to the screen. The scars faded, except for a light one on her forehead, which she covered with wisps of hair.

Ida resumed her screen career playing a princess in *Prince of Arcadia*, a musical comedy featuring Carl Brisson. Then, while filming *The Ghost Camera*, a clever murder mystery, she reached a momentous decision. Paramount talent scout Donovan Pedelty was impressed with her acting in *Money for Speed*, specifically the scene in which the teaser played by Ida feigns sweetness. He sent the scene to Paramount officials in America, and a lucrative offer was presented. For Ida, there was a drawback. Paramount wanted her to play the lead in *Alice in Wonderland*.

"I could never feel Alice," she lamented to her father. "I've never been Alice's age." "That's quite true," he answered. But Stanley advised her to go to America. He felt that the finest training was to act with the biggest stars. Ida would follow Stanley's advice.

Ida was thrilled when Ivor Novello cast her in *I Lived with You*. Novello was one of England's most prominent talents. Not only was he a handsome matinee idol and accomplished dramatist but a musician, famous for "Keep the Home Fires Burning," a song that rallied the British nation during the Great War. Novello had been Stanley's close friend since their early days in the theater, and he was Ida's godfather. He had written *I Lived with You* as a risqué stage play, and he starred as the impoverished Russian prince who is befriended by a kind working-class family. Sudden wealth, coupled with the dashing prince's amorality, results in the moral disintegration of the family. Ida portrayed a young girl seduced by her benefactor. Novello and Ida had an intimate scene lying on a couch together. "Oh, my Gawd, ducks, I'm mad about you. I've got to have you," said a passionate Ida. "Cut," said Novello. "I can't stand this . . . it's ridiculous, what with my godchild lying on top of me trying to rape me." The film was a smash, and Ida Lupino became England's youngest star.

By 1933, all the Lupinos were before the camera. Connie and Rita appeared in *Following in Father's Footsteps*; Stanley was ready to begin *You Made Me Love You*, his clever adaptation of Shakespeare's *The Taming of the Shrew*. Stanley would play a songwriter whose fiery bride marries him only to pay her father's debts. Director Monty Banks suggested that an American comedienne play the bad-tempered wife. Ida recognized the shapely blonde from her comedy roles with Laurel and Hardy and the Marx Brothers. Thelma Todd soon became a close friend of the Lupino family.

Toward the end of the production of *You Made Me Love You*, Thelma collapsed before the camera. She was carried, unconscious, into a dressing room where the studio physician examined her and suspected heart problems.

On a warm August day in 1933, the Lupino clan assembled at Waterloo Station. Flashbulbs popped, and well-wishers bid Ida farewell. She didn't enjoy the fuss. She was especially tense since she knew she was going to Paramount with no intention of playing Alice.

At the Southampton docks, Ida embraced her father in a tearful good-bye. She and Connie boarded the *Berengaria* and stood on the deck waving their handkerchiefs until England was far behind them. Stanley wiped his eyes. It was a sad but triumphant moment for him. In the fifteen years since her birth, his daughter had become everything he had wished for her. During a worldwide economic depression, she had a contract that would pay her six hundred dollars a week, and her future looked spectacularly bright.

When Stanley returned from Southampton, his home seemed desolate. He wandered the garden until he came to the Tom Thumb Theatre, now renamed the Stanley Royal. Pasted to the wall was a weather-beaten playbill announcing Ida's appearance in the Little Company's dazzling revue. Stanley sat in the empty theater remembering his daughter as she had first glided into the spotlight. Above him was a portrait of George Lupino, reminding him of the family's duty to entertain.

Later, a morose Stanley admitted his unhappiness to a reporter: "They cannot pay me enough for the parting. But I cannot stand in my daughter's light. I'm telling you it's lonely without them." He planned a trip to Spain with Rita, but he pined for his eldest daughter.

On August 29, 1933, the *Berengaria* landed at Hoboken Docks in New Jersey. Ida was welcomed like a little queen. Paramount representatives met her with bouquets and a shiny limousine. Ida and Connie were driven to the plush Waldorf Astoria. Ida was splashing in the marble bathtub when the telephone rang and she learned of a reception in her honor. Orchids were hurriedly pinned to a new dress and a publicist whispered to Ida that she was now *sixteen* years old. Reporters flocked to her suite, eager to meet Paramount's newest discovery.

Questions were hurled at "the possible Alice." Ida disarmed the hardened journalists by addressing them familiarly as "uncle." She merely raised an eyebrow when a reporter remarked that she resembled. a blonde Clara Bow. Ida portrayed herself as a sophisticated woman: "So you don't like Shaw? Oh, he's priceless." Before the party ended, the hard-boiled newsmen agreed that Ida was "a swell kid." Frank Nugent, movie reviewer for the *New York Times*, predicted: "Alice or not, Miss Lupino may be a great star."

At dawn, a limousine festively decorated with paper streamers took Ida and Connie to the airport. The exhausted travelers boarded their flight for a forty-eight-hour journey. A week after departing London, Ida arrived in Hollywood.

The following morning, her photograph appeared on the front page of the *Los Angeles Times*. She was dressed in a stylish cape and beret and beamed a radiant smile. The accompanying article stated that she and fifty other hopefuls would "vie for the part of Alice." Hollywood's newcomer, blonde and innocent, was on the front page amid stories of a gang murder, a narcotics arrest and celebrity domestic disputes. She didn't mind a bit. But the information that she had come from London just to play Alice left her steaming. She would straighten that out at a later date. She wrote to Stanley: "By the time we landed we looked like a couple of dead seagulls." After a short stay at the chic Garden of Allah on Sunset

Boulevard, she and Connie moved to a spacious colonial home at 1749 North Fairfax.

At Paramount, Ida rubbed elbows with Marlene Dietrich, Mae West, Carole Lombard, W.C. Fields, Claudette Colbert, and the Marx Brothers.

The studio arranged for an immediate makeup and wardrobe test.

Ida posed as the camera crew photographed her from various angles. With her deep voice and sophisticated attitude, it was apparent that she was no Alice. To Ida's great relief, the role went to unknown Charlotte Henry, who was soon forgotten.

Paramount executive Emmanuel Cohen summoned Ida to his office for a conference. After her rather surprising screen test, he explained what the studio had in mind; Ida would be molded and shaped as a "potential Jean Harlow." She listened enthusiastically; better a sexpot like the platinum blonde Harlow than a boring Alice. Cohen said writers were at work on a special story "just for her."

Paramount decided that Lupino's screen debut would be in *Search for Beauty,* a romantic comedy about Olympic champions who became entangled with con men. The studio had conducted an international contest with thirty winners awarded screen appearances. Co-star Buster Crabbe was an actual Olympic swimmer whose superb physique won him a role in the 1933 *Tarzan the Fearless.* Character actors Robert Armstrong and James Gleason played fast-talking crooks who decide that sex will sell their phony health magazine since "either you've got it, or you go looking for it."

Ida displayed a smooth and confident acting technique. She had a knockout scene: dressed in silk pajamas, she danced a snake-hips atop a table to save voluptuous Toby Wing from a roomful of evil-minded drunks.

Ida befriended a contest winner from Denton, Texas, Clara Lou Sheridan, a former teacher who felt out of place. Both girls were homesick and unhappy.

At the opening of *Search for Beauty*, spotlights swept across the sky as fans crowded the Paramount Theater at Sixth and Hill streets, gaping at the starlet in the white fur and gown. Ida and her escort, Jack La Rue, were surprised to see erotic fan dancer Sally Rand onstage performing nightly to boost ticket sales. As for England's Lupino: "Fine possibilities," predicted *Variety.*

Only a month later, in March, Ida's second Paramount release was in theaters. The studio's "special story" had not materialized; instead, Ida found herself in *Come on Marines,* in which Richard Arlen gallantly leads an armed squad into the jungle to rescue beauties from a Paris finishing school.

Ida was aghast, realizing that her contract left her vulnerable to future casting in such potboilers. Her fiery temper exploded in print. In her first newspaper interview in Los Angeles she bristled over the demeaning role. Reporter Alma Whitaker got an earful. First, Ida scoffed at reports that she had come to America just to play *Alice in Wonderland.* She had known she would never be Alice. "You cannot play naive if you're not. I never had any childhood," Ida said. As for her father, "He kicked me out to make my own way when I was twelve and I have supported myself." She described Connie as "terribly pretty," and said, "I boss her, choose her clothes and everything." As for Rita: "She is different from me. I insisted upon her going to a convent in England." Ida stressed that she had starred in English films since age fourteen and had no intention of getting stuck in ingenue parts. About her friends, she said, "I cannot tolerate fools, won't have anything to do with them. I only want to associate with brilliant people." Whitaker wrote, "She left me a little breathless, this deliciously arrogant child."

Ida's fierce determination to display her acting prowess was evident in her work with Paramount's stock theater, where studio personnel came to see what new players could do. Phyllis Loughton, a prominent diction coach, rehearsed Ida and other newcomers in *Double Doors*. A measure of Ida's artistic confidence was her decision to portray a seventy-year-old woman, even though she would be unrecognizable in thick makeup and gray wig.

Toby Wing became Ida's friend. She found Ida full of fun. Paula Stone was another young actress who came to know Ida quite well. Paula was the daughter of Fred Stone, the original scarecrow in the Broadway production of *The Wizard of Oz*. Ida would accompany Paula to the beach, where they would stretch out in the warm California sun. Connie once told Paula, "Your family is just like ours."

"Yes," said Paula, "we go back in the theater two generations." Ida, who had been listening, remarked, "Ours goes back *seven*." She could just as likely capture a listener by proclaiming, "A lot of my ancestors were crooks . . . con men."

As months passed, Ida began to fear that Paramount had written her off as a serious actress. She longed for an artistically fulfilling picture, something similar to Evelyn Venable's role in *Death Takes a Holiday*. Mitchell Leisen had directed this remarkably creative film about death appearing on earth to discover why he is feared. The same month Paramount released this visually and intellectually stunning film, the studio also gave audiences *Come on Marines*, in which Ida Lupino prances about in her underclothes. Ida's ruffled feathers were smoothed when she was handed the script of *Ready for Love*. Cast as the mischievous daughter of a flamboyant actress, she brightened. She would have a chance now. But as the cameras were about to roll, Ida faced a crisis that plummeted her to the depths of despair.

June 1934 was a month of sweltering heat; it was also a time of terror. For months, poliomyelitis had taken a mounting toll of victims. The disease had no known cure and even healthy people could die or be severely paralyzed in a matter of hours. In the first three weeks of June, four hundred citizens of Los Angeles had contracted the highly infectious viral disease. Fear was rampant. The epidemic was so severe that delivery men left groceries outside the doors of the ill, and doctors and nurses were dying. While visiting a doctor's office with her sister, newly arrived in America, Ida browsed through a medical textbook reading about the disease that terrified everyone.

Three nights later, Ida went on a date with actor Tom Brown. When they returned, she and Tom amused Connie by tap-dancing until midnight. After an hour in bed, Ida awoke, bathed in sweat with a thumping head, sore limbs, and fever. She tried to call Connie, but her voice was barely a whisper. Her right arm stuck out at an angle to her body and her right hand was balled into a fist; the soles of her feet felt as though they were on fire. She tried to stand but slumped to the floor. She painfully crawled to her mother's bedroom, struggling for twenty minutes to move twenty feet. When medical help arrived, Ida was in terrible pain. The mental anguish was even worse. Her physician, Dr. Percival Gerson, confirmed she had polio.

Ida pondered her future in despair. Paramount had advanced her salary and held up *Ready for Love*, but her moments were dominated by fear that she faced a life confined to a wheelchair. Equally devastating were black thoughts about how her illness would disappoint her father. She resolved to wait. But by the sixth night, there had been no change in her physical condition. Panic began to gnaw at her. She contemplated suicide.

"Suppose I can never walk again?" she cried to Connie.

Dr. Gerson arrived. He pinched her body from the right shoulder to the right toe, but Ida felt nothing. She began to sob hysterically. Connie took Ida in her arms, carried her to a rocking chair, and tried to comfort her with words of hope. As her mother rocked her, Ida quieted. Her side began to tingle. The paralysis vanished. She could move her hand.

Dr. Gerson brought Ida to the balcony where the cool air refreshed her. She was thrilled to step onto the balcony. She was out of danger. That night Ida hesitantly sat at her piano; joyous music flowed from her fingertips. Connie's rocking had returned feeling to her limbs. She had stared death and disease in the face, and she had won. Ida renewed her career with *Ready for Love* and obtained good reviews as a naughty girl mistaken for the mistress of a deceased playboy. Audiences laughed as she created a scandal at the Puritan party picnic, where she was accused of nude swimming and punished with an ancient dunking stool, not unlike her ancestor Charles, who had spent time in the stocks for the sake of art.

When the production ended, Ida immediately sailed for England, still reeling psychologically from her bout with polio. The British press interpreted her return as a retreat. Critics had not been impressed by her American films and claimed that the Hollywood grooming process had merely turned her into yet another Hollywood blonde. Stanley leapt to his daughter's defense and responded that her career was progressing. He had seen *Search for Beauty* six times in different theaters to evaluate Ida's acting. After each screening, he was satisfied that Ida was doing fine. He told the press that Paramount was building her until they found the role that would make her a sensation. He emphatically denied that Ida had permanently returned and said that she was in England only for a rest.

But Ida was in a deep depression. When the liner had berthed at Southampton, the person she most wanted to see wasn't waiting for her on the pier. She waited under the enormous "L" where her baggage had been carried, but Johnny wasn't there either.

While Ida was in America, her first love had gone bicycling in Austria and Germany. He had been severely injured in a highway accident. Before his death, he had left a message. A close friend brought Ida a cablegram at her home later that day. As she scanned it, the date gave her a jolt.

She remembered the day Johnny had died. She had returned from the set with an icy fear that something had happened to her father. A transatlantic call reassured her. She had gone to bed, but several hours later Connie had discovered her in her room, standing before a window sobbing and murmuring about Johnny, her face twisted with pain. As Ida read the cable, the terrible dream came back to her. "Tell Loops to carry on," she remembered Johnny saying. The very same words were on the cable.

Stanley consoled his daughter as only he could. As it had when she was a child, his voice painted for her a picture of another realm of existence beyond this world; he told her that the spirits of the dead often return.

Ida felt that she and Stanley shared strong psychic powers. She marveled at his strange ability. She would write a question on a piece of paper, crumple it, and lay it before his pen. He would write the answer. Ida told friends that she had inherited a similar ability from her father. She referred to this ability as "a psychic feeling."

On her last night in England, Ida sat with her father before the fireplace in the library. She asked him what pattern her life would take once she returned to America. Stanley began to write on a yellow pad. She anxiously read the words. By being away from England she had missed much confusion, he wrote, but more lay ahead. He warned her that if she accepted an invitation to go to a party in a horse-drawn carriage, she would become involved in a murder. He predicted that she would make a film for a different studio and that she would be cast in a picture that would not be made.

Stanley understood his daughter very well. He laughed at her bold comments and saucy frankness. He scoffed at writers who called his daughter "Jean Harlow's English rival." He didn't want her compared with anyone. "You may call Ida a star," Stanley said, "a starlet or anything else you like. All I know is she's got something and knows how to deliver it."

When Connie and Ida returned to America, Stanley found himself alone and lonely once more. As usual, he immersed himself in his work. While searching for a young actress to appear in his film *Cheer Up*, he became entranced by a hazel-eyed blonde he'd seen dancing in the chorus of a stage musical. John Glidden, a prominent theatrical figure, introduced the teenager to Stanley, and she was cast as the lead in *Cheer Up*. Later they would star together in the musical *Over She Goes*. Stanley and Sally Gray soon became a famous team, and Stanley fell in love with his partner.

3

LOUIS

She and Louis were a stunning couple, so filled with the joy of living. —HARRY MINES

Ida's year in America had made a profound impression; the four months she'd spent in England had done nothing to make her want to stay. She loved the warm California sun and the high studio salary, which brought her independence. In 1934, she would earn $23,400—not bad for a newcomer, though a paltry sum compared to Mae West's $399,166 or Marlene Dietrich's $145,000. Yet Ida was quite comfortable, and her income allowed her to purchase a car and a small trailer that she used for jaunts in the country.

On her return from England, Ida brimmed with eagerness. She told reporters that if all went well this trip she would become an American citizen.

When she reported to Paramount for her next assignment, her enthusiasm waned. In *Paris in Spring*, Ida was third-billed to Mary Ellis and Tullio Carminati in a trite tale of romantic revenge. In her minor role, she played a naive girl who falls for dashing Carminati. Her next role, in *Smart Girl*, didn't offer much of an acting challenge either. Ida and Gail Patrick played wealthy sisters who find themselves destitute after their father's suicide. Made at the peak of the Depression, the story was filled with jibes at big business and fraudulent mortgage companies. *Variety* had praise for Ida: "A personable girl, Miss Lupino does an elegant job of trouping; far ahead of the material offered."

For *Cleopatra*, she was given five lines and expected to stand behind Claudette Colbert waving a large palm frond. Ida refused. Studio officials pointed out that she was under contract, but she held her ground. When she was suspended, she surprised the studio by asking for a small role in *Peter Ibbetson*, a supernatural romance based on George du Maurier's novel about childhood lovers, played by Gary Cooper and Ann Harding, whose lives are intertwined in life and death. The studio readily agreed to Ida's request and cast her as a flirtatious tart.

The story was close to Ida's heart. There were moments during the production when tears would fill her eyes. Gary Cooper would try to cheer her up. "Don't look so sad," he would say.

But the thought of her first love remained with her. Portraying a little vixen, Ida came close to finding her true screen image in 1935. "Excellent in a brief part," noted the *New York Times*.

Ida kept company with a circle of young friends. She heard the backstage gossip that passed around the lot. She carefully avoided the more aggressive directors and producers who offered their attentions.

Connie kept a sharp eye on Ida and accompanied her to the studio. She was quite aware of the intrigues of show business and understood the difference between public images and private lives. Director Mitch Leisen became a dear friend of the Lupinos and often visited them with his boyfriend, dancer Billy Daniels.

Notice was given that Ida would be loaned to Jesse Lasky and Mary Pickford for their new company, just as Stanley had foreseen.

Even more startling, thought Ida, was her refusal to attend a horse-drawn hayride; a woman in the wagon had been struck by a bottle and nearly died. Ida was amazed by Stanley's uncanny ability to sense the future.

In May Ida's psychic feeling came over her. Jackie Coogan, who had been the child star of *The Kid* in 1921 with Charlie Chaplin, invited Ida to join friends at his family's ranch for the weekend. Ida declined because of a strong premonition of danger. On May 5, newspapers headlined the death of Trent "Junior" Durkin, who had starred with Coogan in *Tom Sawyer* and *Huckleberry Finn*. John Coogan, Jackie's father, was driving a group of youngsters on a country road near San Diego when they were involved in an auto accident that killed four passengers; only Jackie Coogan escaped. As a close friend of Junior and his sisters, Grace and Gertrude, Ida was heartbroken by the tragedy. She attended Junior's funeral on Sunrise Slope in Forest Lawn Cemetery.

Ida was cast in a prestige production, *Anything Goes*, based on Cole Porter's smash musical. Bing Crosby starred as a playboy who falls for Lupino, a runaway heiress. They got along fine, calling themselves "Tipper and Nipper." The studio spent heavily for the luxury liner sets and elaborate musical numbers, but the result was disappointing. The best reviews went to Ethel Merman for her rousing renditions of "You're the Top" and "I Get a Kick out of You." *Variety* summed up Ida's role: "The no. 2 femme is called upon to register adoration while Crosby sings, and that's a thankless task at best."

Ida was dejected over the shallow roles and mediocre films, but soon there was a flame of support at her side. Stanley came to Los Angeles with a plan to advance her career. He had written "a real acting opportunity" for her. They would appear together in his own production. He knew his daughter's mercurial personality was perfect for heavy drama. Paramount obviously didn't recognize her potential, so he would do everything within his power to guarantee her success.

Ida was different, as he explained in a candid article he wrote. He described her as high-strung, sensitive, warm-hearted and generous. One moment she could be a little girl, the next a regal princess. "She is rarely the same for two minutes," he revealed. "She will be sitting down, staring moodily into the distance; then, very suddenly, she will jump up and sing, do a Charleston, or play the piano; a moment later she will sit down again and start to write a play, only to get tired of it after a dozen lines or so."

Movie magazines were also coming to grips with Ida's unique persona. Among her friends, she had acquired the nickname of Lupi; although it was merely an abbreviation of Lupino, it signified she was *loopy* or *loony*.

Drummond Tell, a writer for *Picture Play* discussed her pranks, odd sense of humor, and screwball personality. He titled his article "A Little Bit Cracked." Ida told him why she and Elsie Ferguson, Jr., "once great pals," seldom saw one another anymore. Ferguson had married, and Ida disliked her husband, she explained, so she had brandished a butcher knife and chased him away. The writer stared in wonderment as Lupino spoke, her wild eyes blazing. He had first seen Ida when Paramount had shown the screen tests of potential Alices to the press. Ida said that she "had no recollection whatever of having made that test." The journalist understood that life was never dull around Lupino and that "Loopy has a happy faculty for forgetting things that she doesn't want to remember, and remembering only things as she would like them to have happened."

In interviews, Ida boasted of her eccentric behavior, admitting that many people found her too peculiar. If she had something unpleasant to say, she spoke directly to the person. She asserted that she was one of the most disliked people in Hollywood. "I'm mad, they say. I am temperamental and dizzy and disagreeable. Well, let them talk. I can take it. Only one person can hurt me. Her name is Ida Lupino."

At Paramount, Stanley conferred with studio executives who agreed that Ida could go to England—for a price. But the sum they demanded was more than the budget allowed—in fact, it was higher than Stanley's salary. His failure to come to terms with Paramount was a letdown, but he decided there was plenty of time for him and Ida to appear in a film together. His visit was not wasted. He had enjoyed the reunion with his family, and he had even met Harold Lloyd, a comedian he admired tremendously, on the set of *The Milky Way*.

Stanley wanted his visit to end on a high note. The Lupinos decided to host a lavish party for their friend Thelma Todd as the guest of honor. She had been very kind to Ida and Connie; she had introduced them to influential people in the industry and had made sure they received invitations to elegant parties. She was a frequent Sunday guest at Ida and Connie's weekend gatherings.

Arrangements were made for a dinner party at Cafe Trocadero, a chic nightclub at 8610 Sunset Boulevard. "The Troc" was one of the most famous nightclubs in the world. Celebrities such as Clark Gable and Joan Crawford added glamour to the flashy rendezvous of filmdom's sophisticated and powerful.

A few days before the party, Ida was at the Trocadero discussing the final details when she met Pat De Cicco, Todd's former husband. De Cicco was an actor's agent, a smooth talker, tall and handsome with dark eyes and black hair. He and Thelma had married in Prescott, Arizona, on July 10, 1932. Of the many suitors who had courted Thelma, De Cicco had won her affection, at least for a time. They were divorced on March 3, 1934; she charged him with cruelty. They remained friendly, but Todd had told close friends she had no plans to remarry him. Pat De Cicco asked Ida for an invitation to the party.

On December 14, a Saturday evening, the Lupinos welcomed friends at the Trocadero. The guest of honor arrived alone, radiantly beautiful in an expensive mink coat worn over a blue, sequin-spangled evening gown with blue dance slippers. On her finger was a small fortune in diamonds. Ida hugged Thelma and complimented her lovely appearance. Before dinner, Stanley and Thelma retreated to the cocktail lounge downstairs for a private chat. For dinner Ida placed a chair next to Thelma for Pat De Cicco, but he didn't appear. Guests enjoyed a five-course meal.

While they danced, Stanley learned that Thelma wanted to make another film in England. She explained that she owned the rights to a good story, and they excitedly discussed the possibilities of starring together and agreed to a meeting to work out the details. Ida spotted De Cicco on the Trocadero's upper level, dancing with actress Margaret Lindsay. She was surprised. Though the nightclub usually closed around 2:00 A.M. Stanley and Thelma sat together past closing time, engrossed in their proposed film project. Thelma said she felt tired and, after saying goodnight to remaining guests, she took her chauffeur-driven limousine to Thelma Todd's Cafe at 17575 Pacific Coast Highway, where she lived in an apartment over the business. The driver, Ernest O. Peters, offered to accompany her to the door of the Spanish-style building, but she declined his assistance.

On Monday, the Lupinos learned that Thelma's body had been found in a garage, slumped in the front seat of her twelve-cylinder Lincoln phaeton. A preliminary post-mortem report indicated that her death was a result of carbon monoxide poisoning. According to police, it was accidental. Yet when newspaper articles brought revelations about Thelma's personal life and odd occurrences reported by friends, the disclosures heightened rumors of foul play. Thelma had been deeply attached to forty-nine-year-old Roland West, a former producer and director. West had made his reputation with mystery films but had been inactive for several years. He and Todd operated Thelma Todd's Cafe and lived above in adjoining apartments. The site of Todd's death was the garage connected to a beautiful home where West had lived with his wife, Jewel Carmen, a silent screen actress. The home at 17531 Posetano was occupied at that time by West's in-laws.

When news accounts revealed Todd's relationship with West, gossip and speculation exploded. The mystery deepened when Pat De Cicco left Los Angeles the day after his former wife's body was found. He told reporters he could be of no use to Thelma and he was going to spend the Christmas holiday with his mother.

The coroner's inquest returned a verdict of accidental death but recommended further investigation. As authorities were organizing an in-depth probe, mourners gathered at Forest Lawn to say goodbye to Thelma Todd. On December 23, the grand jury investigation began. Stanley had been forbidden to leave the country until he was questioned. On their way to testify, Ida and her father discussed with reporters details of the Trocadero party. Stanley told detectives and the press that Thelma was in high spirits the entire evening. Ida had also seen Thelma in a gay mood, but earlier in the evening, she had noticed sadness. Ida recalled that Thelma had been her happiest when she spoke of romance. They had been at the bar when Thelma suddenly asked in a jocular way, "Well, Ida, what are you doing about your love life?"

"I'm too busy working right now," Ida had replied.

"Oh, well, I'm having a wonderful affair with a San Francisco businessman," said Thelma.

Stanley corroborated the conversation and clarified that it had been spoken in a hasty, joking way. But whether Thelma was kidding or not, speculation grew about "the man from San Francisco."

Ida related that she had met Pat De Cicco at the Trocadero and that he had asked for an invitation to the party. Reporters flocked to actress Margaret Lindsay as she approached the grand jury room.

While dancing, she said, she and De Cicco had learned that Thelma was downstairs in the cocktail room, but De Cicco didn't want to see his former wife. Later, as Thelma danced with Stanley, she had stopped at their table to ask if Pat had informed Ida that he would be a guest. De Cicco said he had telephoned that afternoon explaining he had a previous engagement. "With me," said Lindsay.

By the end of December, the grand jury had heard the testimony of twenty-four people. De Cicco returned to Los Angeles and was met at the airport by an investigator from the district attorney's office, who handed him a summons to appear before the grand jury. Before entering the jury room, he made a statement to reporters that he and Thelma were good friends, but they did not plan a reconciliation. He insisted that his request for an invitation to the party was merely a joke.

On January 2, 1936, the probe resumed. Ida Lupino was the star witness. The *Los Angeles Examiner* tagged her "the most glamorous witness to appear so far . . . from the richly full, red lips of the actress . . . came words with a sensational import." Ida's anger with Pat De Cicco was evident. She made clear that De Cicco had wrangled an invitation for himself. She said she had telephoned Thelma, who had seemed pleased that he was coming. At Thelma's suggestion, a place was arranged next to her. The Lupinos had regarded him as her escort. Thelma had decided they would arrive separately. When Pat De Cicco didn't show up for the party, Ida said she and Thelma were surprised and hurt. They had been even more surprised when he was discovered upstairs at the Trocadero with Margaret Lindsay. "Thelma bawled him out," said a vexed Ida. None of the Lupinos had received his regrets nor had their Japanese butler.

Ida testified that while making *You Made Me Love You* Thelma had collapsed and had been warned that she must give up motion picture work for her health due to a bad heart. This is why, said Ida, she often remarked she didn't have much for which to live.

Ida explained Thelma's reference to "the mystery man." She suggested that Thelma hadn't meant that he was a San Franciscan, but only that he was in the city. The press reported that the investigation would enter its "ugly phase," digging deeper into Thelma's personal life and pursuing the theory of foul play. It was rumored that "well-known figures," whose names had not been revealed, would be called to testify. Pat De Cicco was expected to return and to explain the conflict between his story and Ida's version; Roland West would be grilled about the "persistent rumor" that a new upper floor of the cafe was to be used for gambling.

West publicly expressed his indignation and anger at the possibility of a continued probe. He had already provided eight hours of testimony to the panel and was the main suspect in discussions of murder. West insisted that Thelma had accidentally been locked out of her apartment and had simply gone to the garage, not wishing to disturb anyone, to wait until morning. West publicly stated he would not answer any questions which might reflect on Thelma Todd's character, since he was determined to protect her memory. "I will tell the jurors anything they want to know about my own life. But they cannot force me to besmirch Miss Todd's character," said West.

There was dissension within the panel as to whether or not the investigation should end. Thelma's mother was furious over any continuing probe; she felt her daughter's death was a clear case of carbon monoxide poisoning.

The grand jury investigation came to a close, and the death of Thelma Todd slipped out of the newspapers. The jury panel was uncertain whether the death was suicide or accident, and everyone else had their own opinion.

On January 10, 1936, a press conference was held to launch *One Rainy Afternoon*. The weather was perfect—it was raining. Producer Mary Pickford posed beneath an umbrella and announced that Ida and Francis Lederer would co-star in a remake of the famous French farce *Monsieur sans Gene*. This would be Lupino's most prestigious film to date. Francis Lederer became a friend who greatly admired Ida's acting prowess. Born in Austria and raised in Czechoslovakia, Lederer had gone to London to begin a theatrical career. Lederer was handsome and romantic. While they worked together, he became smitten; impressed by her beauty and talent, in time, thought Lederer, she would prove herself. He compared her acting to "an artist, with every emotional color on her palette within easy reach." For Ida, Lederer was "a friendly heart." A romance might have grown, except that Ida had found her man, and no one could match him.

The man in Ida's life was Louis Hayward. Tall, dark-eyed, debonair Hayward possessed good looks, impeccable manners, and immense charm. His real name was Seafield Grant. Nine years older than Lupino, he had been born in Johannesburg, South Africa, then educated in England and France. His thespian training had been in the London theater. A chance meeting with famed playwright Noel Coward in a nightspot led to a small part in the 1931 stage version of F.P. Huntly's *Dracula*. His stage success led to his first film, *Sorrell and Son*.

The initial encounter of Lupino and Hayward had produced "tangible hostility." While studying a script on the set of *Money for Speed*, Ida had looked up to see a stranger watching her. Always uncomfortable when stared at, she had felt uneasy. As she struggled with difficult dialogue under the hot klieg lights, her nerves frazzled and the young man's scrutiny continually broke her concentration. When they were introduced afterward, Ida was icy. "He bored me to extinction," she later recalled. "It was strange but the dislike for each other . . . amounted to contempt." Hayward sized her up as "just another dizzy blonde." He came to America and found success on Broadway, winning the 1934 New York Critics Award. Soon he began a film career in Hollywood.

Since her boyfriend's death, Ida had experienced an intense emotional emptiness. In the middle of a party, she would burst into tears. And there were eerie occurrences. "I saw him at night; I have that sort of mind. I wouldn't be asleep, but he'd be standing there suddenly, talking to me. I'd answer and we'd remember the old days and—I swear it—he'd tell me not to be lonely."

While Ida sat in the studio projection room watching a private screening of *Anthony Adverse*, she recognized Hayward's face. This time, though, she was impressed. "He's magnificent," she thought.

Ida had numerous admirers. For a while she and Tom Brown were serious. On her sixteenth birthday, Howard Hughes arranged a party for her. He asked her what she wanted. "Binoculars," answered Ida.

"What on earth do you want binoculars for?"

"To look at the stars."

Hughes gave her the most expensive pair he could find. But presents never won her heart.

In the summer of 1936, the Lupinos resided at 2307 Chislehurst Drive. One afternoon Ida returned home from walking her dog to find Felix Tissot standing at the door. Tissot was an aspiring actor who had formerly been a French textile manufacturer Ida had met at Paramount. He said he lived nearby and was sharing a place with Louis Hayward. Ida was suddenly curious. Tissot asked if she would care to meet Hayward, but Ida recalled their mutual animosity on the Elstree sound stage. Though secretly attracted, she declined. In the following weeks, she often saw Hayward walking his dog.

One warm evening while Tissot was visiting, Hayward called for his friend. He spoke briefly with Ida, then said: "I haven't anything to do, I feel pretty rotten, why don't we all go down to Ocean Park together?" The threesome sped off to the seaside amusement park. The simmering attraction between Lupino and Hayward became evident to Tissot, who was soon left alone. Ida and Louis tossed pennies into little rings to win kewpie dolls and hurled balls at canvas curtains to bring live pigs sliding down a chute. When they jumped in the roller coaster, Ida and Louis were in the first car; they huddled together as they slowly ascended the steep slope and paused briefly on the incline high above the ocean. They stared at each other. Louis excitedly tossed a popcorn bag into space. At that precise moment, Ida later recalled, "something snapped in both of us." They were soon deeply in love. Despite their initial dislike, Lupino and Hayward were a fine match; both were sensitive, emotional, and inclined to melodrama.

Hayward was also outspoken. After they began dating, he happened to see Ida without her makeup and was charmed. Thereafter, when she put on the "war paint," he voiced his disapproval. Ida was stunned by his directness. No one but Stanley had ever talked to her like that. Louis calmly expressed a mature authority, and Ida listened.

Since her arrival in Hollywood, she resembled a little doll with a chubby face, penciled eyebrows and bleached hair. Ida felt her face lacked character. When she stared in the mirror, she was disappointed; her face was too round to have distinction with too high a forehead, besides, "My eyes are set frightfully far apart with too flat a space between them." She lamented that her mouth was too large and her nose was too small. Hayward's searing comments had touched a sensitive nerve. She began to think about remaking her entire image.

Late in 1936, Ida was again a loanout to the Pickford-Lasky company. She starred opposite unknown opera singer Nino Martini. Jesse Lasky had big plans for Martini. Lasky had earlier asked Rouben Mamoulian to direct his Italian discovery in Gounod's *Faust*. Mamoulian was at the time considered one of Hollywood's most creative directors. His fame had soared after his work with Greta Garbo in *Queen Christina* in 1933, and he had just finished *Becky Sharp*, the first feature shot in three-strip technicolor. Exhausted, Mamoulian had traveled to Mexico to rest and ponder an operatic film starring Martini.

On his return, he told Lasky that the *Faust* script was unsuitable for a motion picture; however, he did have an alternative story, a comedy about Mexican bandits who, after seeing an American gangster film, imitate the screen hoodlums. Mamoulian believed that this satire on the popular gangster movie would cleverly allow Martini to display his fine operatic voice. Ida was fiery as a young girl captured by the clownish bandits. In a wild scene, when Martini made amorous advances, she whacked him and they fought like wildcats. Then he bashed Ida over the head with a large flower pot. No stand-ins were used. When Ida first slapped a stunned Martini, a visible splotch appeared on his cheek.

To her misfortune, the flower pots that crashed on her head were supposed to be made of thin wax but were actually constructed of heavier material. When she finished the fight scene, she was woozy and had bumps on her head as big as robin's eggs. She received high accolades from Mamoulian: "I have worked with many stars in my time—this Lupino child is the finest trouper of them all. What an actress she is." This praise came from a renowned figure who had directed Garbo, Marlene Dietrich, Myrna

Loy, Miriam Hopkins, and Anna Sten. *The Gay Desperado* was a commercial and critical success, and Mamoulian was honored by the prestigious New York Film Critics as best director of the year.

Despite the fine reviews, Ida was furious to discover that she was being loaned to RKO for a cheap action programmer. She was growing extremely impatient with Paramount's handling of her career. Though only eighteen, she was already a sophisticated screen veteran, and she understood that quiet desperation was a main part of an actor's life. Ida witnessed first hand how desired roles were fought over by major stars. She saw how unexpected flops could leave top-billed stars without lucrative contracts, without a job, without a career. "You're only as good as your last picture" was the Hollywood adage. If your film failed, then you were a failure. Who wanted to hire losers? Bruised egos often resulted in shattered self-images. Intricately blended with the glamour and glory were alcoholism, broken marriages, and suicides.

During the three years that Ida had been in Hollywood, several notables had died by their own hand. Director George Hill, famous for his 1930 gangster movie *The Big House* had "practically everything that makes life attractive" but blew his head off in his Malibu home. Lou Tellegen, a famous matinee idol in silents, was just starting a comeback when he ended his life with a pair of nail scissors. James Murray, star of King Vidor's memorable *The Crowd* in 1928, died as a derelict, his body found floating in the Hudson River. John Bowers, husband of Marguerite De La Motte, had been a prominent actor until the arrival of sound. Then he dove in the Pacific Ocean and drowned himself; his tragic death became the basis for *A Star Is Born*. Actress Aleta Freel shot herself, and not long afterward her husband, Ross Alexander, noted for his role in *Captain Blood*, put a gun to his temple. The list went on.

Ida's friends Junior Durkin and Dorothy Dell had their brief lives snuffed out by auto accidents. Thelma Todd had died tragically at the height of her fame. Ida soon learned how celebrities attracted unbalanced fans who pursued stars for autographs and made pleas for assistance, proposals of marriage, and claims of parenthood. In addition, con men, phonies, blackmailers, hangers-on, and genuine weirdos lurked in the shadows, ready to fleece and harass the celebrated. Fame did indeed have its price. Though only eighteen years old, Ida had become suspicious and tough, and she relied on her psychic instinct for protection.

Though never hesitant about expressing her opinions, Ida often resented having her innermost feelings exposed and especially resented questions about her first love. "It hurts to talk about it," she said. "That's one of the things I resent the most violently. To have to take your own life and give it away to the public, in pieces." Ida admired the press-shy Garbo. "I am a fan. Not because she is a great actress, but because she has dared the wolves and kept her splendid isolation."

Ida felt that Louis Hayward was one of the few people who truly understood her. She defined her concept of love as "blind devotion." In interviews, she said she had few illusions about life but simply followed the conscious instinct of self-preservation. "I never expect anything to last . . . neither success nor love . . . I can't be hurt."

But she was deeply in love with Louis Hayward.

The Lupinos rented a home at 6950 Oporto Drive, high in the mountains above the Hollywood Bowl. In the summer, Ida enjoyed sitting in her yard, listening to the classical music that wafted upward from the concerts below. Ida's restless spirit ascended to an even higher aerie when she found a residence on Lookout Mountain that was on a knoll at 8761 Appian Way and commanded a beautiful view of Los Angeles far below. The neighborhood was a showbiz colony, and the Lupinos were popular hosts.

Actor William Bakewell was a neighbor. Ida nicknamed him "Billy the Bake." He found the Lupinos a madcap family; they always seemed to be hosting a party. He introduced Ida to Lew Ayres, who lived across from her. Since Ayres was always walking in the hills, Ida called him "the old man of the mountains." He marveled at her high level of energy, as well as her vivacious charm and sense of humor. He had an enormous organ installed in his home, and Ida was thrilled when he played a waltz she had written. "Ida, you'll never learn to take it easy," he chided.

Harry Mines, drama critic for the *Daily News*, was reviewing a Nino Martini concert when Louis Hayward sat in front of him with his lively date. An attractive girl flashed a smile. Mines, an affable fellow with a pungent dry wit, knew everyone in the arts. Being drawn to colorful types, he found Hayward's girlfriend immensely exciting. A few days later they suddenly appeared at his home with an enormous stuffed cat, which Ida thought was a great joke. He was charmed: "She burst with emotion; that's what fascinated me."

"Minesy," as Ida called him, became one of her most intimate friends. His first Christmas dinner with the Lupinos was a memorable event. When he arrived, Connie was in the kitchen preparing dinner. Guests were seated around the table when Connie made a grand entrance, then a speech: "We are so far from England, thousands of miles away. But here is my little Ida, and here is my little Rita, and dear Louis. God bless them." She acknowledged guests until she came to Mines's unfamiliar face. "Who in the hell are you?" she asked. After an introduction, Christmas dinner commenced. Then the front door suddenly flew open. A tall figure stood tottering in the doorway. In a stentorian voice, he bellowed: "Be it man, woman or dog, I throw it on the bed!" Stricken dinner guests glanced at each other. Connie stood up. "Sit down and shut up!" she ordered. Noel Langley, a British writer, reeked of alcohol. He took his seat, but only a few minutes passed before Hayward and Langley were arguing. When Langley left, he released the brake of Louis's car "so it went sailing down the street," says Mines. Later, Connie did a tap routine to "Tea for Two," her theme song. Mines came to idolize Connie. "Ida and Connie were so close, they reminded me of sisters. They looked alike and Ida let her mother into everything."

Paula Stone was also taken with Connie, whose warmth and friendliness endeared her to everyone. Connie taught Ida's young circle "the Lambeth Walk," a dance made famous by Lupino Lane.

If Ida's popularity was growing daily, her film career was slowly fading. She began 1937 with *Sea Devils*, a B-film loanout for RKO. She was then sent to Columbia for *Let's Get Married*, in which she was cast as a society blueblood who falls for weatherman Ralph Bellamy. Her career had sunk to its lowest level, and Ida plunged into a depressed state. She had a nice salary and had attained fine reviews in a string of forgettable pictures. Her modest success would have satisfied many entertainers in Depression America. Lookout Mountain had its share of wealthy stars, but it had hungry ones too. Peter Lind Hayes and his mother, Grace, ran a poker game in their playroom just to survive. They admired their neighbor, Ida, because she was always working. But mediocre acting roles couldn't satisfy Ida. In December, she was featured on radio with Robert Montgomery in *The 39 Steps*; she then took a few steps of her own. Rather than renew her contract, she left Paramount, refusing to work for the sake of her $1,750 a week paycheck. She was determined to gain recognition as a serious actress. If Paramount didn't care enough to cast her in quality roles, she was certain other studios would have her.

Like a woman possessed, she began remaking herself. The heavy makeup, which Louis detested, was already gone. Her hair had returned to a natural soft shade of brown. She lamented that it was thin and wispy, damaged by the studio peroxide.

She pushed herself relentlessly. She had arrived in Los Angeles weighing 127 pounds, a trifle plump but healthy. Paramount asked her to reduce and her weight dropped to 102 pounds. Slimming before a film left her nervous and irritable. Now Ida's fierce will power brought further weight loss. Her five feet, four inch frame tipped the scales at one hundred pounds; her waist measured twenty-one inches. "I ripped everything out of me," she said. "Slowly, I began to feel attractive again."

Ida honed her acting expertise, rehearsing scenes before a mirror. Evenings were spent at the piano, practicing and composing. Her "Aladin Suite" was performed on radio by the prestigious Andre Kostelanetz Orchestra. Other compositions were broadcast by the Los Angeles Philharmonic. She read, gardened, and waited. But the expected calls never came. Her hopes fell and her resolve weakened. "Nobody wants Lupino," she thought.

Ida nervously paced her home. She often called her agent, Leland Hayward. She waited and waited, and thoughts of failure tormented her. The months of being off the screen were unbearable. Her name dropped from the publicity mill. From sheer desperation, she had her business manager, Lee Chadwick, quietly pass the word in London: "About Ida Lupino, she's had enough of Hollywood; wants to go back to England to make a picture or two." Ida even offered her services to British producers for half her usual salary, but to no avail. She bitterly resented the rebuff from her native country.

Louis Hayward knew just how she felt. During their courtship, Hayward had climbed the ladder of success one rung at a time, but in 1937 he had made only a single picture. Louis would have proposed, but he first wanted to achieve celebrity status to match that of his fiancée. He feared becoming "Mr. Lupino." In 1938, his luck changed with *The Duke of West Point.* Before the film was released, his acting generated such excitement that he was signed to a long-term contract with Edward Small Productions. Ironically, it was now Ida's inactivity that kept them from marrying.

When Ida had first come to Hollywood, she was ambitious, impetuous, and impatient. Nothing had changed. Unless she fulfilled her destiny as an actress, she was doomed to personal unhappiness. She brooded at home, jittery, given to crying spells, sobbing on Connie's shoulder that she had failed Daddy, and had failed her name as well.

Louis was certain that his agent, Arthur Lyons, could get Ida's career moving again. Lyons had for years been the dynamo who made success stories happen. From his plush office at 356 North Camden Drive in Beverly Hills, he directed one of the most affluent artist agencies in show business. Lyons represented such stars as Jack Benny, Joan Crawford, Lucille Ball, Ray Milland, Sydney Greenstreet, John Garfield, Hedy Lamarr, Cole Porter, Jerome Kern, and Eugene O'Neill.

The short, heavy Lyons took his job seriously: "It is a grave responsibility, you understand, handling the career of an artist. It's a professional life without which the artist would be dead." For more than a year, he had been aware of Lupino's stagnant career. On one occasion, he had noticed Hayward's moodiness and asked his client what was bothering him. Louis replied, "It's Ida. She's got so much energy it's eating her up. She does everything she can—she thinks I don't know when she cries at night."

Lyons agreed that Lupino had gotten bad casting breaks from the start. The veteran agent hesitated to represent her. He knew of their marriage plans; he thought it would be bad business to represent a husband and wife. If one of them became disenchanted with him, he could suddenly lose two clients. But Lyons reached for the telephone and called Leland Hayward. He asked to represent Lupino; Leland Hayward agreed to let her go.

Lyons promptly swung into action. He sent Ida to see Harry Cohn, who ran Columbia Pictures. The tough, crude, astute boss was blunt: "You are not beautiful, Ida, but you've got a funny little pan." Ida must have winced at the comment but eagerly signed a two-picture contract. Her first release would be a modest "B" programmer, *The Lone Wolf Spy Hunt,* a series release starring Warren William as the ace detective and Ida as his girlfriend. It wasn't what she had hoped for when she parted with Paramount; in fact, it was the same type of mediocre film she was usually assigned, but at least she was back on a sound stage.

Ida's depression vanished. Louis proposed, and she accepted. Photographers caught them in municipal court obtaining a marriage license. Ida was casually dressed, a dark scarf over her head. Ida's close friend, actress Frances Robinson, hosted a wedding shower. Among the guests was singer Joy Hodges, who was quite taken with Ida's generosity, especially to her pal Frances. Production was under way for *The Lone Wolf Spy Hunt,* so Ida couldn't be married until Columbia worked out a schedule. Director Peter Godfrey told her: "We'll give you a free day, then you can dash off. But you'll only get a few hours' notice."

On November 17, 1938, Ida became Mrs. Louis Hayward in a quiet civil ceremony held in the Santa Barbara courthouse. Attending were a handful of friends, led by Frances Robinson, Harry Mines, Connie and Rita. Noticeably absent was Stanley Lupino. After their wedding, the new Mrs. Hayward, twenty years old, and her husband, twenty-nine, returned to work the next day. Over the weekend, the newlyweds rented a cottage in Malibu for a brief honeymoon.

Harry Mines visited Columbia the week after the wedding. A costume sequence was about to be filmed, and extras milled about in garish outfits. Mines was startled as an actress passed by wearing a hat with a blood-covered ax on top. Dapper Warren William appeared with a polite smile on his face and an enormous flowerpot in his arms. When Mines found Ida, she was gasping for breath because her face was covered by a huge headdress, which represented a bouquet of flowers. Despite the rigorous schedule, he observed that Ida was very happy, elated to be working again, but most of all, deeply in love with her new husband. "She and Louis were a stunning couple," recalls Harry Mines, "so filled with the joy of living."

But others felt that the marriage would not succeed. British correspondent W.H. Mooring wrote: "An Ida Lupino, if she is to play housewife, had better, for her own happiness, play it on the screen. You cannot domesticate an actress and, if you could, that actress would not be Ida Lupino." Louis gave up his home at 1600 Benedict Canyon and the couple rented a cottage in Beverly Hills that soon proved to be too small. One Sunday afternoon, Harry Mines waited anxiously for his friends to arrive at Vincent Price's beach home for a party. They finally drove up, excitedly telling everyone they had bought a home: "On the way down, on Sunset, we passed a sign. We went up, saw the place and bought it on the spot."

Their new home, discovered by accident and purchased on impulse, was at 1766 Westridge in Brentwood. It perched on a steep mountainside, commanding a magnificent view of Santa Monica Bay in the distance with sailboats drifting in the blue ocean. In the spacious interior, the Haywards created the casual atmosphere of an English country home. The center of the residence was an enormous den with a massive brick fireplace. Beneath the high-beamed ceiling was an unusual chandelier made of two crossed rifles. Along the rustic pine walls, Louis's collection of antique firearms was displayed; over the fireplace were his antique German beer steins and mugs, shaped like gargoyle heads. The living room was Ida's refuge. There was a fireplace, chintz sofas, a piano, and multicolored floral arrangements from her garden. Her collection of expensive porcelain cats and dogs in fantastic shapes and colors brightened the shelves.

Louis designed the dining room, copying the furniture from pieces in an English pub. Husband and wife each had their own bedroom to prevent lost sleep because of conflicting studio schedules. Ida's was painted gaily in pastels. She slept beneath a satin bedspread with Rowdy, her wire-haired terrier, always nearby.

The Haywards preferred to entertain at home and employed a cook and a houseman on a full-time basis. Guests were treated to candlelit dinners on their eight-foot antique oak table. The menu was usually roast beef, potatoes, and Ida's favorite dessert, trifle, a sponge cake soaked in sherry and covered with custard, whipped cream, nuts, raisins, and fruit. Ida disliked cooking but supervised the meals. She personally arranged the table settings, filling crystal bowls with daffodils and roses. To insure peace and quiet during dinner, there was an ironclad rule that no one, whether guest or host, could be disturbed by the telephone, an intrusive instrument that Ida thoroughly detested. Informality was also enforced, as the Haywards did their best to make friends feel comfortable. After dinner, the group would retire to the den, where the hosts would often surprise everyone by playing tapes of conversations made during dinner. Ida thought it was a great gag. Sometimes she would entertain the gathering with her impressions, performed expertly, especially her imitation of Greta Garbo. On occasion, Ida would invite friends to accompany her up a ladder to the roof to view Mandeville Canyon and the faraway ocean, city lights, and stars.

Harry Mines learned that the Haywards heard many eerie sounds in the house. Ida told him that the residence was built over an ancient Indian burial ground. While Louis was away one evening, Mines chatted with Ida in her bedroom. She stretched on the satin bedcover while her lanky friend sat comfortably on the floor. They heard a sudden thumping noise in the hall.

"Who in the hell is coming to call now?" asked Mines.

"Never mind, it's only them," replied Ida.

"Who?" asked a puzzled Mines.

"You know, the ones who have been around here."

The Haywards were certain that spirits inhabited the home, especially the living room. As Ida explained: "Twice a very dear friend of ours came to the house and was taken deathly ill in that room. He told me, 'There is something evil in this room.' Well, we ripped it to pieces." Louis later told Mines that ice tongs in a champagne bucket had suddenly shot across the room toward him. "It was really a creepy home," says Mines.

When she reached her twenty-first birthday, Louis arranged a surprise party for his wife at the fashionable La Maze restaurant on Sunset. Louis was delighted to see his little "poppet," as he affectionately called her, so happy as she sliced her birthday cake. On the surface, Ida's domestic life was tranquil, but she worried constantly over her career, especially after Columbia cast her in *The Lady and the Mob*, a routine gangster story. After her brief, two-picture comeback, the terrible lull returned. Columbia made no mention of further work, and Ida's hopes vanished.

Despite her inactivity onscreen, Ida was increasingly in demand for radio shows; her distinct mellifluous voice was perfect for the airwaves. Ida suddenly felt that radio would bring her good fortune. In May, she boarded a flight to New York for a guest appearance on *Mercury Theater on the Air*, starring opposite Orson Welles in "The Bad Man." After the broadcast, a representative of Twentieth Century-Fox telephoned, impressed by her radio acting. She was asked to return to Los Angeles for a dramatic role in *The Adventures of Sherlock Holmes* starring Basil Rathbone.

Ida portrayed a terrified woman who comes to Holmes with a strange drawing that threatens her brother with death. The film was enhanced by a somber London setting, shadowy and mysterious, created by art directors Richard Day and Hans Peters. Cinematographer Leon Shamroy captured the eerie atmosphere, which was enhanced by the music of Cyril J. Mockridge, who composed a haunting Inca funeral dirge. Ida's emotions were on the mark as she portrayed a woman stalked by killers. A crucial scene in which she weeps over the body of her slain brother was beautifully played. As she sobs, she hears the faint tones of the frightening Inca dirge, the harbinger of another murder; fear, then stark terror, sweep over her, culminating in a shrill, blood-curdling scream.

A new Lupino had emerged on the screen. The early image of the painted plump doll was gone forever. During her years without employment, she had reached deep within her psyche to remake herself, both physically and emotionally. She was more mature, tougher, and permanently scarred by the indifference shown to her during her year without work. Movie audiences and critics alike were struck by her superb portrayal.

Trade publications heralded the news that William Wellman would direct the Kipling classic *The Light That Failed*. When Ida got wind of the news, she was ecstatic. She had long dreamed of playing Bessie Broke, a hot-tempered streetwalker. From childhood, she had known Rudyard Kipling's famous novel, the story of artist Dick Heldar, who strives to paint his final masterpiece before losing his sight. In London, he meets Bessie, a surly street girl who is faint from hunger, and is taken with her "marvelous eyes . . . with terror in them." She becomes his model for "Melancholia," his final painting, which will express the anguish of mankind through the eyes of Bessie Broke.

Heady with excitement, Ida vowed that she would win the role of Bessie Broke. She devised a wildly ambitious plan to convince "Wild Bill" Wellman of her expertise. Ida had met Wellman in 1935 at a party hosted by producer Walter Wanger. A photo shows Wanger, Gail Patrick, Alice Faye, Henry Fonda, and Ida next to Wild Bill, who jauntily displays a cocktail glass.

Wellman had a reputation for being a hellraiser and a demanding director. He had started in silents, making a name for himself with the 1927 aerial spectacle *Wings* and later the famed gangster epic *Public Enemy* in 1931. Paramount had announced that Wellman would direct Gary Cooper in *The Light That Failed.* Ida had asked for the role of Bessie, but plans for the picture had fallen through. Now, she was determined to succeed. There was fire in her eyes when she walked through the main gate of Paramount Pictures, her former home. She knew this role would bring her the success that had eluded her for six years in Hollywood.

Wellman was taken by surprise when Ida burst through the door of his office. Overwhelmed with excitement, she proclaimed: "You're doing Kipling's *The Light That Failed,* and this is my part. You have got to give me a chance. I know it right now. I know the whole script, because I stole it!" The startled director didn't even recognize her; slowly he realized who she was, the little blonde he hadn't seen in years. Wellman said she couldn't read the part since the star, Ronald Colman, wasn't there. Undaunted, Ida insisted that Wellman read with her. She wanted to act the most difficult scene, in which Bessie becomes hysterical as the artist verbally torments her. Impressed by her display of guts and self-confidence, Wellman agreed to play the scene.

Ida suddenly transformed herself into the feline Cockney slut. She was a veritable madwoman, savage and frightening. Wellman was spellbound, marveling at her acting prowess, which reached a powerful crescendo of hysteria and mad shrieks. He had never seen anything so terrific in his entire life. He immediately took Ida to see B.P. Schulberg. Her repeat performance was as magnificent as the original and Schulberg agreed that she was indeed Bessie Broke.

Wellman's strong belief in Ida's ability was tempered by a strange threat that she never forgot. Wild Bill said, "If you aren't as good on the set, I'll take a .22 and blast you!" Then something unexpected happened. Schulberg balked at hiring Lupino. Ronald Colman wanted his friend Vivien Leigh to play Bessie. Wellman refused to budge.

Schulberg relented, and agreed for the second time that Lupino had the part. Wellman rehearsed Ida at his home and cleverly kept her from learning of Colman's resentment. Once filming was under way, Ida found Wellman "a tower of strength." Colman was sullen over losing Vivien Leigh. When the moment arrived to play the most difficult scene, the one in which Bessie becomes hysterical, Ida was extremely nervous. Wellman yelled "Action!" Colman twice flubbed a line in the middle of Ida's big moment. Wellman believed he had done this on purpose.

"Cut!" he yelled. He signaled for Colman to follow him. He walked behind the set, then faced the star. Wellman threatened to make Colman a character actor if he blew the line again. The cameras rolled, and Ida did the scene. She played it beautifully, and Colman was on the mark.

Wellman had great faith in Ida and, fortunately, didn't have to use his rifle. He knew that Lupino was destined for star billing and made sure that the studio acknowledged her new stature. This surprised Ida. Her usual dressing room was "the size of a closet, three floors up." One day, on her way to her dressing room, she heard a car horn. It was Wellman, who shouted, "Hey, baby, over there. You got a star dressing room, shower and tub." Ida was wide-eyed. She was near Marlene Dietrich "and all the big stars."

Anxiously awaiting the release of *The Light That Failed*, Ida awoke on September 1, 1939, to discover that Germany had invaded Poland. On September 3, Britain and France declared war on the Nazis. The western democracies were stunned by the deadly might of the blitzkrieg as it demolished everything in its path.

What will happen to Stanley? worried Ida.

Speculation was rampant that it was just a matter of time before Hitler invaded England. British actors were packing their bags. Ronald Colman and his wife Benita were prominent figures in Hollywood's British colony who hosted many prestigious parties, where newly arrived Britons were introduced into their elite circle. After his rather cool disdain, Colman warmed to Ida, and she and Louis became regular guests at Colman's dinner parties. Ida was saddened that two of her new friends, David Niven and Robert Coote, were joining the military. Louis had applied for American citizenship but was torn between fighting for the British Empire or remaining in his adopted country. Ida agonized about the future.

Ironically, in the midst of her deep concern, she was to triumph. Ida was so nervous over the release of *The Light That Failed* that she refused to attend the lavish premiere in Westwood.

Afterward, an excited Harry Mines drove straight to Ida's home to telephone his review to the *Daily News*. He had loved the film and had thought Ida's performance was wonderful. As Mines spoke, Lupino sat listening. He described Ida, as Bessie, as "a portrait of ugliness." When he hung up, he was surprised to see her glaring at him. "You panned me in my own home," she said angrily. Mines was taken aback, until he realized that Ida thought he had criticized her magnificent performance. Ida calmed herself. For a moment, Bessie had come to life before the movie critic. It wasn't the last time he would see the hair-trigger temper.

During the Christmas season, audiences lined up to see *The Light That Failed*. Colman, who was forty-eight years old, had given one of his best performances. Not only was the picture a success at the box office, but so was Lupino. The *New York Times* said it all: "A little ingenue suddenly bursts forth as a great actress."

4

THE YEARS OF GLORY

Raft and Bogart honest men but Lupino steals picture.

—NEWSWEEK

Mark Hellinger waited anxiously in a studio projection room. As expected, a grinning Jack Warner swept in with his aides. He eased himself into a seat, and the room darkened. Hellinger was producing *They Drive by Night*, and he wanted Ida Lupino for the lovely murderess. Director Raoul Walsh was ready to sign unknown Catherine Emery, so Hellinger had to move quickly. Impressed with Lupino in *The Light That Failed*, he had arranged for her to make a test with George Raft. Designer Milo Anderson had created a breathtaking dress to enhance Lupino as an alluring seductress. Hellinger had spun his web and was determined to snare the powerful man beside him.

Hellinger was a fast talker. With his breezy New York manner of speech, he displayed a brash style and confidence. He had made his reputation as a reporter, columnist, and writer and was lauded as a master of the short story. He was known to stand out on the Warner lot, attired in a dark suit, black shirt, and white tie, tangling with Jack Warner and his subordinates. But the powerful studio chief had the upper hand, and he would make the final decision regarding Lupino.

Jack Warner was a man always full of good humor, without any guile. This, at least, was the character he wished to portray. Behind the smiling mask was a domineering mogul who expected his executives to laugh at his corny jokes. But Warner was no fool. As he watched the girl in the tight-fitting gold lamé dress, he was pleased. "Let's sign her up," he commanded.

Lupino was summoned to Warner's office and offered a seven-year contract. He told her she would be "another Bette Davis." Davis was the studio's most valuable star and the most difficult. In 1936, she had gone to court to free herself from what she considered an unfair contract. Though she had earned three thousand dollars a week, she had bitterly complained that she was forced to work fourteen-hour days and was often handed second-rate scripts that demeaned her screen stature. Most unfair, she told the press, was the crippling suspension clause, whereby any performer who refused an assignment was placed on suspension; the time absent from the assigned role was added to the studio contract. A seven-year contract could stretch into eternal servitude. Davis failed in her lawsuit and was compelled to return to Warner Bros., known among the rank and file as "the San Quentin of studios."

Ida recognized Warner's transparent strategy. If the queen of the lot refused to do a picture or caused trouble, Lupino would be at hand. She had fought with Paramount over decent roles, and she didn't want to be a slave like the wealthy but unhappy Davis. Seven years was a long time. She would have to think it over, she told a surprised Jack Warner. Stanley and Connie had taught their daughter that show business was a struggle, and Ida turned to her agent.

Arthur Lyons began negotiations with Fox. The strategy worked.

On May 3, 1940, she signed a one-year contract with Warner Bros. that permitted her to freelance elsewhere. Her salary would be two thousand dollars a week for two pictures. Lyons won the right to three outside films and shrewdly negotiated radio appearances without studio control. The contract was an ironclad agreement that placed golden handcuffs on those who signed. The thirty-one page document was minutely specific regarding what "the artist" was expected to do while receiving a Warner paycheck: "The Artist hereby grants to Producer the right during the full term hereof his name and to use and/or distribute his pictures, photographs or other reproductions of his physical likeness for advertising, commercial or publicity purposes."

Errol Flynn and Olivia de Havilland puffed Chesterfield cigarettes— "The right combination satisfies millions." Of course, the advertisement plugged *Dodge City*, their new movie. If Warner stars were slaves to the studio, they were certainly wealthy ones. Weekly salaries for 1939 were, for James Cagney, $12,000; Paul Muni, $11,500; Edward G. Robinson, $8,000; Claude Rains, $6,000; George Raft, $5,000; Errol Flynn, $5,000; Bette Davis, $4,000; Pat O'Brien, $4,000; John Garfield, $1,500; Olivia de Havilland, $1,250; Ann Sheridan, $500; and Jane Wyman, $200.

Lupino's first release would be top quality, a solid screenplay based on A.I. Bezzerides's novel *The Long Haul*, a taut drama about "road slobs" hauling freight. Warner Bros. excelled at presenting celluloid slices of working-class life, and *They Drive by Night* was first-rate.

Production began on April 22, 1940. The screenplay was shot in sequence, making it easier for the cast to develop full-bodied characterizations. Ida's first scene sizzled. Hearing a fight below his trucking office, her loutish husband, played by Alan Hale, cheers the brawlers. At a different window, cleverly underscoring the emotional distance between husband and wife, Ida appears as Lana, with an expression of boredom and disgust. In a voice as sharp as a scalpel, she berates her husband for his uncouth behavior: "Stop yelling out the window! You're not a truck driver anymore!" Lana oozes subtle malice toward her buffoonish husband but projects sweetness when Raft walks into the office. The obvious phoniness makes her all the more sinister; by the time she murders her husband, she is molten fury. On May 24, Ida paced the courtroom built on Stage 17, emotionally primed to play her most difficult scene. She remembered the advice Phyllis Loughton gave her while she was in the play *Double Doors*, in which Ida played a woman of seventy who finds herself deserted and utterly alone, with nothing left but the strand of pearls around her neck. Loughton had told her that mad people are often childlike. She told her to think back to something pleasant in her childhood, something she had wanted very much and had received. In the play, Ida fondled the pearls against her throat as a child fondles a new toy. In *They Drive by Night*, "When I was on the stand, I did much the same thing. I wasn't maniacal. I was quiet. I was simple. I was a child who was not a child. That's madness." Wearing scant makeup with her hair swept back, revealing the light scar on her forehead, she clutches a handkerchief and begins speaking softly. Gradually her hollow voice turns shrill, and she madly screams her confession.

They Drive by Night was completed in thirty-three working days, for $498,000. Even before its release, Warner Bros. knew it had a winner, thanks mainly to Ida Lupino. Hal Wallis, head of studio production, wanted her signed for a third film. On July 8, a preview was held at the Warner Theater on Hollywood Boulevard. Ida ignited the screen; she projected a fascinating blend of beauty, danger, and deceit. *Variety* reported that the audience had twice broken out with applause. *Newsweek* proclaimed, "Raft and Bogart honest men, but Lupino steals picture."

Other reviews were equally laudatory: "Miss Lupino goes crazy about as well as it can be done," noted the *New York Times*. The *World Telegram* stated that she finally had gotten the break she deserved "and the result is a performance so superb that she immediately becomes one of the screen's foremost dramatic actresses."

Not only did she receive rave reviews for her acting, she was hailed as a fashion queen. Magazines were filled with Lupino posing in elegant Milo Anderson creations. The most sensational gown was the sleek gold lamé dress she had worn in the test and onscreen in a seduction scene with George Raft.

Ida soon discovered that her screen hysteria in *The Light That Failed* and *They Drive by Night* had made her the talk of Hollywood. At parties, guests were often asked to sing, dance, or play the piano. The host would turn to her and say, "Ida, go crazy."

Mark Hellinger chose Lupino for his next film, which he described as "a great yarn." The studio had paid twenty-five thousand dollars for *High Sierra* by W.R. Burnett. Although the era of the gangster film had peaked, Hellinger was enthusiastic about the story, but Warner stars shied away. The lead was turned down by James Cagney, George Raft, Paul Muni, and Edward G. Robinson; but there was one player on the lot who badly wanted the part. He even sent a telegram expressing interest.

> Hal Wallis May 4, 1940
> Dear Hal: You once told me to let you know when I found a part I wanted. A few weeks ago, I left a note for you concerning *High Sierra*. I never received an answer, so I'm bringing it up again as I understand there is some doubt about Muni doing it.
> Regards, Humphrey Bogart.

Bogart had yet to break out of third-billed character roles. In 1936, he had thrilled audiences as cold-blooded killer Duke

Mantee in *The Petrified Forest*, then he had drifted back to minor parts. In 1939, Vincent Sherman began his directing career with *The Return of Doctor X*, a B-film. Sherman recalls, "He was just a heavy and nobody thought he could do anything else. Warner said to me, 'I'm giving you this guy Bogart, and for God's sake, see if you can get him to do something besides Duke Mantee.'"

Like Lupino, Bogart never stopped trying for better roles. Since nobody else wanted the lead in *High Sierra*, Bogart won it by default. Mark Hellinger's persistence brought W.R. Burnett's novel to the screen. A decade earlier, Burnett had risen to fame with *Little Caesar*, a crime novel based on the life of Al Capone, and in 1931 the book was brought to the screen in a sensational portrayal by Edward G. Robinson. Gangster movies became popular. Too popular.

In 1934, the Production Code was adopted by the Motion Picture Producers and Distributors of America. Religious groups, such as the Catholic Legion of Decency, had put intense pressure on the industry to insure "proper morality" on the screen. Joseph Breen, a Catholic, went to work for the MPA to enforce the formidable code. Breen and his staff did not see themselves as censors but rather as "self-regulators." Under the Code, motion pictures were expected to avoid brutality, swearing, and especially the supreme taboo—sex.

The restrictions were oppressive as far as writers were concerned, and were especially difficult for those wishing to depict realism onscreen. W.R. Burnett and John Huston collaborated on a dynamic screenplay, but Breen condemned *High Sierra* because of the suggestion of the illicit sexual relationship. He also directed that the words "punk," "damn" and "tramp" were to be eliminated as offensive. Roy Earle couldn't even use a machine gun. Despite the restrictive guidelines, Burnett and Huston completed a masterful script—the simple yet compelling story of an Indiana farm boy who turns to crime. Bogart plays Roy "Mad Dog" Earle, and Ida plays Marie, a young woman picked up at a dime-a-dance joint, who begs to stay with Earle because she has nowhere else to go.

Production began August 5; the company assembled for exterior scenes at the mountain resort of Big Bear. For four days, Raoul Walsh filmed the meeting of Roy and his henchmen. Initially, the relationship between Lupino and Bogart was cool. As she later disclosed, "I have a way of kidding with a straight face; so has Bogie. Neither of us recognized the trait in the other. Each of us thought the other was being nasty, and we were both offended."

Matters were complicated by Mayo Methot, Bogart's wife. As the picture progressed, Ida and Bogie established an onscreen rapport and an off-camera friendship. The volatile Mrs. Bogart constantly hovered about the set, making her husband nervous. Dialogue director Irving Rapper knew why Mayo was there, as did everyone else. "Mayo was very jealous of Ida," says Rapper.

The Bogarts were famous for their noisy fights. On a *Dodge City* publicity tour, they had argued violently, and Mayo had broken a bottle over her husband's head. Bogart was on edge as his wife patrolled the film set, watching his every move. Walsh tried to outmaneuver her, telling the crew, "Let's be ready before Mayo starts in."

Ida created the portrait of a woman who feels a fierce loyalty and love for the only man who has ever shown her kindness. Bogart created a multidimensional screen character who is much more than just a common hoodlum.

In early September, the company motored to Calabasas to film the highway farewell scene. The script called for Lupino to cry, but the tears wouldn't come. Bogart took her to the side and, glancing at director Walsh, told her: "Listen, doll, if you can't cry, just remember one thing—I'm going to take this picture away from you." Ida laughed, just as Bogart had wanted.

"All right," he said, "now you're relaxed. If you can't relate it to me or the character go back to your childhood," he counseled. "Can you remember when you had to say goodbye to somebody, somebody you loved? And you thought you weren't going to see them again?"

"Yes," responded Ida.

"Well, think of that, baby, think of it!"

Ida saw tears in his eyes. Before she knew it, she was crying too.

Shortly afterward, the company traveled 230 miles to Lone Pine to create the dramatic climax. On a steep slope of Mt. Whitney, fifteen miles west of the small hamlet, Walsh and stunt-man Buster Wiles scouted the rugged terrain. Wiles, who usually doubled for his friend Errol Flynn, had been chosen for his dare-devil expertise. Walsh pointed to a steep crag and asked if he could fall from there.

"Yeah," said Wiles, "but I'd be dead when I landed."

The director pointed to another peak. "Can you tumble down that slope?"

"If I can't, I'll eat Mt. Whitney," said Wiles confidently.

For days, teams of crewmen worked to clear a path up the steep slope. Equipment was hauled up the mountain using mules and pack horses. Wiles doubled both Bogart and the actor who was to shoot Roy Earle. "So I shot myself off the mountain," says Wiles.

Walsh constructed an elaborate death for Roy Earle. At the shout of "Action!" Buster Wiles began his death descent. As he careened down the slope, he rushed past two lifelines; a third saved him from plunging to his death. It was a stunning sequence, earn-ing Wiles the admiration of the spectators, especially Lupino.

The final scene called for Marie to cry over the broken body of her dead lover. As before, Ida's tears wouldn't come. She was emotionally drained, and her eyes were weak and irritated. Buster Wiles lay in the dust, as impatient crewmen grumbled and cursed, discussing ways to make her cry. Insults were not appropriate, said Walsh. Finally, Ida delved into her private thoughts; the stuntman felt the warm tears on his cheek.

The final scene of *High Sierra* is powerfully moving. Marie's tears of sadness are transformed into tears of elation as she realizes that the tortured soul of Roy Earle is finally free. The production closed on September 26, nine days over schedule but $35,000 under the allotted budget of $455,000. For their creative efforts, the principals did well. Mark Hellinger earned $21,452; Raoul Walsh, $17,500; John Huston, $15,667; Ida Lupino, $12,000; Humphrey Bogart, $11,200; W.R. Burnett, $3,750.

Hal Wallis was extremely impressed by Lupino's fine performance. He sent a memo to Jack Warner asking if Lupino shouldn't be billed first instead of Bogart. "Lupino," he reasoned, "has had a great deal of publicity on the strength of *They Drive by Night* whereas Bogart has been playing the lead in a lot of 'B' pictures." Despite his second-billed status, Bogart sent a telegram to Wallis thanking him for the role.

Some took exception to the much-praised film. Moral watchdogs felt that the depiction of gangster Roy Earle was too sympathetic, too human. In response to the Better Films Council of Milwaukee, the studio sent a defense, explaining that the picture could not have been made had it been in violation of the Production Code. "This type of picture does not tend to make crime attractive . . . this type has a cathartic effect upon young minds with an incipient criminal tendency." As for the sympathetic depiction of Roy Earle, the studio's position was that "were he to be portrayed only as a vicious and completely unsocial person the tendency upon the part of the audience would be to make it impossible for them to identify with such a character."

High Sierra was to remain one of the greatest pictures of Ida's career and quite memorable personally for her experience with

Humphrey Bogart. Initially, Ida had found Bogart's pleasure in needling people upsetting, but by the film's end, she understood that he, like herself, was a person with many sides, some of them contradictory. She grew to like Bogart and never forgot his unexpected support when the tears wouldn't come. As she was to remember: "He was the most loyal, wonderful guy in the world."

Though Ida was finally achieving the screen recognition she deserved, her personal life was deeply troubled. In May, the Germans had conquered Europe. England stood alone. In August, the Battle of Britain began with hundreds of Nazi aircraft nightly dropping bombs on London. She and her father exchanged precious letters, giving Ida direct insight into the terrible destruction. Stanley had one of the most dangerous jobs a civilian could undertake. He was an Air Raids Precautions Warden, escorting Londoners to shelters, extinguishing incendiary bombs and, most hazardous of all, locating time bombs that could explode at any second. In October, he penned a poignant letter to his wife: "Dearest Connie, The Germans are trying all the devilment that hell can supply."

Stanley showed the Cockney spirit beneath the rain of Nazi bombs. He worked from sunrise to sunrise with two hours sleep, completing his rounds with the sky aflame. He described life in his shelter: "In the dim light of a hurricane lamp, I see a girl sleeping on a mattress and a dog curled up with its head on her chest. Two months ago she was starring at His Majesty's Theater. Now she had not been able to eat or bathe properly for a week without shells screaming above . . . I am doing my bit. But so is all Great Britain and never was the word 'great' so truly applied. When it's over, we can face the world and if the word British doesn't open the doors to all the world's hearts, then I shall be glad to put my tin hat on again to help prove it. Daddy."

Such letters brought tears to Ida, as well as a deep hatred of the Germans who made her father's life so miserable. In contrast to

Stanley's dangerous existence, Ida's life was spectacular, as hundreds of fan letters poured into Warner Bros. each week. She was recognized and mobbed wherever she went. Flashbulbs exploded in her face, proposals of love were slipped into her hand and her mailbox. As fans gawked and pointed at her, she felt uncomfortable; the trappings of fame left her uneasy. With her phenomenal success, her anxiety level rose. A mentally unbalanced veteran harassed Ida by repeatedly hovering about her home, finally breaking inside. She feared strangers lurking in the shadows.

She also worried about making sound career decisions. She wanted only top-quality scripts, and she wanted her acting to be perfect. The tension and the sleepless nights increased.

She and Louis lent their presence to many benefits to raise money for British War Relief. Sundays were sacrificed for entertaining visiting British military men, who were welcomed with delicious meals that included steaks, kidney pie, berry tarts and crullers. Guests were surprised to meet the Haywards' "adopted son"—six foot, two inch Peter Cushing, who was employed in a film at RKO.

Warner Bros. made no mistake when casting Lupino for her third release of 1941. She would again play a "bad girl," this time in *The Sea Wolf*, a script based on the classic novel by Jack London. The studio had paid producer David O. Selznick fifteen thousand dollars for the rights to the story, the tale of a cruel captain who torments his crew and passengers. Before filming, the Breen Office informed Warner Bros. that Ida's character could not be a prostitute nor could she be referred to as a slut. A revised script made her "a fugitive from justice."

Ida rehearsed daily with co-stars Edward G. Robinson and John Garfield. Robinson considered twenty-seven-year-old Garfield one of the best young actors he had ever encountered. Ida was also enthralled. "His real name was Julius Garfinkle. He was wonderful and I loved him. He and I were like brother and sister." She admired her new friend and the passionate political beliefs that led him to champion the economically disadvantaged. Garfield's political boldness and his cocky spirit matched Lupino's innate rebelliousness.

Hungarian-born Michael Curtiz, who would direct *The Sea Wolf*, was one of Warner Bros.' finest. Although he had the reputation of being a tyrant, he knew how to make great films. Curtiz directed Errol Flynn in *Captain Blood* and *The Adventures of Robin Hood*, which were responsible for the actor's rise to stardom. He had just completed *The Sea Hawk* with Flynn, an action picture about Elizabethan buccaneers. For *The Sea Wolf*, Curtiz used the same set, located on cavernous Stage 21. It was an architectural wonder. The stage had a tank five feet deep. Norwegian shipmaster James Madsen had supervised construction of a three-masted schooner, which measured 150 feet long with a 32-foot beam. A special thirty-eight-thousand-dollar rocking mechanism was installed in the tank, providing the realistic motion of a ship at sea. Cinematographer Sol Polito had designed a gyro camera for shooting aboard the tilting *Ghost*.

The film belonged to Robinson, but Lupino and Garfield asserted their artistic integrity, defiantly complaining when promised rewrites were not delivered on time. Ida was so upset that she traced Arthur Lyons to New York and voiced her disappointment in the studio. Lyons fired off a telegram of complaint to producer Henry Blanke. This was the first clash Ida would have over scripts. To his dismay, Jack Warner discovered that Ida was, indeed, another Bette Davis—talented and fiercely independent.

Once production was under way, Ida found Curtiz haughty and disinclined to listen to any of her suggestions. After fifty-four grueling days aboard the *Ghost*, the traditional closing party afforded a golden opportunity for revenge. The autocratic Curtiz, immaculately dressed in a white sweater and matching pants, stood on the damp set.

The crew grumbled about having the party on "this rotten tank." Someone suggested the high and mighty should get wet.

"You're looking at the two newcomers," offered Ida. She and Garfield exchanged glances.

"We'll do it!" they chorused.

They pushed Curtiz into the foul water. "Boom! He was wet," recalls Ida. The partyers grabbed drinks and food and dashed from Stage 21 as an angry Curtiz spluttered in the tank.

Reviews praised *The Sea Wolf* for its sinister and moody atmosphere, which reflected the shadowy figures who sailed aboard the doomed *Ghost*. As expected, Robinson, as the bestial yet intelligent Wolf Larsen, dominated the picture. "I'd rather rule in hell than be a servant in heaven," he says. One reviewer called the picture "Little Caesar at sea." Though overshadowed by Robinson's masterful acting, Lupino was praised as "excellent . . . the girl with a past. Her intelligent and forthright playing gives complete conviction to the role."

By the beginning of 1941, Ida Lupino was proclaimed "Hollywood's Hottest Star." Her phenomenal success had amazed both Louis and Connie. Her first year at Warner Bros. surpassed even her personal expectations.

Author William Saroyan was so impressed that he wrote, "Give Miss Lupino something to act in and there's a fifty-fifty chance that she will be the finest actress in the world."

Louis had scored high in *The Man in the Iron Mask* and *The Son of Monte Cristo* but had not come close to his wife's spectacular acclaim. Ida's triumph cast a long shadow over their marriage. She wanted to be recognized as a fine dramatic actress, but she also wanted to be a good wife; she was aware that her sudden fame denied her husband a solid identity. When Louis returned from the studio, she patiently listened to his complaints.

In interviews, Ida insisted that her marriage was more important than her career. She espoused the view that "the man is the master of the house," insisting that marriage wasn't an equal arrangement, that instead "seventy-five percent is up to the woman." She understood this wasn't a popular view. Ida professed devotion to Louis: "My husband, when I was down, was the best, most understanding person in the world." If one of them were to achieve stardom, leaving the other behind, "We'd quit," she said. "I'd still be Mrs. Louis Hayward."

Lupino's comments on marriage were quite revealing. As the precocious offspring of indulgent parents, she had never really been disciplined. As the world revolved around her, she was accustomed to getting her own way. She inherited strength and inflexible will. Only her father exerted any type of firm guidance. She believed that her willfulness argued the need for a strict hand, a male presence, so she made her husband the king of the household.

Emotionally, Ida was a jumble of contradictions, infused with the polarity often present in intensely creative individuals. On one hand, she wished to be regarded as down-to-earth, just plain Ida, the good wife; but she also wished to startle, to shock and to dominate. Her inconsistency was a personality trait that her intimate circle came to accept. As fame threatened to overwhelm her, she retreated, secluding herself at the Westridge home. The Haywards shied away from nightclubs and preferred to entertain on their own turf. Ida veered away from the starchy Hollywood circles; she viewed formal parties as dull and preferred to romp with her terrier Rowdy. She was also accompanied everywhere by a German shepherd named Duchess, a beloved pet that slept protectively at the foot of her bed.

Listening to classical music soothed her. Her record collection numbered in the hundreds; Mozart, Debussy, Beethoven,

Sibelius and Tchaikovsky were her favorite composers. She and Louis often listened to Bloch's *Hebrew Symphony*, a theme they considered romantic.

Ida loved the night, which she found to be a magical time for reflection and inspiration. She admitted: "I'd rather work all night and sleep all day . . . perhaps I was a mole in my last incarnation." She would sit at her piano in the late hours, softly inventing melodies or stretch outside in the moonlight with Duchess alongside, while Louis slept. When engaged in a film, Ida immersed herself in the characterization, adrenaline flowing, emotions charged, sleepless night after night.

Collier Young was a frequent guest at Westridge. He was Louis's friend, a witty conversationalist and a story editor at Columbia. Ida also readily welcomed Reginald Gardiner, a thespian pal and suave raconteur, who charmed people with his droll humor and sophisticated erudition. The owlish-looking Gardiner had become famous on the British stage with his clever imitation of trains, lighthouses and other objects. Ida would convulse with laughter whenever he emitted his weird noises.

Ida could be wickedly funny herself, but she publicly acknowledged her "terrible temper," and explained that she tried to control it but found that "keeping it back sometimes upsets me." Louis discovered he could lure his wife from her black moods by laughter, but her volatile fits and evanescent rages caused slammed doors and marital scars.

Ida felt more comfortable around men. The distance she kept from her fellow females masked a grave insecurity and a fear of competition. But for Ida, women, especially actresses, were a curious breed: "A woman in show business isn't honest with herself . . . so how can she be honest with another woman? We are all of us acting every minute of the day and night."

Despite her comments, Lupino's contradictory nature brought exceptions. Ann Sheridan was always a dear chum because she was "honest, feminine and yet had masculine directness." Frances Robinson was another actress Ida could count on. Robinson had been making films since the age of four, when she played in D.W. Griffith's *Orphans of the Storm* in 1922. From her office at 8619 Sunset Boulevard, Helen Ferguson represented such stars as Lupino, Barbara Stanwyck, Robert Taylor, Henry Fonda, Joan Bennett and Jeanette MacDonald. Ferguson was privy to intimate knowledge about her celebrity clients but prided herself on never betraying confidential information. Her sole responsibility was to publicize her stable of stars. She once told a reporter: "We don't deal in fiction, but we certainly present the facts as dramatically as possible." Rena Cournyn, daughter of singer Helen Morgan, was also Ida's good friend. Rena met the Lupinos through a bridge club frequented by her mother and Connie. Teenager Rena was used to show-biz glamour but found Ida entrancing: "She was so vivacious and one of the kindest people I've ever met."

In 1940, the year of Lupino's shining glory, Rita introduced her sister to a friend, Diane Meredith, a fellow dancer in Mitch Leisen's review at the Coconut Grove. At the Westridge home, Ida lounged in her dressing gown, staring with her enormous blue eyes. Recalls Meredith: "She seemed to look into my shy seventeen-year-old soul, then said, rather dramatically, 'My dear, you have something.'" Ida liked Meredith's lovely voice and looks and immediately began coaching her, giving her advice to enhance her appearance.

Meredith was admitted into the intimate Lupino circle and became a frequent guest at the informal parties Ida held at her beach home in Malibu. Meredith found Louis Hayward "reflective and poetic, too gallant, too beautiful to be true."

Meredith found the entire household a delight. Dancing was a major form of recreation. Connie daily performed her tap routine to keep fit. Rita, a magnificent dancer, would bring her mother and friends to the Westridge home for an evening of fun. After dinner, the group, led by Ida, would create and compose ballets that would be executed throughout the house. Candles would often be carried from room to room as the cast worked on pas de deux, solos and company dances. The high point of the evening was a vaudeville dance line, in which each performer would emerge and render a specialty. Ida and Connie loved to imitate the ridiculous motions of the English stage comedian, which always got laughs.

Meredith, also an actress, noticed Ida's film scripts, carefully marked with bold writing, evidence of Ida's method of developing portraits of the characters she played. All comments were carefully considered and delved deeply into the motivations and lives of those she created. Ida told Meredith that the villainess roles left her very depressed at the end of the day. "Getting in the mood of the murderer makes it very hard to get out of. I really think black thoughts, murderous thoughts," she said.

Ida could be extremely warm and confiding with her circle of friends, but, just as easily, she could display a cool reserve and an air of secrecy that kept others at a distance. Those who grew close to her were easygoing personalities who seldom ignited sparks.

Ida's best friend was her husband. They amused themselves at home, entertaining their circle with recordings of radio plays they wrote and recorded on wax discs. Ida would forward the records to friends Robert Coote and Colin Tapley, both Royal Air Force flying instructors in Saskatchewan. The airmen would then transmit the plays to Stanley in London. As 1940 came to a close, Stanley Lupino reveled in the screen triumph of his daughter. Just as he had predicted, Ida's success had been as a great dramatic actress.

Ida's first film of 1941 was slated to be *Out of the Fog*. The script was based on Irwin Shaw's successful drama *The Gentle People*, the hard-hitting story of an arrogant extortionist who terrorizes a fishing community and of Stella, a young telephone operator, who falls for Harold Goff, the smooth-talking hoodlum. The play had achieved great acclaim because of the expertise of the Group Theater, with Franchot Tone and Sylvia Sidney as leads.

When Barbara Stanwyck turned down the role of Stella, Ida jumped at it. Producer Henry Blanke asked George Raft to play the heavy, but he declined. Bogart asked for the role, but Lupino used her influence and Blanke agreed that her pal John Garfield would play the extortionist. Thomas Mitchell was cast as the victimized father and Eddie Albert was Lupino's tossed-off boyfriend. Anatole Litvak, highly regarded at Warner Bros. for such successes as *City for Conquest* and *Confessions of a Nazi Spy*, would direct.

Ida pored over her script, quite excited by the fine writing and drama in Shaw's play—an honest depiction of social injustice, a study of "gentle people" who are pushed so far they rise up to exterminate the aggressor. The screenplay by Robert Rossen, Jerry Wald and Robert Macaulay remained true to the play, maintaining as much realism as possible. However, even before the script was completed, the Breen Office reviewed the drama and found it "unacceptable . . . because it is the story of murder, which is allowed to go unpunished . . . there are, too, a number of vulgar and blasphemous lines, such as Jesus Christ, son-of-a-bitch, God-damn, lousy, bastard, etc." For the screenplay, the Breen Office sharpened its scissors. Breen sent a five page letter to Jack Warner detailing the violations.

Not surprisingly, lines such as "We can wake up in the morning with our arms around each other" and "When I get to first base, I'm going all the way home" were to be deleted. The Breen

Office objected to scenes that contained drinking, goosing, a "hot dance number" and a "toilet gag." They cautioned that if violence became "gruesome" or was "shown in frame" it would be objectionable to "political censor boards." They also asked that "Coca-Colas" be changed because use of the word violated "industry policy regarding advertising."

All references to killing a man had to be expunged and, in a final two-page critique, the office wrote, "In order not to give undue offense to the banking profession in this country, the comedy references to banks in general will be changed to a specific reference to one banker."

The Breen Office sliced the screenplay until it was a pale reflection of the original stage drama; the potent ending of justified revenge was altered so that Goff dies by accident rather than by planned retribution. When Lupino was handed the final rewrite, she complained angrily to Arthur Lyons that she had been double-crossed; though she was ill, Ida's temper flared as she expressed her bitterness. She was appalled that her character had been changed from the obviously superior original and that integral scenes had been eliminated. Lyons conveyed his client's disappointment and resentment to producer Blanke, who, fearful that Lupino would walk off the picture, told Lyons to get her ideas.

On the morning of February 14, the first day of production, Lyons spoke with a smoldering Lupino. At first Ida denied that she had any suggestions about the script. "It is not my place to make suggestions or to try to rewrite in any way," she said. When Lyons had coaxed her sufficiently, she showed her flare for analysis of character and she detailed ways in which the script could be improved. "Well, for instance," she said. "The opening scene in the cafe . . . when he is playing cards and she gives the spiel to George? That scene was taken out . . . It was a great opening for the two characters."

Ida discussed in detail specific scenes she felt enhanced the picture; she argued passionately about the original Stella. Her cruel boyfriend, Ida pointed out, is "an absolute mania with her—an absolute fixation in her mind. He is life to her . . . her whole existence. He typifies everything she has wanted," she told Lyons. "It was a wonderful scene that Jerry Wald wrote which they took out. Something like this: 'Are you in love with him?' 'I think I'm nuts about him. Every time I walk down the street beside him I feel hot all over—because I feel every minute might be his last.'"

Ida described for Lyons Stella's motivation. "That builds the whole character about this girl—it doesn't make her a bitch. It isn't because she wants to get out of Brooklyn. She is crazy about him. She is crazy about the exciting life he can give her. She probably knows he won't marry her and she might wind up taking dope in China, but she would have gone with him anywhere and he gave her everything she wanted."

Lyons transcribed the conversation and forwarded it verbatim to Henry Blanke. The producer agreed that Ida's comments were astute. Deleted scenes were returned. Lupino went to work with earnest inventiveness on Stage 21, which had been transformed by art director Carl Weyl into a block of buildings resembling Sheepshead Bay, Brooklyn. Blowers were positioned sixty feet above the huge tank to release carbon dioxide vapor, which created a heavy fog. Cinematographer James Wong Howe had the water dyed; the blue-black waves reflected light better and photographed more realistically. When it came to photographing Lupino, he was just as precise. His strategy was designed to enhance her beautiful eyes. He took the point off her chin by high-angle lighting and broadened her cheeks and throat by the artful creation of shadow. Ida appreciated Howe's painstaking efforts to make her look good. He would thereafter be her favorite cinematographer on the Warner lot.

By March 4, director Anatole Litvak was causing headaches for the studio's front office. Hal Wallis had been viewing the footage and didn't like what he had seen. He sent a memo advising the director to restrain Garfield's acting, which Wallis felt was exaggerated; he suggested that Garfield was reaching for his lines, an indication that the actor did not know his dialogue.

Jack Warner had also been scrutinizing the daily production reports, and he was amazed. Litvak's technique of shooting the same scene over and over drove Warner into a frenzy. He wrote to Litvak: "It is ridiculous that you, as an important director, cannot understand that if you get the scene right the first time, stop and go to your next scene." Warner accused Litvak of "wearing out the actors, causing a furor" and forcing Warner himself to leave the city "to get my nerves together after going through two weeks of pressure that I have never gone through before."

In March, Ida became seriously ill with a streptococcus infection and broke out in a rash and suffered from a fever. Warner Bros. sent a studio physician to verify her illness. When it looked as though she would have to be replaced, she recovered and was able to continue with the project.

Veteran character actor John Qualen enjoyed watching from the shadows as Ida acted before the camera. "When she goes into a character, it's not like she's acting. It is like she is really that person."

During production John Garfield received a congratulatory telegram from Eleanor Roosevelt commending him for his assistance to the Committee to Aid Chinese Industrial Cooperatives, one of his many efforts toward social improvement.

On the film's release, the publicity department proclaimed "Lupino and Garfield—Most Exciting New Screen Team!" *Out of the Fog* opened to good reviews. "A moving and thought-provoking drama. . . . Lupino created another outstanding character in her repertoire of tragic and oblique women, etches unforgettable. John Garfield makes his satanic portrayal the essence of symbolic villainy," said *Variety*. Warner's avalanche of press releases concentrated on Ida's peculiarities, with her approval. "Ida Lupino is afraid of the dark, picking up germs, being locked in a room. . . . By her own admission Miss Lupino is forever dramatizing herself—even in private."

Dramatizing life, Ida explained, kept her interested in it.

5

THE HARD WAY

We are making the pictures and financing them and, in our opinion, she is not miscast. —HAL WALLIS

Ida was chosen for the plum role in *Ladies in Retirement*. The play was a well-crafted psychological thriller starring Flora Robson as a murderess. The lead role was that of a woman of sixty, but producer Lester Cowan decided to take a chance on twenty-three-year-old Lupino. Harry Cohn exploded: "You are out of your mind choosing this child to play that role." Ida was taking a big risk. Robson had been acclaimed on Broadway, and comparisons were inevitable. Director Charles Vidor wanted Ida to appear about forty years old. Ida wore scant makeup, pulled back her hair in a severe style, and cinematographer Charles Barnes lit her face with a high light to wash out the softness. "I'll do what I can with my camera," he told her, "but nearly everything depends on your performance." Outwardly, Ida was calm, but within were jangled nerves and a touch of fear. Louis Hayward was also in the picture, but Ida distanced herself from competing with her husband. She explained that acting techniques were different. Hayward simply memorized his lines, then depended on inspiration. As for Ida: "I take a script and mull over it and underline the bits I want to emphasize. When I go to the set, I know exactly what I want to do." She insisted both methods seemed to work and that they never argued about it.

The cast of *Ladies in Retirement* included Isabel Elsom as Miss Fiske, the tyrannical proprietress of a gloomy farmhouse. Elsa Lanchester and Edith Barrett were mad sisters, and Louis played Miss Fiske's dashing, worthless nephew.

Ida's performance was one of her greatest. Her restraint as the cold-blooded Ellen made her all the more frightening. The most memorable scene is Lupino dispatching the giddy blackmailer, who sits at the piano playing "Tit Willow." From behind, she approaches with a rope, steely-eyed and calm. A gasp is heard. The pearls from Miss Fiske's necklace fall to the floor, one by one, like drops of blood. Lupino's masterful acting left audiences spellbound.

Ida, now a spectacular success, renegotiated her contract with Warner Bros. Her salary was boosted to three thousand dollars a week, and she had won the right to appear in four outside pictures. Her triumph was sweet until July 1, when the studio assigned her the role of Cassie in *King's Row*. She read the script, then ruefully responded that the part was too small and the billing too low.

A few days later, Ida injured her knee. Warner Bros. sent its own physician to Ida's home; his opinion was that she could return in eight to ten days. Ida was furious, incensed at suspicions that she was malingering to avoid the unwanted role. She protested that she had already missed a Fox picture that would have teamed her with Tyrone Power. She was then assigned to *Captain of the Clouds*, a James Cagney action spectacle. She refused to do it, complaining that the part was insignificant.

Arthur Lyons came to see his stubborn client and advised her in a fatherly fashion that she should cooperate with the studio and have confidence in casting decisions. Lyons departed at two o'clock in the morning, beaten by her arguments. By the end of August he was again trying to persuade her to appear in *King's Row*. He spoke with her for two hours on the telephone, urging her to break the impasse and return to work. She seemed to bend a little, but the agent's hopes were shattered when she called back, and repeated her argument. She said she could not feel the part of Cassandra, nor could she see herself doing it.

Warner Bros. placed her on suspension. Ann Sheridan was assigned the lead role with Ronald Reagan as co-star. Betty Field played Cassandra. Based on Henry Bellamann's bestseller about the decadence of a small community, *King's Row* became a box office success. Reagan, who played the victim of an unscrupulous doctor, who had needlessly amputated his legs, uttered the memorable lines: "Where's the rest of me?" Sheridan, as Reagan's poor but honest girlfriend, made the role one of her best. Ida later wrote in a telegram to Arthur Lyons, "Having my professional linen washed in the press concerning Cassandra—has been embarrassing and uncalled for and is about all I care to take."

The remainder of Ida's telegram was about *Juke Girl*, a script of which she'd received in September. She said she found it interesting but that the character she was being asked to play was "something I am totally unfamiliar with. Neither am I physically right for it or my accent." She tried to soften her criticism by saying, "However, I am so fed up with being a supposed heavy that anything will do."

She didn't mean that, though. The next day Ida sent Lyons another telegram. "I am so sorry to have put it this way," it read, "but if you think enough of me as you say you do, do not think I could do that picture." She sent Lyons back to Warners for more negotiations. "I cannot face another Warner Bros. session," she concluded.

Ida could be adamant, as Lyons discovered. He forwarded the telegram to studio executives. Shortly after his return to Los Angeles, he opened his door one morning to find Ida. They went over the script for *Juke Girl*, and Lyons agreed that his client was miscast and that the character was completely foreign to her. Lyons composed a three-page telegram to Hal Wallis detailing his client's reasons for refusing to accept the role; specifically, that she could not protect herself intelligently "so as to be able to uphold her position in the industry and turn in a part which would be a credit to her and to Warner Bros." Lyons backed his client forcefully, charging that the studio had failed to give Lupino the recognition that was due her as an actress and had made the conflict public unnecessarily.

Lyons pointed out that every time the studio used Ida in a picture, it made a cash profit of sixty thousand dollars and that outside producers were offering her as much as seventy-five thousand to do a picture. In fact, said Lyons, even these high sums were rejected by his client if the scripts did not suit her.

When Lyons's telegram reached the desk of Hal Wallis, the situation became even more heated. Wallis felt that the gauntlet had not only been tossed but flung in his face. He instructed attorney Roy Obringer "to reject categorically and individually" the arguments Lyons had put forth. Wallis even gave Obringer a list of specific points to mention in his reply.

Two days later, Obringer sent Lyons a stern letter threatening to cancel Lupino's contract. Wallis had directed Obringer to convey, in response to Lyons's claims that Ida had been miscast, that "in the last two pictures she played the part of a murderess and I cannot believe that Lyons would want to intimate that she did know about a murder but would not know about a juke girl." He questioned Lyons's professional judgment and criticized Ida's unwillingness to cooperate "despite the fact that she does not have story approval, and also the fact that recognized artists are playing both parts rejected by her." He pointed out that Ann Sheridan, who was "in a fairly good position insofar as her career is concerned," had accepted the part of the juke girl. As for Lupino, "Whether or not she is miscast is a matter of opinion, and we are making the pictures and financing them and, in our opinion, she is not miscast." Finally, Wallis refused to consider how valuable Ida might be to the studio in terms of profits generated. "We do not deal in cash profits on artists' salaries."

Ida was not fazed. She refused to be intimidated into playing a part she didn't like. Ann Sheridan and Ronald Reagan made *Juke Girl,* but this time the magic was missing and the picture was a dismal flop and an embarrassment to both performers for years to come.

The friction began to dissipate when Ida was allowed to appear in *Forever and a Day,* a star-studded tribute to Britain's wartime courage. Actor-director Cedric Hardwicke had personally asked Ida to join the production and had gone to Jack Warner himself for approval. The studio had agreed to allow Ida to participate if she worked for free with American profits donated to charity.

Warners hoped to force their recalcitrant actress to return to the fold by penalizing her monetarily. Though Ida was on suspension, she was nonetheless earning a considerable sum of money from radio shows and outside movies, to the studio executives' consternation. One radio performance could bring her as much as six thousand dollars. Despite the suspension from Warner Bros., her 1941 income was $106,333.

Lyons met with Jack Warner for a crucial summit. Warner pulled out a photograph of Abraham Lincoln. Lyons read the quote emblazoned on it: "You can only fool some of the people some of the time." Unlike the brilliant but autocratic Hal Wallis, who wanted to terminate Lupino's contract, Jack Warner could be flexible when he felt it was in the studio's interest. He left Lupino on suspension and agreed to find a script they both liked. In December, Ida received a script of *The Hard Way*; she was enthusiastic. By the end of the year, her career crisis at Warner Bros. had ended. But Ida had other worries.

The Haywards felt that America would soon be at war. Ida studied nursing and enlisted in the Women's Ambulance and Defense Corps. She immersed herself in first aid and studied medical textbooks late into the night. Ida impressed her friends with her vast knowledge of diseases and cures. On December 6, 1941, Louis Hayward became an American citizen. The following day the Japanese bombed Pearl Harbor. Without fanfare, Louis quietly enlisted in the U.S. Marines. Now, not only her father, but her husband, would be dodging bombs. But Stanley Lupino's days were numbered.

Stanley confided to Ida that he had cancer. He asked her to keep the news a secret. Ida now grew anxious with the fear that her father might never recover. But Stanley carried on, as he always did, entertaining his besieged countrymen. In August, he launched *Lady Behave* with Sally Gray as his co-star. The show was London's first major musical since the war began. During the early weeks of German bombing the theaters had been closed; theaters in the West End were pitted with shrapnel. Despite the rain of terror from the skies, the Lupinos were in the forefront of entertaining the nation. Lupino Lane was a smash as Bill Snibson in *Me and My Girl*; the musical comedy had opened in December 1937 and ran for 1,646 performances.

The British revered their entertainers, who kept the spirit of the nation high. The esteem and affection felt for Stanley Lupino brought reports that he would soon be knighted. The public was aware of his sacrifices as an air raid warden. In fact, he had written *Lady Behave* in his assigned shelter. As he labored on a scene, a wounded boy lay quietly at his side, his head resting on the manuscript. Stanley took the script, blood-stained and flecked with candle wax, to his church for a blessing. *Lady Behave* was the tale of a struggling actress who refuses to marry her stuntman boyfriend until she becomes a success. The comedy opened to a packed house at His Majesty's Theatre, a wonderful triumph. Stanley was hoisted atop the shoulders of elated fans and paraded through the aisles as a hero. Even the king and queen attended, and they invited Stanley into their private box to thank him personally for braving the blitz, onstage and off.

Despite his advancing cancer, Stanley courageously tried to continue in the show. He fought constant pain. His concentration wavered. Several times, the curtain was brought down prematurely, which must have pained Stanley dearly, for he believed fervently that he must never disappoint the audience or his fellow players. In September, he was forced to quit the show to undergo a serious operation. Stanley Lupino would never return to the stage again.

While Ida had been waging her war with Warner Bros., her friend Mark Hellinger had packed his suitcase. After *High Sierra*, the disgruntled producer, feeling unappreciated, sought greener pastures. At Twentieth Century-Fox, Darryl Zanuck handed him *Moontide*, a script by a first-time writer for which he had paid thirty thousand dollars. The author, Willard Robertson, was a character actor who had penned his book to escape boredom while on location in *Brigham Young, Frontiersman*. *Moontide* was the tawdry tale of an alcoholic Frenchman who falls for Ada, a hashhouse waitress.

The melodrama appealed to Ida, who readily agreed when Hellinger asked her to play Ada. Darryl Zanuck personally selected rugged Jean Gabin for the role of Bobo, the dock worker who falls in love with Ida's character. Gabin spoke little English but was famous for the 1936 *Pepe le Moko* and *Grand Illusion* in 1939, Jean Renoir's famous antiwar masterpiece. Gabin's hard-edged face and solid physique gave him a distinctive working-class image and considerable romantic appeal. Hellinger cast Thomas Mitchell as Tiny, the sly blackmailer who tries to extort affection from Bobo's wife; it became the distinguished actor's first "rat role."

To prepare for portraying his seedy character, Gabin wanted to explore the underbelly of America. Ida led him on a rather dangerous tour of Main Street in Los Angeles, where he got a firsthand look at vice and violence. They began at a training gym for boxers, then drifted through bargain shops where the poor pawed over cheap items. On the sidewalk they passed drifters, derelicts, alcoholics and prostitutes. They paused in a skid row bar to observe the clientele. A drunken ex-dancer accused them of slumming. The woman stumbled through a dance routine, then, in a sudden fit of anger, emptied a bottle of cheap perfume in Ida's lap, ruining her dress. The pitiful denizens of the bar returned to their booze. Ida and Gabin continued their tour. In a park inhabited by winos they studied a filthy elderly man, bearded and broken in spirit. Lupino and Gabin had seen what they wanted.

Moontide was adapted for the screen by noted author John O'Hara. Fox asked for permission to set up cameras in San Pedro harbor, but because of strict defense preparations, the request was denied. A forty-seven-thousand-dollar harbor was built on the studio back lot. Ida found the picture tough work. Director Archie Mayo insisted on realism, to Ida's despair. The worst moment came when the blackmailer beat her, then stuffed her into a tank filled with live bait. Ida's reaction to the stench was exactly what Mayo had hoped to capture.

Another difficult scene called for Ida to struggle in the ocean. Early one morning, attired in a cheap gingham dress, she eased into Fox's expensive harbor, into an oily scum that floated on the surface along with chunks of watermelon rind and seaweed. The foul water was disgusting. With paddles attached to their feet, prop men churned the muck to make it seem that waves were rising. Only after gulping a shot of brandy was Ida able to play the scene.

Thomas Mitchell was working simultaneously in *This Above All*, another Fox picture starring Joan Fontaine, an actress Ida had known and liked since Louis appeared with her in *The Duke of West Point*. Fontaine and her hairdresser, Irene Beshon, were on their way to lunch when Beshon tripped over a cable and injured her leg. Ida examined her and discovered a sliced vein; she improvised a bandage, then had her patient carried inside Fontaine's dressing room to await the studio doctor. Ida was immensely proud of the help she'd been able to offer.

While working on their respective films, Lupino and Fontaine met regularly, sharing laughs and the latest news. They wrote amusing accounts of each other, profiles that were subsequently published in the movie magazine *Hollywood*. Lupino's comments: "I started off not liking Joan Fontaine a bit. I don't know why I disliked her. Perhaps it was because I suspected that her demure manner covered a penetrating directness. It shocks me when I meet someone as direct as I am. Now that I know that she is strictly mad, I like Joan very much." Fontaine wrote: "Ida Lupino is the nearest thing to a caged tiger I ever saw outside a zoo. I don't think she has ever been still a whole minute of her life. At midnight she still burns with energy that won't let her rest. She wanders about the house from couch to couch. Nobody knows where she will be found in the morning. Of course, Ida isn't normal. No one ever accused her of that. One of her peculiarities is that she does everything well."

Lupino's career sailed aloft as *Moontide* was praised for cinematic power. After the bitter rift with Warner Bros., Ida knew that *The Hard Way* was a critical juncture in her relationship with the studio. She studied the script late into the night, memorizing every line to perfection. She wanted to please and assured Arthur Lyons that all would go well, that she felt the role was ideal for her. Outwardly, she exhibited a cool facade of self-assurance, but inwardly she churned with worry.

Stanley had returned home a convalescent, his health in obvious decline, although he told family members that the operation had been trivial. But when he failed to return to his beloved stage, Ida knew that he was very ill and was hiding the facts of his condition. She suffered fits of anxiety, sleepless nights and guilt.

Ida had not forgiven the studio's treatment of her, but she felt lucky to receive a role in *The Hard Way*. Jerry Wald had written an intriguing story about a vicious, domineering woman who ruthlessly advances her younger sister's career in show business. Rumor circulated that the story was a thinly disguised version of the life of a famous actress. Wald chose Irwin Shaw to write the screenplay, then struggled to generate interest in the script. The project had a circuitous history. Wald had sent the script to Ginger Rogers, but she turned it down in favor of a Leo McCarey film. In December, Wald sent the script to agent Frank Vincent as a possibility for Cary Grant and Rosalind Russell. Wald asked powerful Hal Wallis to help him interest Grant; to the producer's surprise, Wallis responded that he had tried for months to interest Grant in *The Man Who Came to Dinner* and *The Constant Nymph* without success. Warners announced that the production would begin with Olivia de Havilland and John Garfield in the lead roles, but the casting fell through.

Vincent Sherman found the script in his hands. After directing *The Return of Doctor X*, he was regarded as a marvel. The studio had considered *Doctor X* an insignificant "B" film, but it had filled theaters, prompting Jack Warner to sit up and take notice. Sherman, a native of Georgia, had given up a law career to become an actor. While he was performing at the Biltmore Theater in Los Angeles, producer Bryan Foy came backstage; Sherman interested him in a few story ideas and was offered two weeks of writing work at Warners. He stayed for fifteen years. As a former actor, he had a great affinity for his casts, and after *Doctor X.* he was especially favored by Humphrey Bogart.

Sherman was a director on the way up. After completing *Underground,* he was crossing the lot when Mike Curtiz, a man he regarded as a genius of the cinema, approached. In his thick Hungarian accent, the gruff Curtiz exclaimed: "I see this picture you make—very good! Full of vitality!" Hal Wallis also recognized the thirty-three-year-old as a bright talent. He assigned *The Hard Way* to Sherman, to the latter's surprise.

Sherman and Danny Fuchs did a rewrite, but a month before production began, the Breen Office performed its usual purification and complained of "sex affairs." The expression "bore the pants off me" was cited as unacceptable. Even after filming began on March 5, 1942, further rewrites were necessary. When Irwin Shaw learned of the rewrites, he was furious and demanded that his name be removed from the credits.

The final story unfolds with beautiful Helen Chernen; she walks to a pier, tosses her fur coat into the water, then jumps, in an attempt to commit suicide. From a hospital bed, she recounts her struggle to help her sister Katherine escape the soot and coal dust of a dirty mining town.

At the studio, Ida felt that Jack Warner eyed her as though she were a convict on parole; she was eager to get under way. But Ida's relationship with the director rapidly began to slide downhill. Sherman wanted her to be tough and nasty.

"Oh, I'm such a bitch in this," she complained.

"That's what I want," he assured her.

Joan Leslie, only seventeen years old, had a true challenge portraying the talented sister who becomes bitter and corrupt. Despite her youth, Leslie had played James Cagney's wife in *Yankee*

Doodle Dandy. Sherman asked if the young girl could handle such a difficult part. Cagney expressed reservations; he thought she would be ideal for the first half of the story but was skeptical about the transformation into a dissolute woman of the world. Sherman, though he had doubts, kept her in the picture.

Lupino and Leslie, as screen sisters, had to develop a rapport. The film contained moments of great drama, such as the scene in which Helen convinces her naive sister to leave her vaudevillian husband for greater success.

Lupino's worry manifested itself in illness. Only a week after *The Hard Way* began, she was admitted to Cedars of Lebanon and diagnosed as suffering from exhaustion and emotionally drained. For two years she had mercilessly pushed herself, working steadily. Her father was dying, and she couldn't tell Connie because she was sworn to secrecy. The studio was told she needed a six-month rest. Jerry Wald tried to coax her back to work. But Ida pleaded for time to rest.

Wald arranged for two weeks off. On leave from the Marines, Louis took his exhausted wife to agent Noll Gurney's home in Palm Springs. By April, Roy Obringer suggested that Lupino be replaced by Ann Sheridan. Jack Warner didn't agree and allowed Ida to remain in the film; he even sent flowers, a kind gesture that Ida genuinely appreciated.

After a brief rest, she penned a note to Jerry Wald, thanking him for the vacation. Ida informed Wald that she was working on a story in her isolated desert cabin. The quietness of the desert brought thoughts of her father, ill and far away.

Wald wanted everything to go smoothly for Ida's return on May 4. When he got news that James Wong Howe was being taken off the picture and assigned to *Casablanca*, he went directly to Jack Warner and explained that Lupino had pleaded to have Howe as cinematographer. Warner sent Howe back to *The Hard Way*. But only a day later, unit manager Al Alleborn was prodding Howe to rush things. Reported Alleborn: "I explained to him that he must step along and not pay much attention to the photography in this picture and that it is not a cameraman's picture."

Problems were mounting for Vincent Sherman. Joan Leslie, still a minor, could only work until 5:00 P.M., with four hours off for schooling each day. The picture was slipping behind schedule, and the situation was made worse by Ida's poor health. On May 8, Al Alleborn recorded: "Ida is in one of her spells today, and very difficult for her to memorize lines."

Sherman asked his cast for a great deal of trust. In the early scenes, he wanted to capture the bleak atmosphere of the dreary coal town; he insisted on realism even to the point of asking cinematographer Howe to place agricultural smudge pots on the set so the cast could smell the unpleasant odor and feel the griminess of their empty lives. Sherman insisted that Lupino wear no makeup for these scenes. Ida reluctantly complied, but she felt lost, as if her character were one-dimensional. Sherman asked for faith in his judgment. He knew how good she was; he praised her skill and insisted her portrayal was right on the mark.

Day after day, Ida struggled through her scenes; she developed a bad cold and sore throat. She came to work anyway. The front office sent a nurse to the set to insure that she remained before the camera. As the days dragged on, Ida grew more irritable and tense. She carried in her heart pain and anguish caused by a terrible burden.

On June 10, Stanley Lupino died. Though he had known the end was near, he had continued working. His last weeks were spent completing *The Love Racket*, a stage drama he wrote for Ida. He signed it with a pseudonym, avoiding his own name because it was associated with comedy. He became critically ill and lay down his pen forever to enter a hospital in Balham. Three days later, at age forty-eight, he passed away.

News of his death reached Connie at her Hollywood home. She hurriedly dressed in the predawn blackness and drove down Sunset Boulevard to Mandeville Canyon and turned up the narrow road to Westridge. She quietly entered the darkened house. Ida was asleep in her bedroom. She tapped on Louis's door and tearfully whispered the news. They huddled in the den. Finally, Louis entered his wife's bedroom. She had an early studio call and the alarm was set for 5:30 A.M. Louis turned off the alarm, then returned to Connie.

"You'll have to tell her," he said.

Connie nodded. They heard Ida stirring in her bed. When her mother came through the doorway, Ida instinctively knew.

"Daddy?" she asked. Connie's response brought a stunned silence, then Ida wept uncontrollably. On June 13, England's most famous comedian was laid to rest. Before the hearse departed for Lambeth Cemetery, the Lupinos gathered at Leigham Court Road. But his wife and daughters were far away. Barry Lupino led the mourners as the cortege slowly wound its way to Tooting where the streets were lined with a vast crowd offering a final tribute. Nearby were the tombs of Mark Lupino and Dan Leno.

Though his death was attributed to cancer, the Lupino clan believed that Stanley had drastically shortened his life by passionate devotion to his country. Ida was immensely proud of her father and believed that he had sacrificed his life as surely as any soldier on the battlefield. She took comfort in a religious poem Stanley had written.

> He gave me all the world and put me in it
> He gave me the use of everything that's there
> The sun, the moon, the starlight and the flowers
> The grass, the trees, the heaven-wafted air . . .

Not only was Stanley gone but the family home as well. Nazi bombers nightly attacked Croydon Airfield, and the neighborhood was in their path. Blasts had severely damaged the foundation; windows had been shattered, and sections of the roof had been blown away. The Stanley Royal, once the Tom Thumb Theatre, was only a shell, soon to be rubble.

Stanley's will left 62,312 pounds, the home and personal possessions. The proceeds of a ten-thousand-pound insurance policy was left to Sally Gray. The young actress had suffered an emotional collapse, reported London newspapers.

A week after her father's death, Ida returned to work. Al Alleborn reported to the front office that Lupino had arrived on the set at 9:15 A.M. and she soon became hysterical. Friends rallied to her side, offering support and sympathy. It was the least they could do, thought Geraldine Fitzgerald. "She always tried to help everybody who was her friend. She was so devoted to her father and shattered by his death."

When she was finally able to return to the production, Ida's relationship with Vincent Sherman worsened. She had viewed the previous footage and was upset, believing that all the characters in the film were too down-beaten. She felt they were all misfits and was perplexed how an audience could ever sympathize with any of the characters. During a critical scene, as Sherman patiently tried to explain what he wanted, she blew up.

"This picture stinks!" she shouted, "and I'm going to stink in it!"

Sherman assured her that she was excellent, but by the last ten days they communicated through an assistant director. The difficult production finally closed on June 27, nineteen days behind schedule.

Ida was emotionally devastated. Not even Connie could calm her. "Poor little thing," said her mother. "She was always like that about her daddy from the time she was a baby. It was like she drew something from him, and when he was gone she was just helpless. Lying there moaning and crying, and I couldn't comfort her."

Ida read and reread Stanley's last letter. He had praised her fine acting in *Ladies in Retirement*, and said that she was truly beginning to fulfill her destiny as an actress. Ida despaired that her mentor and guide was gone. Then eerie things began to happen. Ida vaguely sensed Stanley's presence. As she told Harry Mines, one afternoon she returned home and was told that a stranger had visited. Her maid described a short man with jet black hair and a pencil behind his ear; he had asked for Ida in a voice with a British accent.

From the ashes of her father's death a dream took flight. Ida wanted to be a director. She had worked with the best and had learned from each. She had theories she wanted to test. But she had another reason: "It would give me a chance to take some promising youngster, some girl with talent, and mold her into a fine actress. I imagine there is great satisfaction in something like that." Though she was only twenty-four years old, she knew she could direct a picture and she passed the word on.

Vincent Sherman readied a final print of *The Hard Way*. He knew he had a good picture. Filled with enthusiasm, he and Jerry Wald took the film to Jack Warner's home for a private screening. When the lights came on afterward, Sherman eagerly scanned Warner's face. Instead of joy, he saw a scowl there.

"Holy God," Warner sighed, "I'm afraid we've got a flop on our hands."

Sherman couldn't believe what he had heard.

"Ah, Vince," Warner said, "who cares about these dirty people in the coal mines?"

Sherman's heart sank. This was his chance to move into A-films. He had worked his heart out over the production. The star had been unimpressed, too.

Though Ida was superb as the domineering sister who relentlessly pushes her sibling, at the premiere, she squirmed in her seat.

She had never felt comfortable watching herself, but this was unbearable. "I'm going to leave," she whispered to Connie. She walked
out in the middle of the picture and Connie followed; she was so
angry she would not speak to her daughter for two days.

Ironically, Ida's performance brought her accolades. She won
the New York Film Critics Award for her brilliant performance.
She had triumphed over such contenders as Joan Fontaine in *The
Constant Nymph*, Ingrid Bergman in *For Whom the Bell Tolls*, Claudette
Colbert in *So Proudly We Hail* and Lucille Watson in *Watch on the
Rhine*.

When *The Hard Way* opened to rave reviews, Sherman was
already busy directing Bette Davis and Miriam Hopkins in *Old
Acquaintance*. He had his hands full, with the actresses fighting. Mark
Hellinger telephoned him with the news that *The Hard Way* was
breaking records. Hellinger asked Sherman to patch things up with
Lupino. Despite the live-wire tension during the final days of the
production, Sherman understood temperamental stars. He telephoned. Ida was charming, as if they had never quarreled. Sherman
smiled to himself.

"Oh, darling, how are you?" she asked.

Sherman congratulated her. Thereafter, they became the best
of friends.

6

DEVOTION

I'm coming wherever you are if I can see you for an hour. —MRS. LOUIS HAYWARD

The New York Film Critics Award was, thus far, the crowning achievement in Lupino's career. Yet Stanley wasn't there to share the glory. Neither was Louis, who was on active duty in Quantico, Virginia. Ida burned with an intense hatred of Germany and Japan. She roused herself from the deep lethargy brought by her father's death and devoted free hours to the Women's Defense Ambulance Corps, installing a switchboard in her home to monitor emergency calls. Ida seldom refused any patriotic request; she assisted the Red Cross, the USO, China Relief, Bundles for Britain and other groups. After radio shows, she always urged listeners to purchase U.S. Savings Bonds. When the first contingent of RAF fliers graduated from flight school in Lancaster, California, she braved the cold wind to cheer them. She would have enlisted for combat had women been allowed to risk their lives on the battlefield. She considered joining the service, but Warner Bros. explained that she did more by boosting morale than she would by firing a rifle.

One evening Ida attended a concert conducted by Leopold Stokowski that featured the music of Russian composer Dimitri Shostakovich. The concert was a patriotic event honoring Russia, whose soldiers had valiantly fought the Nazis on their own soil. The honored guest was a young woman whose husband and child had been murdered by the invaders after which she had become a deadly sniper. Ida was amazed by her bravery. "She shot hundreds and hundreds of Germans, God bless her," she said. "But they shouldn't make her wear evening dresses. She belongs in her uniform. I wonder how a woman has been made to feel by those beasts before she can kill and kill like that?"

With the threat of gasoline rationing, Ida moved closer to the studios, relocating to a second home at 1405 Miller Drive in the hills above Sunset Boulevard. Connie and Rita shared the residence, and the women grew vegetables in their Victory Garden. They held open house on Sundays, and guests arrived by the dozens. One afternoon, Harry Mines brought famous ballerina Alicia Markova, who was nursing an injured leg. Ida graciously looked after the lonely dancer.

Ida was enthusiastic about her next project, *Life Begins at 8:30*. The screenplay was based on Emlyn Williams's London play *The Light of Heart*, the story of an alcoholic actor, once famous as "Mr. Theater," who is reduced to playing Santa Claus in a department store. Not long before his death, Stanley had written that he hoped they might one day appear together in the play. Distinguished white-bearded Monty Woolley was cast as the pompous actor who loves the bottle.

Ida was to play his shy, devoted daughter, who is disabled by a clubfoot. The role of Madden Thomas was perfectly tailored for the dapper Woolley, who could portray blustering, self important characters like no one else. On Broadway, he had been acclaimed as the caustic wheelchair-bound Sheridan Whiteside in *The Man Who Came to Dinner.*

At Twentieth Century-Fox, Ida felt more relaxed. By the time the cameras rolled on July 27, she and Monty were fast friends.

Ida's obsession with perfection led to her wearing an orthopedic boot during her month at Fox to enhance the screen impression that she was lame. Afterward, her foot muscles were inflamed and sore.

Diane Meredith had been amazed when she saw Ida's script. It was filled with comments sketching the psychology of the character: "This girl is crippled. She had been crippled since birth; however, she would walk in a way that does not indicate she is aware of it. It has become part of her daily life. Her limp is therefore, ignored." *Life Begins at 8:30* brought a round of bravos to the leads. Lupino was praised for the story's most poignant moment, when she confronts her father with the truth, that he was responsible for her lameness, because he had dropped his baby daughter while drunk.

At Warners, Lupino brightened over her role in *Devotion*, a biography of the Brontë sisters. Ida knew the story of their lonely life in Haworth Parsonage where their stern father was rector. Ida was cast as Emily, with Olivia de Havilland and Nancy Coleman rounding out the trio. Lupino and de Havilland began researching the period, immersing themselves in Brontë biographies. Olivia bought costume designer Milo Anderson a rare, three-volume set of *The World of Fashion, 1834.* Ida's enthusiasm was infectious, until the final script arrived. To her disappointment the screenplay deviated considerably from the facts, resulting in a concocted tale of Emily and Charlotte loving the same man.

Ida and Olivia marched to the front office to argue for historical accuracy. Ida wanted a pet mastiff and a falcon; Olivia insisted on glasses and a blonde wig. But Jack Warner wouldn't budge. The duo roamed the studio mischievously denouncing the cast. Word of their dissatisfaction spread and they became known to the supervisors as "the de Havilland-Lupino underground movement."

Stage 21 was designed to resemble the Yorkshire moors. One of Ida's early scenes called for her to descend a path with her dog. Instead of the desired mastiff, Ida was handed a sheepdog named Veronica. As the cameras rolled, she became entangled with the dog and tumbled wildly. The scene was the highlight of the annual Warner Christmas party, when the studio entertained theater owners from around the country, allowing them to meet the stars whose films they exhibited. The highlight of the party was the screening of outtakes, usually of stars forgetting their lines and cursing.

Despite her personal feelings about the poor script, director Curtis Bernhardt found Ida artistically accessible and liked her sense of humor. De Havilland found her screen sister a hard and faithful worker.

On December 6, 1942, gas rationing began. It was also the day Reginald Gardiner disappeared from date books as "Hollywood's Number One Bachelor." Ida's close friend had romanced such beauties as Hedy Lamarr, Marlene Dietrich and Frances Robinson before falling for Russian model Nadia Petrova. Ida was one of the first of their circle to meet Gardiner's fiancee. Nadia liked her immediately: "When Ida and Reggie got together it was laughter, laughter, laughter." Ida was asked to serve as matron of honor. The aristocracy of filmdom gathered at the Beverly Hills Presbyterian Church on Rodeo Drive to witness the nuptials. Among the many notables were Mary Pickford, Norma Shearer, Greer Garson and Basil Rathbone. Photographers clamored for pictures as Ida and Nadia arrived.

Ida grew nervous when she realized she had to walk alone down the aisle, before the elite. In the church vestibule, she froze.

Gardiner and the best man, director Robert Stevenson, waited anxiously at the altar. As organ music droned on, heads began to turn. Nadia was astonished. The fearless actress insisted they go up the aisle side by side. Seeing Ida shaking made Nadia nervous. Finally, the impatient minister came and pushed Ida down the aisle, to Nadia's relief: "As she walked ahead of me, I could see her little fanny shaking like a leaf."

As Ida toiled on the set of *Devotion*, she received word that Louis would be home for Christmas. She pleaded with the front office for a week off. The studio reluctantly granted her wish, realizing she would simply "get sick" if refused. The blissful week brought dire news. Louis was being sent overseas.

The Haywards had faced many of the hazards inherent in a Hollywood marriage. The survival of their union was no accident; they had made many concessions. They had weathered fiery clashes and a serious separation. But Ida loved Louis very much and was distraught to hear he might soon depart for combat. They said goodbye. Ida told Louis she would think only positive thoughts, but she agonized about the dangers facing her husband.

In the winter of 1943, Ida Lupino was a unique symbol of triumph. She was successful, beautiful and always made good copy for writers. Though she professed to be publicity shy, Ida was quite outspoken. She allowed Adela Rogers St. John, a veteran reporter, to follow her for a story in *Cosmopolitan*. An interview with Lupino was no small feat, as St. John discovered. "Getting Ida on the telephone is one of Hollywood's major achievements and her excuses, conveyed by bewildered maids or her equally bewildered mother Connie, have become collector's items among her friends. The cat is having kittens; Ida is combing the hills for a runaway dog; Ida heard a shot up the canyon and has gone to investigate."

Once inside the Westridge retreat, the journalist felt comfortable. The house lacked the sleek, polished look she had come to expect in the homes of Hollywood stars. The fragrance of eucalyptus filled the den and a fire crackled. Duchess yawned before the flames, and an orange cat, Rimske Of Course Of Course, sat atop a pillow. Books and phonograph records were piled on chairs and on the floor. A typewriter sat on a cardtable, with sheets of paper strewn about. Colorful flowers floated in copper bowls.

Ida sat on a sofa, barefoot, knees pulled up, fiddling with her hair, which she wore in tiny braids with red ribbons. She looked about fourteen, mused St. John. "Her eyes were enormous and desperate . . . tragic eyes." Those making Ida's acquaintance were always startled by her luminous blue eyes; they were so large they seemed to stare, an effect that was enhanced by her habit of locking eyes with the person to whom she was speaking. An adept reporter, St. John simply listened and tried not to miss a detail.

Connie chatted away about the British theater. "The audience roared for Marie Lloyd," she exclaimed. She jumped to her feet. "The way they always did for my Stanley when he kept his theater open every night during the bombing of London. They loved him for that."

"We're all hams," Ida said. "None of us can talk sitting down. Isn't she wonderful?"

The telephone rang. "It's Louis," said Ida excitedly. "Oh, darling, darling, it's really you . . . "

With every word St. John witnessed the change in Ida's face, from joy to grave concern. "You won't get leave?" asked Ida. "Then, I'm coming wherever you are if I can see you for an hour . . . to hell with the picture. It can wait."

St. John left the room with Connie, who was overwhelmed with emotion. "Poor little thing," she said, "with her father gone and Louis fighting, she wants to be a clown on the screen, like her father, making people laugh, and she will. Her heart's breaking, so she will. She'll have Louis laughing before she hangs up."

After Louis's call, her eyes red from crying, Ida welcomed five Marines and sat them down for sandwiches. Ida told St. John that the psychic link with her father had been restored and that she derived inspiration from Stanley, and sensed his presence.

St. John was taken with Lupino's uniqueness. St. John accompanied Ida to Reggie Gardiner's home. Ida selected a Mozart record and lay down before the blazing fire. When tea was served, St. John was amused by Lupino's dexterity. Ida lay flat on her back on the floor and placed the cup and saucer on her stomach. Reggie slipped a pillow under her head, and Ida brought the steaming tea to her lips. She avoided spilling a drop, to her great satisfaction. St. John considered her a delight, calling her "the last of Hollywood's rugged individualists."

With the arrival of the new year, Ida's low spirits received a boost. *Forever and a Day* was finally released after its completion two years earlier. Sixty performers had donated their time to make the "this is what we're fighting for" picture. The story was built around the fortunes of a venerable home in Britain. Ida played a young maid who emigrates to America with coalman Brian Aherne. *Variety* designated them "runners up for top honors."

Other wartime films boasted all-star casts. *Stage Door Canteen* was filled with sixty-five stars paying homage to the centers where servicemen were entertained. Warner Bros. jumped on the bandwagon with *Thank Your Lucky Stars*, produced by Mark Hellinger.

After two years at Fox, Hellinger had grown disenchanted. His agent at William Morris spread the word and, surprisingly, Jack Warner offered the highest bid for his services. Hellinger signed a five-year contract at three thousand dollars a week with a solid guarantee that he would produce quality films. For *Thank Your Lucky Stars*, Hellinger used his abundant charm to convince Warner stars to go before the camera and play roles different from those they usually played. Players donated their services with the stipulation that fifty thousand dollars would be given to the Hollywood Canteen. During the final weeks of *Devotion*, which was still dragging interminably toward a close, Hellinger asked Lupino and de Havilland to put aside their aura of drama and go for laughs.

What emerged was a wild number, a satire of the Andrews Sisters. Ida and Olivia wore garish striped dresses with huge bows blossoming from their heads. Accompanied by George Tobias, they smacked gum, jive sang "The Dreamer" and mugged outrageously.

After their enjoyable comedy scene in *Thank Your Lucky Stars,* the Brontë sisters once again sank into the morass of *Devotion*. Both the cast and the hierarchy knew the results were disappointing. De Havilland did not like the ending. She and Ida argued over camera angles. Tempers flared. By the time production closed on February 25, 1943, everyone was exhausted. The studio shelved the picture.

Though famous for her dramatic acting, Ida refused to alter her public image. Magazine articles were titled "A Little Bit Cracked," "Ida—The Mad Lupino," "She Lives in a Madhouse." When Howard Sharpe interviewed her for *Photoplay*, he tried to provoke one of her high voltage "nervous fits," but Ida remained calm.

Though she was only twenty-five years old, legends had already grown around Ida. An enormous will and a passion to astonish led Ida to public confessions. Revelations in print no doubt tickled her ego.

Publicists and writers followed Ida's lead and seized her eccentricities as themes for potent stories, adding color to her fame. One of the puzzles of Ida's personality was the desire to dazzle, even to the point of falsehood. As a gifted actress, she could easily drop a sensational tale with casual conviction. From youth, she had been encouraged to use her imagination, and her behavior was perfect for Hollywood, where writers were paid huge sums for inventing stories, and actors were paid kingly salaries for pretending. Although Stanley Lupino died of cancer, Warner Bros. released a different account of his demise. "His death was an indirect result of wounds sustained during a bombing of London two years previously." In Ida's mind, she created a hero's death for her father. Even seasoned journalist Adela Rogers St. John swallowed the heroic shading, and wrote that Stanley "was caught by a German bomb while he was among the people as an air raid warden."

Even if Ida, publicists and writers were apt to embroider the Lupino legend, it remained a fact that she was different. Ida's sharp moods created an air of unpredictability.

She would also be so tightly wound emotionally that she would go for days without sleep. If Ida was trying to have a quiet day and friends in the pool were disturbing her, she would complain angrily. "It didn't matter how well you knew her," says Harry Mines. "Boy, you learned to shut up."

Though Ida reveled in her own uniqueness, she was acutely aware that something in her personality was out of kilter. She had a sensitive, high-strung nature and was prone to anger easily. Adela Rogers St. John wrote: "Lupino gets mad at everybody, though she gets over it in a hurry." *Movieland* correspondent Joseph Wechsberg commented, "When Lupino gets mad . . . brother, you better be gone." Ida spoke honestly of her inner demons. "I have my mad moments. There is a little black devil inside me. . . . Sometimes I must fight that devil. It's a terrible fight. Someday I'm going to lose. It will be very bad for all of us. I have moods, lots of moods, and some of them very dark."

Whenever she felt depressed, she busied herself with visits to wounded servicemen. The war came closer when her cousin, Wing Commander James Bradford, was shot down in a bombing run over Bremen and taken prisoner. In April, she was proud to learn that her husband was now Captain Hayward and had been assigned to head a special photographic unit. Louis wrote Ida as often as possible, but there were long weeks of silence, to her despair.

Warner Bros. cast Ida opposite Paul Henreid in *In Our Time*, a historical drama of the romance of an English girl and a titled aristocrat during the fall of Poland in 1939, touching on the corruption of the Polish aristocracy and the consequent demise of the nation. Ida met with Jerry Wald, and both agreed that Vincent Sherman should direct. He selected an international cast, including Michael Chekhov, and Alla Nazimova, former silent screen star. Years earlier, she had cast a struggling actor named Vincent Sherman in *Ghosts*, one of her stage plays. Now he returned the favor. Paul Henreid, a native of Vienna, had fled Austria because of his anti-Nazi beliefs. Before filming began, language expert Daniel Dragen, a professor at UCLA, converted the numerous cast accents to Polish. To guarantee authenticity, the studio hired Dr. Stephen Barasch, a former militiaman in the siege of Warsaw, to supervise historical detail.

Of course, the Motion Picture Administration pointed out that portions of the screenplay were in violation of the Code ("Page 62. 'You should wear a fig leaf on your face.' Unacceptable"). On May 2, the cameras rolled. Ida's role, unlike her usual tough-girl parts, required considerable restraint and subtlety. As the weeks passed, she fell ill with sinus problems and had to have her wisdom teeth removed. Vincent Sherman suddenly had his hands full, constantly rearranging shooting schedules. On her return, Ida was in a dangerous mishap when her horse bolted and dragged her; fortunately, she suffered only scalp lacerations. Paul Henreid became sick with a throat ailment and was given a "miracle drug," sulfanilamide.

During production, Henreid was shocked to hear that his good friend, director Rudolf Beer, had been executed in Dachau on a charge of treason. Another friend, Dr. Paul Bada, author of *Ball at the Savoy*, had been beaten to death by the Gestapo. Because of her personal loathing of wartime enemies Lupino formed a political bond with her co-star.

Henreid found her "sweet" and "vulnerable." Ida occasionally dined with him and his wife, Lisl. He told an interviewer that Ida "works up a terrible appetite by uttering insults against her enemies."

At a party one evening, Warner Bros. costume designer Howard Shoup watched in disbelief as Ida and actress Miriam Hopkins got into an argument about Errol Flynn. The two actresses had to be separated, recalled Shoup.

If Ida could frighten people with her fiery temper, she could amaze them with her uncanny predictions. Harry Mines remembers her at parties, dazzling guests by reading palms. "Ida was just marvelous at fortune telling. But every time it was my turn, she was tired."

Filming of *In Our Time* dragged on into the summer heat. For the dramatic ending—the torching of the aristocrat's estate—Vincent Sherman worked a small miracle in five days on a Chatsworth ranch, employing five hundred cast and crew members to see it through. Everyone was relieved when the production closed on September 3. On its release, critics were unimpressed. *PM* magazine acidly reviewed the film as "Cinderella Plots a Better Poland."

By then, Captain Hayward had come home. So had the real war.

7

THE BREAKUP

It is just one of those things. —CAPTAIN LOUIS HAYWARD

On November 1, 1943, a convoy filled with troops of the Second Marine Corps left New Zealand. The full force of the tropical sun beat down on the men who thronged the steel decks and anxiously pondered their fate. During their nineteen days at sea, strategists had carefully analyzed the course of the attack. The First Division was to storm ashore on New Britain; the Second would invade the Tarawa Atoll; the Third, Bougainville.

Captain Louis Hayward displayed a surface suavity, strong compassion and quiet courage, characteristics that impressed the dozen photographic specialists under his command. The Tarawa plan had fifteen hundred Marines landing in the first three waves of assault. Hayward's unit was instructed to obtain photographs and 16 mm footage for study in future operations. In the steaming heat below deck, Louis gathered his men. "I know all of us are fed up with hearing about the marvelous photography coming out of the European war," he said. "This time let's really give them something to talk about—from the Marines of the Pacific."

On the morning of November 20, an ear-splitting barrage from the convoy and aerial bombings pounded the Japanese strongholds. Inside a landing craft, Louis cradled his 16 mm camera, an expensive gift from his wife. Despite the massive barrage of bombs that ripped into the beaches and blossomed into towers of smoke, the Japanese resistance was fierce. They were solidly entrenched in thick coconut groves dotted with cement pillboxes. Between the hidden defense fortifications and the ocean were fifty feet of white sand, the destination of the attackers.

The amphibious landing craft packed with fully equipped Marines surged toward the beaches. Five hundred yards from shore, they struck a coral reef that lay just below the surface. The boats began churning helplessly, trapped on the submerged reef, sitting ducks. Of the first assault, two of three Marines failed to make the beach alive; only 50 percent of those who did remained unscathed.

Deadly crossfire swept the landing areas, spattering the helpless who staggered in the surf. Shells whistled overhead, then became explosive infernos of death as they dropped into the amphibious boats. The only protection was a long log seawall where men huddled in confusion and fear. As his craft approached the shore, Louis gripped his camera in one hand and his pistol in the other.

As he burst from the craft, the man next to him was shot dead; others screamed in agony. A bullet smashed into his helmet, and his head snapped back. When he found cover, Louis was stunned. He saw dozens of bodies stretched on the glistening sand and bobbing in the surf; just beyond was the ghastly scene of stranded and destroyed boats. He watched helplessly as desperate men, clinging to the sides of landing craft, were shot by camouflaged snipers in high palm trees and slid beneath the waves. He spent the next forty-eight hours filming the carnage, aiming his camera at scenes of horror and death, stumbling over the remains of men he knew. By sunset of the first day, fifteen hundred

Americans had been killed or wounded; thirty-five hundred others were ashore, trying to stay alive. The second day, artillery fire, aircraft bombs, flamethrowers and sheer courage allowed the Americans to advance and secure the beaches.

On his second day in hell, Louis, exhausted from lack of sleep, found refuge in a foxhole. In a nearby crater were fifteen dead Japanese soldiers. Before dozing off, he photographed the grisly scene. When he awoke, his eyes were again led to the gory sight, but there were only fourteen bodies left; one had crawled away during the night. The tenacious enemy fought to the bloody end, refusing to surrender. From below, Louis filmed the dead snipers who had lashed themselves to the palm trees. By November 24, Tarawa was secure, after four days of fierce fighting. Under the pungent smell of gunpowder was the stench of death as corpses rotted where they had fallen. Of the 4,836 defenders, only 17 soldiers remained. On the American side, 948 were dead and 2,072 wounded.

A week after the bloody invasion, the telephone would not stop ringing at Ida's home. A delayed newspaper report had detailed how Louis Hayward and Navy Lieutenant Eddie Albert had participated in the savage combat. Albert had undergone a baptism of fire, evacuating wounded men from the beach as weapons blazed. Ida anxiously read the scant newspaper account of Hayward's and Albert's brief meeting during combat. The last message she'd received from Louis had been from New Zealand. He had jokingly written of his soft life in the service. Then the letters had stopped for several weeks. With the invasion news, she was frightened and worried sick.

The American public was shocked by the reports of the heavy casualties. Admiral Chester W. Nimitz, commander-in-chief of the Pacific Fleet, tried to explain the significance of the victory: they had captured four strategic airfields in the Central Pacific. Despite Nimitz's response, newspapers referred to the invasion as "Tragic

Tarawa" and compared it to the heroic yet suicidal Charge of the Light Brigade.

Marine battlefield commanders had seen the tenacity of the enemy, and they had visual proof. Hayward's unit had compiled hundreds of still photos and thousands of feet of 16 mm footage verifying Japanese resistance and Marine courage. Captain Hayward was assigned to prepare a documentary about "Bloody Tarawa."

The photographic unit had achieved its mission but at a terrible price. They had witnessed unforgettable scenes of horror. Louis was deeply shaken by the experience; as he wrote to Ida: "I wish you could have seen our men going into action. I can't write about it as my powers of expression are definitely limited. I was amazed by the personal courage and gallantry of them. Without asking a damn thing in the way of the slightest credit, they went ahead and did stupendous things. Sometime I will try and talk about it."

Ida was proud of her husband, grateful that he had survived. She expected to wait weeks or months to hear from him, but the week before Christmas, Louis telephoned. He was coming home.

When his plane touched down, Ida's heart was in her throat. She nervously watched as the aircraft taxied to the arrival gate, a throng of newsmen beside her. Louis emerged, neatly dressed in his Marine uniform. As photographers snapped the arrival of a hero, Ida gasped. The boyish, handsome face had vanished; in its place was a mask etched with weariness. Louis managed a wan, empty smile, but Ida instinctively knew that something terrible had happened to him. During the ride home, he was silent. She chattered on with the latest movie gossip, then spoke of her recent trip to March Field. She described how, the week before, she had visited the military hospital nicknamed "the twenty-five acres," meeting hundreds of patients in the huge complex. Afterward, related Ida, she was so tired, a wheelchair had to be brought up, and she was rolled to her car. She had hoped to make him laugh, but Louis was silent, his thoughts a thousand miles away.

Even after a few days of rest, he was moody and withdrawn. He would begin speaking of Tarawa, then suddenly stop, unable to continue. Ida didn't probe. She drove him to Warner Bros. for a reunion with friends, but instead of relaxing, he grew nervous.

Her husband was a changed man. Tarawa had been a living nightmare, and as he supervised the editing of the combat footage, he relived the horror day after day, viewing rough scenes the public would never see, gruesome color film of bodies blown to pieces— the true images of war. Ida saw her much-loved husband disintegrating before her eyes. He suffered from severe asthma attacks aggravated by exhaustion and sleepless nights. But Louis was suffering from something worse than asthma—an unseen malady.

Even before Tarawa, columnist Hedda Hopper had described Louis as "introspective, moody and filled with psychological problems." He had returned from the war physically unharmed, but deep within he carried the emotional scars of having survived while others died. Ida was unable to reach her husband. He was treated at three different hospitals for severe depression. As months passed, Louis drifted further away. Finally he uttered the most terrible words possible. He wanted to start a new life, he told her. Ida listened in shock. For several months they lived apart, Louis residing on Miller Drive, Ida crying nightly in their Westridge home, for she feared her marriage was doomed.

In March, Ida's oppressive worry and nervous tension resulted in a breakdown. Physicians hovered around her bed, reporting to the studio. Warners suspended her contract for three months rather than assign her to a picture she couldn't complete. She tried to rest, seldom leaving her Westridge home. A request to appear briefly in *Hollywood Canteen* roused her broken spirit. Ida had been an early supporter of the canteen, which was located at 1451

Cahuenga off Hollywood Boulevard. Bette Davis and John Garfield had been the dynamic forces in starting the club, and it had become internationally famous. Servicemen could dance with Rita Hayworth or chat with Hedy Lamarr. Three thousand servicemen flocked to the club each night. Thousands of motion picture employees assisted. Ida became a regular, signing autographs, dancing or merely conversing. One evening, Rita and her partner performed a Spanish dance. On one occasion, a soldier spotted Ida and politely asked, "Miss Lupino, please scream for me."

Before Ida could appear in *Hollywood Canteen*, the production came to a halt. A bitter dispute erupted between the studio and the Screen Actors Guild, which complained that performers had been forced to take salary cuts, ostensibly for "patriotic reasons," while Warner Bros. stood to make a profit. Guild representatives noted that there were nine "all-star" pictures ready for production in which actors were requested to take reduced pay. In April, a compromise was reached, and the guild agreed to issue salary waivers if performers were not pressured to appear. Warners agreed to donate $240,000 to the Hollywood Canteen, and the club would receive 40 percent of the film's profits after expenses were recouped. Despite the compromise, many stars hesitated to appear, harboring the sentiment that the studio was still profiting at their expense. On July 19, Ida emerged from her seclusion and appeared as a celebrity who encounters a soldier. She donated her $3,000 to the canteen.

While he and Ida were separated, Louis suffered a physical collapse. On a warm Sunday afternoon, he finally left his hospital bed for Miller Drive. Accompanied by a nurse, he quietly greeted the old friends who had gathered to help the Haywards end their marriage in style with a farewell party. Harry Mines remembers the sadness felt by everyone. Louis said goodbye to each person. When he came to Mines, he glanced about, then said wistfully: "It's a funny thing, saying goodbye in my own home." Mines was speechless. He could only shake his head, "They were so spiritually alike, so perfect for each other."

The official separation came on July 21, as word of their "rift" first made the newspapers. Columnist Louella Parsons spoke with the estranged couple. Louis stilled any unwarranted speculation. "Ida has been a perfect angel to me. There is no one more considerate. I hoped we could work it out. Before I went into the service, we were having a little trouble, but we decided to try again. There is no one in my life and I know there is no one in hers. It is just one of those things."

Parsons reported that Captain Hayward would receive an honorable discharge from the Marines on August 7, because of his ill health. Reluctantly, Ida spoke to the press about her failed marriage; she confirmed the separation, but displayed sympathy and affection for Louis. "He's done a magnificent job in the Marines," she said, "and I feel terribly sorry for him because he's been so very nervous."

"Just one of those things," said Louis.

But to Ida, their love had been everything. She would try to pick up the pieces of her shattered life. She started by hiring a secretary, Leslie Forrest, to organize her household.

Vincent Sherman called her, enthusiastic over an amusing script he had read, a comedy variation of the ribald jokes about the "traveling salesman." Only this script featured a traveling saleslady who can't find a place to sleep because of the wartime housing shortage. Since military men are granted preferential treatment, she pretends marriage to a handsome lieutenant, and they spend the night together. Sherman sent the risqué script to Ida, and she loved it. William Prince was cast as the soldier who innocently agrees to be a husband for the evening.

Ida began the filming of *Pillow to Post* with her hand in a cast. She had returned home late one night after a radio broadcast and had fallen and broken bones in her hand and foot. Her bad luck continued when the cast on her hand was removed; a tendon had grown against the wrist bone and required an operation to correct.

The film contained numerous slapstick scenes, and Ida received the brunt of the visual gags. She willingly accepted such indignities as being drenched by water bags dropped on her head. She was struck with ironing boards and collapsible beds. A huge, slimy bullfrog was thrust in her face. She performed a wild jitterbug routine on a sound stage where the temperature reached 106 degrees.

Life was difficult not only before the cameras but offscreen as well. After one long day of acting, Ida emerged from the make-believe world to find that her prized 1940 Buick convertible had been stolen. A message later came from a fan, who admitted he had taken the car in hopes of meeting his idol. Then came the theft of her front door by souvenir seekers.

Ida's screen work paid off as notices hailed her flair for comedy. *Pillow To Post* was a hit. One scene in particular evoked a strong response in male viewers. Milo Anderson had designed a short, sexy nightgown for Ida. When her character emerges from the bathroom in the daring costume, William Prince sits up in bed, quite taken with the vision before him.

"Holy Mackerel!"

"It happens to be the latest thing in nightwear," says Lupino.

"I suppose it gives you more freedom."

"Well, that's what we're fighting for, isn't it?"

Ida told Vincent Sherman that *Pillow to Post* brought her more fan mail than any other film in her career. Servicemen wrote to her from around the world. They identified with the poor fellows caught in the housing crunch but were envious of William Prince. They wished that they, too, could have spent a night with Lupino.

The failure of her marriage had badly shaken Ida. Her youth and innocence were far behind her. The man she had loved was gone, and her freedom brought maturity and an awareness of her strength but also of her fragility. Lupino was a strong woman and knew it; yet she needed emotional strength from a man. She began dating, but Ida was fearful of even-tempered suitors; she avoided placid men who were charming but easily crushed. The inner disappointment and anger at being rejected led her to seek out aggressive males, lady-killers capable of derring-do and cocky combativeness.

Many suitors sought Lupino's affection, but none really interested her. Then, on the studio lot Paul Henreid introduced her to a fellow Austrian, actor Helmut Dantine. He charmed Ida immediately. Dantine was tough, decisive and exhibited a bravado that other men lacked. They became constant companions, and rumor had it that he would soon be her second husband.

Dantine had been a member of the Austrian diplomatic corps when the Nazis came to power. He had been interned for several months; on his release he came to America in January 1939. Ironically, Dantine began his screen career portraying Nazis in *Mrs. Miniver* and *Desperate Journey*, both in 1942.

Several Lupino intimates were perplexed by the attraction, since Ida's new boyfriend was so unlike Hayward. Beneath the Austrian actor's smooth facade, he was volatile and imperious. Like Lupino, he thrived on drama and dangerous emotions, and was often driven by anger. Where Louis had tried to reason with Ida, Dantine tried to dominate her with Teutonic passion and daring. When others ducked, Dantine charged.

Dantine had a shady reputation. The spring before he and Ida began to see each other, he had been arrested on a hit and run warrant. Though the case was dismissed, he was soon back in court when opera star Miliza Korjus filed suit to recover twenty-two hundred dollars on a worthless check he had given her.

The public became aware of the romance between Dantine and Lupino when it made unexpected news in the early hours of 1945. On New Year's Eve, Ida joined Rena Cournyn and Barbara Reed for a night of celebration. Ida hadn't seen Dantine since they had argued four weeks before. Though Ida had invited him to her home for a reconciliation toast to the new year, he never showed up. Since Ida was slightly ill and taking antibiotics, Connie asked Rena to be the chauffeur for the evening. Ida slumped in the back seat, out of view, as they drove to Hollywood. "I didn't know Helmut was on the warpath," recalls Rena Cournyn. Ida made an appearance at the Hollywood Canteen, then the group went to a party hosted by David O. Selznick.

On their return to the Westridge home, the women soon retired. Dantine telephoned at 3:00 A.M. and said he was coming over. Leslie Forrest told him that Ida was in bed and that the party had ended. Before daylight, Forrest was awakened by a noise in the dining room. She recognized Dantine's drunken voice, asking for brandy. She heard him roaming the house. Dantine broke into Forrest's bedroom and chased her into Rena Cournyn's room. Barbara Reed heard the commotion, jumped from bed and encountered a furious Dantine. He trapped the three frightened women in a corner and, enraged, began to slap them. When Forrest pleaded with him to leave, he bit her on the arm, then slumped to the floor, passed out. The trio rushed into Ida's bedroom. "Ida took too many sleeping pills and we couldn't wake her," recalls Rena. They tried walking her around the room. Dantine rushed in and slapped her, but even that failed to revive her.

When the police came, they arrested Dantine on a charge of battery. When he was released on bail, the contrite hellraiser told reporters: "It was all a terrible mistake. I am going back to Ida's house, just as soon as I get washed up and into clothes, to straighten the whole thing out."

Ida awoke in the morning and was told of the drama that had surrounded her. When Dantine showed up at Ida's house, the women were astonished to see the offender was out of jail so soon. He turned on the charm and apologized for the rampage. He shook hands with Leslie Forrest, saying "it was just a case of too much new year's celebration." All was forgiven. At that moment, the staff of *House and Garden* magazine arrived for a scheduled layout, only to find Lupino in pajamas and the house wrecked.

Dantine's violent behavior didn't faze Ida. In fact, she was thrilled by such emotional fireworks. As she told the press: "He's full of enthusiasm, which I like because, as you know, that's the way I am. He's very sensitive, which I also like. Helmut is the only man, except for Louis, of course, of whom I have been really fond in more than ten years."

Ida said she wasn't after a wild romance but marriage and a family. "Definitely," she insisted. "Come hell or high water, adopted or my own. I am going to have, I *must* have some kids."

Reporters took note of Louis Hayward's dates with socialite Peggy Morrow Field, the former wife of wealthy Julian Field. On January 27, Ida telephoned Hedda Hopper with the news that she was instructing her attorney, Joseph Dubin, to begin divorce proceedings. She stressed that it was Hayward who had prompted the legal termination of their marriage. Technically, Ida's action was based on a complaint of extreme cruelty, with no specifics mentioned. She petitioned the court to approve a property settlement, amicably agreed upon.

On March 15, *With the Marines at Tarawa* won an Oscar as best documentary of 1944. Ida was the first to telephone and congratulate Louis. The award was a significant triumph. He had already been given the bronze star from Admiral Nimitz for "meritorious conduct in the performance of outstanding service." Richard Wheeler wrote in his authoritative *A Special Valor*, the history of

Marine combat in the Pacific, that the Tarawa footage shot by Hayward's unit was "the finest and most startling record of combat ever obtained." At the time of its release, correspondent Robert Sherrod asked Brigadier General Robert Denig what effect the remarkable film had on the Marine Corps.

"A strong one," replied Denig. "Enlistments are down 35 percent."

On May 11, Ida was in court, nervously testifying about the demise of her marriage. Tense and twisting a handkerchief, she answered questions from the witness stand. "My husband told me that he didn't want to be tied to one woman and that he wanted a divorce. . . . I was so emotionally upset that I suffered a nervous breakdown."

Louis was absent from court, permitting Ida to win the decree by default. The six-minute hearing ended six years of marriage, but it did not end their friendship. Ida never blamed Louis for the collapse of their life together. After a year, the divorce would become final and she would be free to remarry.

Years later, when she looked back on her marriage to Hayward, she said she was too young and full of life to have married then: "Louis had a lot of tragedy in his life and would call himself a manic depressive. He would say life stinks, don't ever love anything too much because it will always be taken away from you."

Ida knew exactly what he meant. Though she never blamed Louis, for her, wartime passion would never fade.

8

DEEP VALLEY

You'll never work for Warners again. —JACK WARNER

"Lupino Sisters Wed and Shed" reported newspapers. While Ida's marriage had ended, Rita married Enrique Veledez, her dance partner.

Shortly after giving her divorce testimony, Ida left for a six-week tour of military hospitals on the East Coast, accompanied by Frances Robinson. In the hospital wards Ida brought smiles to hundreds of recuperating servicemen. Warner Bros. hosted an expensive party in her honor at the Sherry Netherland Hotel. Among the guests were Helmut Dantine, Faye Emerson and her husband, Brigadier General Elliott Roosevelt.

A few days later, while attempting to move a large trunk in her suite, Ida strained a stomach muscle. This injury, combined with severe exhaustion, brought a physician's order to stay in bed. But she wasn't lonely. She had found a half-starved kitten, which she named Socrates after his habit of staring with philosophical disdain at food he had no intention of eating.

By July, Ida had started a new life in a home at 917 North Beverly Drive. It was just in time, recalls Harry Mines, because "Socrates had become a mother." Ida rejoiced over the kittens, the first residents of what was to become known as "the hotel." The residence would become a human menagerie as well. "It was open house twenty-four hours a day," says Mines.

Warner Bros. announced that Ida would star in *The Man I Love* based on Maritta Wolff's novel *Night Shift*. The studio had first tried to bring the story to the screen with Ann Sheridan, but script trouble had forced a halt. The screenplay was retitled and rewritten and circulated as *Why Was I Born?* Raoul Walsh felt he could make the melodrama come to life. He convinced Ida to accept the role of torch singer Petey Brown. Playing opposite Lupino was handsome Robert Alda, portraying a smooth nightclub racketeer who was out to seduce Petey's naive sister. While singing in the racketeer's nightspot, Petey falls for her pianist, who, unfortunately, is still in love with his wife. The novel was controversial, and the screenplay was carefully scrutinized.

The Breen Office found the story unacceptable because of "the low moral tone . . . of adultery and illicit sex on the part of the principals." They objected to the locale for one scene, stating that it must "be established as a room where both male and female employees keep their hats and coats, without a toilet cubicle. It should not in any way suggest the ladies' washroom." A reference to a slot machine was deemed objectionable, as well as "reference to any crookedness on the part of the Desk Sergeant" and the "action of Johnny feeling along the blankets to find out whether the diapers are still dry." Of course, double entendre and all scenes that seemed to "encroach too closely on the intimacies of married life" were scrapped.

The script was finally accepted, and shooting began on July 18, in the midst of stifling summer heat. Although the story took place in winter, the set was steaming; huge blocks of ice were placed on the sound stages with fans blowing over them. The title was finally changed to *The Man I Love*—from the haunting 1924 ballad. The studio felt that Ida's voice was unimpressive, so singer Peg La Centra actually recorded the song. The front office grew apprehensive as Ida appeared weak and irritable and complained about her makeup and costumes. Fear spread that the picture would be too much for her.

Actress Andrea King found Ida and director Walsh a memorable duo, who reminded her of a father and daughter. Walsh was all business on the set, but after the day's last scene, he relaxed. "Cut! Print!" he would shout. "Now it's time for some cooking sherry." "I didn't know what that meant until I was invited to join him for a glass," King remembers. King was amazed by Ida's artistry and felt she had "a magic glow."

Ida's health soon failed, just as the front office had feared. Her salary at the time was four thousand dollars a week, and executives were alarmed when she began arriving late. Only four days after she started, she became bedridden. On July 26 she sent an apologetic telegram to Walsh at Warner Bros. "Sorry I am laid up," it read.

"Wanted to come to work but doctors said absolutely no. The hypos are hyping. The dogs are barking. The cooking sherry does not do any good and I just shot my aunt Kate. Will do my best to make it Saturday."

By the beginning of August, the front office was complaining of slowness. Frank Mattison, studio production manager, attributed the snail's pace to constant rewrites and "war hysteria." The cast and crew were engrossed in the news reports about the atomic bomb that had devastated Japan.

When the surrender came on August 16, war-weary Americans were ecstatic. Ida had prayed nightly for the war to end.

The Man I Love dragged on, to the agony of all concerned. Catherine Turney, the author of the screenplay, visited the set and was greeted by Ida's lament, "You know, I turned this down once. I don't know what happened." In a dramatic scene with Robert Alda, Ida fainted. Alda caught her before she hit the concrete. The blackout was caused by the fierce heat and aggravated by the tight-fitting Milo Anderson evening dress, which had to be snipped off to revive her. On another occasion, during an emotional scene, the stillness was shattered by a loud snore. High above, on the catwalk, an electrician had fallen asleep.

"Well, it's the first time my acting has made the rafters snore," quipped Ida.

The production closed on September 21, nineteen days behind schedule and one hundred thousand dollars over budget. Ida threw a lavish party for the cast and crew, and more than two hundred laborers, grips, prop men, makeup artists and other technicians turned up for the event. Ida insisted on dancing at least once with all the men, until she twisted her ankle. She was sidelined for weeks on crutches.

Ida had worked tirelessly during the war and her efforts on behalf of America's fighting men were well-appreciated. In October, she was selected "Queen of the Castle" by military engineers. The following month, the Australian government honored her for the outstanding contributions she had made to their loan drives.

The Man I Love premiered in February 1947. Critics judged it lachrymose, the story reminiscent of radio soap operas. But Lupino fans, especially women, lined up to see it. When hard-edged Petey Brown, tough but emotionally vulnerable, finds herself alone when her man sails to sea, a responsive chord was struck in many a woman's heart.

Lupino's creative impulse was growing stronger. She wanted to do more than just act. For several years, composing music had been a major outlet for her artistic expression. By 1945 she had written dozens of songs. Ida and Nick Arden had collaborated on "When Our Fingers Meet," "Leave Me Alone," and "Storm In My Heart." Louis had introduced her to a Marine with musical talent. Bill MacIlwinen was a North Carolina teacher who impressed Ida with his melodies. Many of their songs were recorded by conductor Opie Cates and broadcast over NBC radio.

Ida was also writing stories and screenplays. For *All Our Yesterdays* she used the pseudonym "William Threely." It was the story of British street musicians who entertain as German rocket bombs explode in London and had been written with Monty Woolley in mind. Ida and Barbara Reed collaborated on *Miss Pennington*, a screenplay they optioned to RKO for five thousand dollars.

The home on Beverly Drive was always a hive of activity. As many as fifteen people occupied the residence, and guests came and went. The household included Connie, Leslie Forrest, housemen and a variety of pets. Visitors were tucked away in quarters above the garage. Ida called her select group of friends "the Chums." Charter members were Reginald and Nadia Gardiner, Harry Mines, Frances Robinson, Ann Sheridan, Rex Harrison, Geraldine Fitzgerald and Barbara Reed. The home was their private club; each knew where the key was hidden. Ida frequently returned to her living room to find it filled with guests; she merely waved and went to bed. Needy servicemen were also welcome and were often starstruck by the ebb and flow of celebrities—Bing Crosby crooning at the piano, Errol Flynn clowning or Ida serving coffee.

Kindness was a Lupino trait her friends admired. This was most apparent when tragedy struck David Niven. In August 1940, he had married Primula Rollo, a beautiful blonde aristocrat. After five years of military service, including combat with British commandos, he had returned to America with his wife and sons and took up residence near Ida's home. Primmie Niven struck up a friendship. When invited to a barbecue at John Huston's home, Ida asked the Nivens along. Primmie said that they already had plans to attend a party at the home of Tyrone Power and his wife Annabella; she told Ida that she preferred to go with her but that they were expected. Ida remembers arriving home from Huston's with a strange sensation, a feeling that something terrible had happened. It was around one o'clock. Connie was still awake.

"Did you have a good time?" she asked

"Yes, I did, darling, but I've got one of those funny Lupino feelings on me, like Stanley. Something has happened to Primmie Niven."

Forty-five minutes later the telephone rang. Bob Coote said he had bad news.

"It's Primmie, isn't it?" asked Ida.

Coote was astonished that she already knew. He explained that Primmie was in St. John's Hospital with a skull fracture. At the Powers' home, at 139 Saltair, the Nivens had joined guests Gene Tierney, Oleg Cassini, Cesar Romero, Rex Harrison, Lili Palmer, Richard Greene and others. While playing "sardines," a hide and seek game, the lights went out. A scream cut through the darkness and chilled the guests. Primmie Niven had fallen down the cellar stairs and suffered serious head injuries. Her husband kept a constant vigil at the hospital, where the medical team predicted she would improve. Instead, she took a turn for the worse and, unexpectedly, she died. For Niven it was a cruel irony that he and his family had survived the blitz and combat only to have a tragedy strike his wife while playing a game in Hollywood.

Ida was heartbroken over Primmie's death. "She had the feeling that something was going to happen, too. Niven took it very badly. He loved her. He didn't seem to have any interest in anything after that."

Niven withdrew and was a changed man. Harry Mines would sometimes see him at Ida's home, as one of her Chums. "Ida was very kind to him. She even took the boys in her home for a while. Ida suggested that we just let him be himself and he'd come out of it." David Junior would always remember Ida's home and the colorful murals she had painted in his bedroom: "Elephants with their smiles and the funny adorable mouse they were chasing."

Niven often came to Lupino's home with Clark Gable, whose wife Carole Lombard had died in an airplane crash. Gable would talk seriously, reminiscing about his wife, one of Ida's childhood screen idols. He lamented to Lupino that he had no children. One evening she was Gable's date for a party at Niven's home. She volunteered to make scrambled eggs, her specialty, and disappeared in the kitchen. When she came back, her date had nodded off. Ida placed gladioli flowers in his hands. In a half-hour his eyes opened, and he looked at the flowers and laughed.

Ida, with her mischievous nature, often surprised her friends. Harry Mines was walking through Lupino's upstairs hall one evening when he was "nearly knocked off my feet by the most repellent picture I'd ever seen in my life." In a corner, practically hidden, was a portrait of a beautiful Mexican girl, her throat slashed. John Decker, Hollywood's eccentric and popular artist, had gone to a morgue and painted the gruesome portrait for Ida's birthday. He inscribed it: "To Ida on her 70th birthday. I hope this never happens to you." Decker's macabre sense of humor matched hers. Ida was fascinated by stories of murder and enjoyed the thrill of being frightened. She wondered how it felt to kill. If Ida was feeling particularly mischievous—which was often—she would show the strange painting to visitors, despite her mother's objections. As she told a reporter: "Lots of people can't stand looking at the picture. Seems to give them the willies. Personally, I like it, but I have to keep it in seclusion."

As a member of "the Insomniac Club," Ida started the day at three in the morning or four in the afternoon, depending on when she had managed a few hours of sleep. Friends were often invited at 3 A.M. for predawn cocktails. For a time, Ida even refused to have a telephone because she did not want her privacy interrupted. If she needed to make a call, she would walk to the nearby Beverly Hills Hotel. Then Connie insisted she install a telephone. Strict routine was foreign to her normally busy existence. The lack of organization and her overwhelming schedule brought about forgetfulness.

Ida enjoyed puttering around her home, rearranging furniture, hanging drapes or gardening. One evening Harry Mines and Louis Hayward stopped by "the hotel" for a visit. They were startled by what they saw. Recalls Mines: "As we got out of the car we looked up and saw a man climbing up the side of the house. 'What is that?' asked Louis. We found out it was Helmut Dantine, trying to get in. He hadn't seen her in a long while." Ida's romance with Dantine was an increasingly stormy affair. He would be welcome at her home one moment, turned away the next.

One afternoon the Chums gathered for a pool party. Harry Mines noticed the lovers embracing passionately, holding hands, gazing in each other's eyes. The next moment a heated argument exploded. "You dirty Nazi!" shouted Ida. They whacked each other with towels in a fierce quarrel. Ida hated being single, but life with Dantine became more unpleasant every day.

When the studio cast her opposite Errol Flynn in *Escape Me Never*, she was elated. She had met Flynn and his first wife Lili Damita in Palm Springs in 1936. At Warners, Ida, Flynn and Raoul Walsh formed an elite triumvirate dedicated to fun. Each had a nickname: Ida was "Little Scout"; Flynn was "The Baron"; and Walsh was "Uncle." Even Connie was part of the group. She loved Flynn like a son, and he dubbed her "Connetta Moonstone." The charismatic Flynn charmed everyone. Says Harry Mines: "There was a wonderful exhilaration being around Errol. You became as bold and as wild as he was." Ida saw that beneath the devil-may-care surface was a troubled man.

Like a skyrocket, Flynn had burst into international stardom at the age of twenty-six. He had a hedonistic streak that led him to indulge in all the pleasures of life, including alcohol and drugs. The discrepancy between the actor's heroic screen image and his failure to serve in the military had puzzled everyone. How was it that the seemingly robust Flynn was not in uniform? Warner Bros. released the information that he had a heart murmur. FBI director J. Edgar Hoover was so curious, he sent an agent to examine Flynn's medical records. The medical report verified that Flynn was worse off than the public knew. He had tuberculosis. In the 1940s the disease often caused death. Only a few close friends knew the truth. Though disqualified for military service, he was nonetheless sought out by spymaster William O. Donovan to embark on a secret mission to the Republic of Ireland to negotiate the use of naval bases. The mission never reached fruition, but he had lined up a job as a war correspondent. Unfortunately, the actor was charged with rape, and the writing assignment fell through. Ida publicly proclaimed his innocence while others cooled their friendship with the accused star. Ida was aware that Flynn was besieged by women day and night. Flynn was exonerated of the charge, but the legal ordeal had brought embarrassment and personal anguish. Ida had loyally stood by him during the trial and was overjoyed by his acquittal.

Escape Me Never would offer Lupino and Flynn a change of pace from their standard roles. The story was a light, rather creaky plot about an English girl in love in turn-of-the-century Venice. In a case of mistaken identity, brothers in love with Lupino and Eleanor Parker become confused. The Breen office was perturbed by the film's implications that Flynn's character was "an apron chaser" and pointed out that the actor "has the same reputation in life."

Lupino and Flynn enjoyed making the picture; their friendship deepened into romance.

Escape Me Never was a disaster at the box office. Critics found the tale contrived, sentimental and replete with cliché-ridden dialogue. Flynn fans weren't excited about their hero in Alpine shorts. As Ida admitted, to her dismay, "The postman and I became strangers." The real drama was offscreen, but the Lupino-Flynn romance was short-lived. Ida adored Flynn but knew he would never be content with any one woman. She was alone again.

In April, *Devotion* finally made it to theaters; in the interim, a lot had changed with the Brontë sisters. Olivia de Havilland had filed suit and won a precedent-setting contract agreement against Warners; Ida had welcomed Louis home, only to have her marriage unravel; Nancy Coleman had married and given birth to twins.

Warner Bros. hadn't even notified Olivia of the premiere. The following morning, Ida telephoned to compliment her work in the film. De Havilland was surprised by Lupino's unexpected thoughtfulness, despite the tiff they'd had while filming. This was a gracious act, Olivia felt, and quite unique in her career.

The Brontë sisters had accurately predicted the outcome of *Devotion*, a mediocre picture that failed. But it does contain a classic mistake that made audiences laugh. In one scene, Olivia de Havilland opens a door and enters a room; a prop man's hand appears from nowhere and closes the door.

Lupino felt that Warners had failed her. While the studio seemed to forget about her, she busied herself with radio shows. For *Request Performance* she shared the microphone with W.C. Fields and Reginald Gardiner. Fields even had his fellow cast members laughing as he delivered a facetious lecture on temperance. By May 27, 1946, the first of Lupino's yearly films should have commenced, but she hadn't been assigned to anything. Because of this scheduling mistake, the studio was legally obligated to pay her for five weeks' work. She was handed a check for twenty thousand dollars. Her second pay period was to begin at the end of August; still there was no production scheduled. Ida didn't care. She went on her merry way, starring in lucrative radio shows. The studio tried to recoup some money by product endorsements. She was photographed with Zippo cigarette lighters and Barrington Hall instant coffee.

To prevent another free paycheck for Lupino, the studio hastily dusted off an old script, *Deep Valley*, which had originally been announced in 1942 as a film starring Humphrey Bogart, John Garfield and Ann Sheridan. Now the billing was Lupino, Dane Clark and Wayne Morris. Ida played a shy country girl disabled by a speech impediment who resides with her surly parents in a secluded farmhouse. The unhappy woman befriends escaped convict Dane Clark; his affection helps her overcome her stammer. Then a posse corners the convict, and he dies trying to escape.

Director Jean Negulesco hurriedly put together a shooting schedule. *Deep Valley* was destined to be the most physically grueling picture Ida ever made. On September 23, the company began filming on a rugged section of coastal bluffs known as Surfboard Point in the Palos Verdes Estates. Convicts were depicted as laboring on a highway, but no artificial perspiration was necessary because of a fierce heat wave.

In mid-October, the cast and crew traveled to the mountain resort of Big Bear and stayed at the Paramount Lodge. Ida wore a sixty-three-cent wardrobe of old jeans and a work shirt. The scenes called for summer shots, to match the previous footage, but the mountain air chilled Ida to the bone and she caught a bad cold. Accident prone as ever, she was being photographed at Bartlett Cedar Lake running barefoot over rocks when she sliced her toe. An infection developed, and her ankles began to swell from the physical stress. Although she could barely stand, she insisted on remaining at Big Bear to avoid delaying the picture. Her fragile health worsened when she suffered a flare-up of chronic bronchitis.

While Ida struggled with *Deep Valley*, Arthur Lyons was negotiating with Warner Bros. Both the studio and Lupino were dissatisfied with her present contract. In 1944, Warners had offered to pay her fifty thousand dollars per picture, *if* Lupino agreed to terminate her Fox contract. But Jack Warner, again, proposed an exclusive seven-year contract. Warner was acutely aware that the present contract allowed Lupino to do outside pictures and prevented the studio from exerting tight control. Lupino had adamantly refused to go along with such an arrangement. Jack Warner refused to renew her contract unless she met his terms; his assistant, Steve Trilling, insisted that before any new deal be struck, a mutual cancellation of contract take place. Lupino had another film on schedule at Fox; she refused to be a slave, fully aware that Jack Warner wanted her under his thumb artistically. Ida fumed over Warner's craftiness. She told Lyons she would never sign a long-term contract with Warners, so the negotiations dragged on.

After a month of shivering and suffering at Big Bear, the company departed the frigid resort, to Ida's great relief. A personal tragedy befell Ida when her German shepherd, the beloved Duchess, elderly and arthritic, suddenly died. In December, plagued by worry over her contract and pain from the loss of her pet, Ida toiled at the Warner Ranch in a flimsy wardrobe that was small comfort in the chill weather. Just before Christmas she strained her back and was carried from the set on a stretcher. A physician gave her an injection to ease the spinal pain, and she gallantly returned to complete the day's shooting. Stanley had taught his daughter well; she was, first and foremost, a trouper.

In spite of her numerous ailments and personal woes, she dutifully reported daily, winning the admiration of Frank Mattison, a tough company production manager. Mattison informed studio executives that Lupino deserved a medal for sticking it out on location. By December 1946, Warner Bros. was forced to pay Lupino another twenty thousand dollars, since the starting date of a third picture had come and gone. One evening, when she was nearing the end of her contract, she encountered Jack Warner outside his office. Lyons had yet to reach an amicable arrangement. Uneasy at meeting her adversary, Ida didn't know what to expect. "We can have you take Bette Davis' place," the studio had already propositioned, without success. But Warner seemed friendly and flashed his pearly smile.

Then he got down to business. He asked her to sign a four-year exclusive contract. Ida refused.

Warner's sharp retort was like a stiletto in her breast. If she didn't sign a long-term contract, she was finished at Warner Bros. On January 25, 1947, *Deep Valley* closed production, forty days behind schedule. Four days later, Ida signed the mutual cancellation of her contract. Lupino's impressive career at Warner Bros. was over. She ended her years of cinema glory on a high note; she was critically acclaimed for her fine acting in *Deep Valley*. She cleared her dressing room at the studio, then walked away, filled with bitterness.

9

COLLIE

George Gershwin seemed put on earth to write the music that expressed him. —ARMAND S. DEUTSCH

Lupino at twenty-nine years old was at a crossroads in her career. Being unshackled from Warners gave her a sense of freedom and independence. The art of acting before the camera was no longer a personal challenge. Had she remained with Warner Bros. she would have guaranteed wealth. But money was secondary to her. What she wanted, more than anything, was artistic freedom. Her yearning to be her own boss led to a hasty partnership with Ben Bogeaus, an independent producer. They formed Arcadia Productions with offices at the General Service Studio and in a press release announced that Ida would star in a picture a year. As their first release, they acquired the rights to *Early Autumn*, Louis Bromfield's Pulitzer-Prize-winning novel. Ida brimmed with enthusiasm for her new venture. She read voraciously, searching for good scripts and new talent. She preferred stories about "poor, bewildered people. That's what we all are," she said.

In interviews, Ida described herself as a "bachelor girl." She spoke longingly of finding a mate. Fame and fortune were satisfying, she said, but "the security of being someone's beloved wife sounds more attractive right now." Louis had married Peggy Morrow Field in May 1946. He had resumed his screen career and seemed happy. Ida saw him occasionally at the Chanteclair Restaurant on Sunset Boulevard where he was part-owner. Ida was a sought-after date, seen with the most eligible escorts, including David Niven, attorney Greg Bautzer and singer Tony Martin.

She relaxed with Frances Robinson and Sandra Perry, a lovely socialite and the former wife of tennis star Fred Perry. The trio spent their weekends sailing the *Bahia*, moored at posh Newport Beach. When the subject of men arose, each morosely discussed her failed marriage and her hopes for the future. The first of the group to remarry was Sandra Perry, who became the wife of cinematographer Henry Freulich. Ida and Frances Robinson continued their leisurely hours in Newport and were frequently guests aboard Sterling Hayden's sixty-three-foot schooner, the *Quest*. Ida was thrilled whenever Hayden let her take the wheel on the high seas; she loved to hear the mastline whistling as the *Quest* rose on the waves then plunged into the trough, showering the deck with plumes of glistening sea water. Ida scampered over the deck barefoot, joyously riding the foaming ocean; she found sailing both exhilarating and frightening. Hayden told his passengers that they had to work aboard ship. Ida had trouble furling the jib, but she happily served vegetable soup in the galley. Hayden kept a small library aboard his sailboat, and Ida was impressed by his knowledge of international affairs and national politics. Once moored, Ida and Frances would dutifully scrub down the ship. As twilight fell, Hayden would convey his amorous mood, suggesting that Ida remain aboard overnight. She eluded her suitor on such occasions, playfully dubbing him "old scrub and screw."

In Hollywood circles, marital fidelity was not particularly prized. Many actors, insecure in their own lives, had become performers to bask in the glow of worshipful admiration. If they were besieged by those who loved them; how could they say no? For the studs, there was always a pretty young thing eager for a private rendezvous. And the queen bees had their discreet strings of lovers. Though single, and undeniably lonely, Ida preferred emotional security to uninhibited affairs.

Approaching the seemingly ominous age of thirty, she succumbed to anxiety and worry that she would never find the right man. Though young, she was acutely aware of the rapid passage of time and the brevity of existence. On June 7, her dear friend John Decker died at age fifty-two. His colorful career had come to a sudden close. Friends crowded into his large studio at 1215 Alta Loma Road to pay their respects. Among the grief-stricken were Ida, Errol Flynn, Red Skelton, Vincent Price, Thomas Mitchell and Anthony Quinn. Decker lay in an open casket, surrounded by wreaths of gladioli and dahlias, his palette and easel nearby. Behind the casket was "Clown With Cabbage," a painting of his friend John Barrymore. Even in death, Decker's startling originality shone forth. After a simple eulogy, mourners sat quietly as the casket was moved out of the studio. Then, as they were about to depart, Decker's voice boomed out from beyond the grave: "To sing, to laugh, to dream, to walk in my own way, and be alone," reciting the famous speech from Rostand's *Cyrano De Bergerac*, from a recording he had made six weeks earlier. The audience of two hundred sat stunned, inwardly smiling at Decker's farewell. Ida shed tears for her friend; she admired his unmatched style, even in death.

While at a party one evening, bored and ready to leave, she spotted Collier Young. They had met a decade earlier, introduced by Louis. Collie, as he was known to friends, had always found her "tremendously feminine and blindingly bright." He liked her rapier wit and her delicate frame, which reminded him of fragile porcelain. There was an instant attraction between them. He drove her home.

Connie joined them, and they chatted until dawn. Ida and Connie felt it had been a rewarding encounter.

Collier Young had an abundance of charm. His elegant style and witty sophistication attracted women and made him popular with men. He was thirty-nine years old, handsome with exquisite manners. Born into a prominent North Carolina family, he was often described as an F. Scott Fitzgerald character. While he had attended Dartmouth, the stock market crash had triggered the Depression, but the irrepressible Young had a knack for rising to the top. After college he started as a copywriter for Young and Rubicam, an advertising firm in New York, then became a literary agent for Brandt and Brandt. In 1935 he moved to Los Angeles and worked as an agent for Myron Selznick's firm. Next, he spent two years as a story editor for Sam Goldwyn. He worked briefly as an assistant for Jack Warner. By 1947 he was executive assistant to Harry Cohn. Like Lupino, he was alone. After he returned from serving in the military as a navy commander, his marriage to model Valerie Edmonds had failed.

Though a capable studio assistant, he was a frustrated writer and unhappy under the boot of Harry Cohn, a mogul who made underlings cringe with his insults. Young had just sold *Act of Violence*, a story he had written, which was to be produced by MGM. He was eager to write and produce his own films. With their shared ambitions, Ida and Collie became fast companions. She loved his wild sense of humor, which matched hers. He had a colorful streak that led him to outrageous moments, such as his yearly re-enactment of a Civil War battle. Dressing in a Confederate uniform, he would imbibe spirits, then whoop it up on his horse, Traveler, named after Robert E. Lee's steed.

Ida and Collie were devoted to sailing and both shared a passion for reading. Collie, nine years her senior, displayed erudition that impressed Ida, especially his knowledge of contemporary literature. He had a convincing, fatherly way of assuring her that he was an experienced man of the world, well versed in life and, more important, in the motion picture business.

Collie was soon in love with her and hinting at an engagement. He was captivating, thought Ida, agreeing with his friend Armand Deutsch that "George Gershwin seemed put on earth to write the music that expressed him." But they had just met. Should she marry so soon?

As always, Ida relentlessly pushed herself, avidly poring over dozens of scripts, original stories and novels. One evening over dinner, she mentioned that she had come across "the most wonderful book," one that would make a great film. Collie was taken by surprise, for he had the very same idea about *The Dark Love*. They were definitely on the same wavelength, thought Ida. But where Collie dreamt, Ida acted. She was being pursued by agent Charles K. Feldman. Arthur Lyons had sold his company to David L. Lowe, but smooth-talking Feldman asked to represent her, and he proposed a fabulous deal. Feldman, who bore a striking resemblance to Clark Gable, was a business genius, a gambler and a playboy. He bought *The Dark Love* for twenty thousand dollars, just for Ida. In September, he sold the rights to Twentieth Century-Fox with the stipulation that Lupino play the lead. The deal was concluded for $130,000. Ida was paid $95,000 for the role, with twenty thousand deducted for the story purchase. The remaining fifteen thousand dollars profit on the story sale was also hers. Feldman waived all commissions so Ida could receive a substantial income for 1947. Not surprisingly, the bold maneuver won Lupino to his Famous Artist Agency. Fox retitled *The Dark Love*; it became *Road House*.

Collier Young waged a determined battle to win Ida's affection. She was the most amazing woman he had ever met, and after several months, she was deeply attached to him. He had a reassuring air that calmed her when she became anxious. His most attractive feature was his ability to make her laugh. But when he proposed, she hesitated. He gave her thirty days to decide; on the twenty-eighth, she agreed to be his wife. In November she made the announcement: "I'm in love and this bachelor girl existence is too lonely. I can't tell you the date yet. Collie's divorce won't be final for four and a half months. We'll also have to find a place to live."

Wearing her new engagement ring, Ida reluctantly told Ben Bogeaus that she had a new partner. Arcadia Productions was dissolved as she and Collie laid plans. She placed her house on the market with a sigh of relief; she had often found it nerve wracking to have the place filled with people day and night.

As a superb conversationalist and Ivy League man, Collier Young had impressed Sam Goldwyn. He had long been a weekly guest at Goldwyn's dinner parties. Ida now accompanied her fiancé to the Saturday night soirees. Although Collie could charm listeners with stories, he could not convince the studio moguls to let him produce motion pictures.

On one of Collier and Ida's dates, they decided to see *Kiss of Death*, a thriller with Richard Widmark as a psychopathic, giggling murderer. Ida was impressed with Widmark.

Fox then announced that the cast would be Lupino, Widmark, Cornel Wilde and Celeste Holm. The cigar-chomping Zanuck was filled with confidence, but four directors turned him down. Charles Feldman got the job for his client Jean Negulesco, who had also departed Warners, but with less dignity.

While on location for *Johnny Belinda*, Jack Warner had become incensed when he thought Negulesco was indulging in too many pictorial shots, one of Warner's pet peeves. He cabled a fiery order to producer Jerry Wald: "Fire the Rumanian jerk!" Wald threatened to quit if Negulesco went. Warner let the director finish the picture, then gave him the boot. Ironically, *Johnny Belinda* received several Oscar nominations, winning Jane Wyman the best actress award for her fine portrayal of a deaf woman. Negulesco got a phone call from an exuberant Jack Warner: "Kid, we did it again!" But Negulesco never returned to the Warner lot.

In *Road House*, Ida plays Lily Stevens, a sultry nightclub singer caught in a dangerous love triangle. Richard Widmark is the club owner who falls for her, though she is taken with his partner, Cornel Wilde. The film is a tight, well-crafted melodrama filled with tension as Lupino's character is stalked by her insanely jealous boss, who is mad with love and capable of frame-ups and sadistic violence.

From the very first day, the production was a physically demanding experience for Ida. During a brawl scene, a three-hundred-pound wrestler left her heavily bruised, then she wrenched an ankle fleeing from the maniacal character played by Widmark. She was accidentally knocked down in a fight scene and suffered a pulled neck tendon and painful back injury. She was called on to scream so much at her sadistic boss that her voice eventually faded.

Cornel Wilde was equally delighted to work with Lupino. "She was so real, offbeat and just lots of fun." But what impressed Wilde most was her serious side. As he remembers, "We were, a lot of us, very much against that louse, Joe McCarthy." Both Lupino and Wilde were alarmed and angered about the creeping political hysteria sweeping the nation. Fear of "the red menace," promoted by politicians such as McCarthy, flamed obsessive anticommunist sentiment to the point of reckless hysteria and empty allegations against the innocent. Soon, the pervasive terror of being labeled a fellow-traveler, a pink, a sympathizer or a Communist would permeate Hollywood, as Lupino would intimately discover.

Ida courageously accepted the challenge of singing in *Road House*. She could carry a melody but didn't have much confidence in her voice, once described by a writer as sounding like a nutmeg grinder. But musical director Lionel Newman felt her husky tones conveyed a distinct, sexy quality. "Her voice was so right; it wasn't any great singing, but it was just perfect for the picture."

Lionel Newman wrote "Again" for Ida. She also recorded "The Right Kind" and the haunting "One for My Baby" by Johnny Mercer and Harold Arlen, half-speaking, half-singing the classic song. As director Negulesco aptly put it: "No-voice Lupino sang them and placed them first on the hit parade."

Road House was a phenomenal smash. Under Negulesco's direction, the veteran Lupino and the rookie Widmark created vivid characters that held audiences spellbound. Widmark's sinister psycho shocked viewers with his suave, frenzied evil. One reviewer called him "Frankenstein minus makeup." The vote was unanimous that Lupino had delivered one of her most memorable performances, and she received high acting marks for believably showing the transition from a lonely singer to a radiant woman in love. Ida always raved about the powerful ending. As she and her lover Wilde are pursued by Widmark, who is insane with jealousy, a fight ensues. She grabs a .38 pistol. As she holds the smoking revolver over Widmark's punctured body, he smiles fiendishly and murmurs his last words: "I told you she was different." This is exactly what Lupino had been telling audiences for years, and she loved the powerful ending.

John Franco, a college student and a struggling musician, was trudging through Laurel Canyon in search of work. Collier Young found his business card and summoned him to his residence on Stanley Hills Drive. As Franco approached the house, he saw an attractive woman leaving. She seemed alarmed by his unfamiliar face and roared away in a green Cadillac. Later, Franco's new employer told him he had given his fiancée quite a scare. A few nights later Franco offered to cook dinner for the couple. "She likes boiled lamb chops and homemade dessert," Young told him.

Ida arrived, stylishly attired. In a deep voice, she introduced herself. The couple asked Franco to sit and dine with them. "They were really just beautiful people," says Franco. "They never treated me like a servant. I was more like a member of the family.

Franco, who had been crippled by polio at age fifteen, walked with a limp, which concerned Ida. "It was very close to Ida's heart seeing anybody with a disability. She sent me to her doctor and paid for it herself."

At first, Franco didn't realize his new friends were in the motion picture business. One day he had noticed on a wall an etching of Ida by Jean Negulesco.

"Is she famous?" he asked.

Collie laughed, "Around the world."

On June 28, 1948, Ida proudly became an American citizen. A year earlier, she had eagerly appeared at the U.S. Department of Naturalization for a history exam. For months, she had studied intensely and had impressed her examiner by knowing the vice-president who served under President Harrison. Though she was elated to have become an American citizen, Ida was reluctant to join the noisy celebrations on Independence Day. She puzzled over why Americans celebrated severing ties to England, which for her remained a great and good nation.

In August, Ida and Collie were married in the chapel of the Presbyterian Church in La Jolla. Harry Kurnitz, a wit and bon vivant, was the best man. Harry Mines gave the bride away. Ida wore a high-necked Adrian gown of heavy white silk. Her light brown hair was arranged in bangs beneath a halo hat of white lace edged with burgundy. She wore white satin slippers and carried a bouquet of magenta orchids.

As guests filled the chapel, Ida and Mines became anxious. Three times they mistakenly started down the aisle. At the altar, Mines waited for his big moment. The preacher looked at him. "I

DO!" he blurted loudly. Ida doubled up laughing. Thirty guests attended a lively reception on the warm outdoor patio at the Casa de Mañana Hotel. Ida was ecstatic, happily hugging everyone, sipping champagne and showing off her new ring, an expensive antique that glittered with diamonds and rubies. As the party progressed, Connie, Rita, Reggie Gardiner, and newspaper columnist Harry Crocker put on an impromptu dance. The chorus line kicked up a storm of laughter as the press clicked photographs. After the reception, the bride and groom boarded the *Malibar II*, a yacht on loan from radio comic Ed "Archie" Gardner, and sailed for Catalina's Toyon Bay for a week-long honeymoon.

The newlyweds settled into a home resembling a New England farmhouse at 13030 Mulholland Drive, off the main road, high in the Santa Monica Mountains. They had purchased the unusual structure from Sandy and Henry Freulich. They enjoyed a spectacular view of the San Fernando Valley and the majestic Santa Susana range in the distance. Dubbed by Ida "the Mouse House" because of unexpected, four-footed visitors, their new residence, surrounded by a white picket fence, was the picture of rustic privacy.

Remodeling began immediately, and Ida served as interior decorator. She supervised every detail, carefully watching as carpenters hammered and sawed. When she could no longer resist, she jumped up and began painting. She enjoyed mixing the whitewash for the fireplace bricks, then going to work with her brush.

The home was on a single level, except for an upstairs bedroom where Ida and Collie slept on a canopied, four-poster bed, the jewel in their vast collection of early American antiques. Ida skillfully blended her treasures with Collie's, adding her special touches. She transformed a cobbler's strongbox into a magazine rack; a Franklin stove was painted white and crowned with cascading philodendrons in an antique vase, a Pennsylvania Dutch dresser became a bookcase for Collie's rare tomes. One of her husband's sentimental pieces was his childhood school desk, sent by his mother as a wedding gift. Ida moved it next to a huge wing chair, a perfect place for the telephone. In the library were Ida's high-backed "prayer chairs," the seats at kneeling height. Carefully arranged throughout the home were her pewter tankards, Sheffield plates and valuable Meissen figurines. Ida hung her New York Film Critics Award in the guest bathroom above the toilet.

Just when friends thought the extensive remodeling was finished, Ida surprised everyone. She asked John Franco to help her paint the house red. Franco remembers the disaster: "At night, when it was lit up, it looked like the house was on fire. Later, she couldn't stand it, so we painted it white."

Ida's final task was erecting a sign, clearly visible from the steep driveway. It warned: "Visitors Don't Drop In. Please Call First." The open house policy of past days, prompted by her loneliness when Louis left, was gone forever.

Collier Young soon discovered that he was wed to "nine wives" who had "nine personalities." When asked what life with Lupino was like, he said: "One of the exciting things about Ida is her unpredictability." One evening she played a recording of a drama she had written, a romance about the love between a Cockney bus driver and a spinster. The story had half a dozen characters. When he finished listening, Collier asked Ida why she hadn't had a part. She smiled. She had played all the roles and had even written the music.

The newlyweds' domestic tranquillity in their mountain haven soon vanished. Collie returned to twelve-hour days at Columbia, enduring long hours of orders from Harry Cohn. Ida agreed to appear in Columbia's *Lust for Gold*, a rugged western based on the legend of the Lost Dutchman Mine. Ida chose the script because, as she said, "I thought I could at least have lunch with Collie." To her dismay, most of the film was shot on location in Arizona. The cast and crew, led by F. Sylvan Simon, headquartered in Phoenix. Each day the company drove miles into the stifling desert, often mounting mules to reach isolated areas. Opposite Glenn Ford, Ida plays a scheming woman who commits murder for gold, only to die in a mine during an earthquake. Assistant director James Nicholson watched Lupino closely and admired her professional expertise in the parched desert under a burning sun. What Nicholson found most curious was her constant presence. Rather than retreat to town once her scenes were completed, she remained. She watched the director, the cameraman and crew technicians.

Ida's careful observance of the technical aspects of *Lust for Gold* was for her a final lesson in the motion picture arts. As the forties came to a close, she and Collie had plans to strike out on their own. A decade earlier she had proved to the world that she could act; now she was just as determined to show the world her own films.

At a party about this time, Ida met Roberto Rossellini, hailed for his stunning *Rome Open City*, a major film in the history of international cinema. Rossellini had attempted to express life as it really was, creating a true window into the lives of simple everyday people. When Lupino spoke with Rossellini, he complained, "In Hollywood movies, the star is going crazy, or drinks too much, or he wants to kill his wife. When are you going to make pictures about ordinary people, in ordinary situations?" Rossellini's question made a profound impression on Lupino.

10

FILMMAKERS

Everyone clamored to see Not Wanted. *Joan
Crawford called me and asked if I could bring a
print to her house. Lupino was hot.* —HARRY MINES

Ida had read countless scripts in search of the perfect project.
Finally, she found something that spurred her to a momentous de-
cision. She was wildly enthusiastic over a story written by Malvin
Wald. According to writer Paul Jerrico: "I was approached by Jerry
Wald, then a producer at Warner Bros. and Malvin's brother, who
asked me if I could develop an original story about unwed mothers.
There wasn't a hell of a lot of time. He said it was for Ida Lupino."
Jerrico, an accomplished professional writer, was a solid construc-
tionist who turned in a tight, gripping first draft. Ida added a few
touches written with a shrewd eye for camera angles. She and Collie
felt the moment was opportune to launch the project. Collie showed
the script to Harry Cohn, seeking support and financing.

Cohn refused to provide any money or even permit his assistant to produce the picture for Columbia. Cohn had superb
intuition about what would make a good film, but he also had
a sadistic streak, a cruel penchant for belittling subordinates,
especially when they were married to beautiful actresses. Collier

Young was livid. Rather than accept the brutal rejection, he quit. The unexpected move caught Ida by surprise; not only had her husband failed to convince Cohn, but he had allowed his anger to deprive him of a job and an income.

Yet Ida understood the depth of her husband's bitterness. Cohn's lack of vision epitomized for Ida the rigid studio mentality of slave and master. Both she and Collie were sick of "front office domination." They joined with fledgling Emerald Productions, whose president was thirty-five-year-old Anson Bond, a specialist in low-budget films. Bond had honed his craft in the armed services, where he had produced documentaries.

In January 1949, the company released *The Judge*, a film that was written in two days and shot in five. Lupino and Young had invested money in the picture, which made quite a profit. Ida and Anson Bond struck a deal to co-produce *Not Wanted*. Collie was handed the lesser title of "production supervisor."

The Mouse House was soon awhirr with activity. As Ida plunged into a frenzy of production details, Collie found her an assistant, Robert Eggenweiler, a former office boy for Jack Warner. Eggenweiler would arrive early at the Mouse House and share breakfast with Ida, who always started the day with sole and scrambled eggs. Ida preferred to work near the pool, basking in the sun. She had usually been up all night. She dictated a multitude of ideas, correspondence, dialogue and production details to Eggenweiler in an amazing flow of creative thought. He came to idolize his boss as a brilliant woman.

Ida had long dreamed of discovering new talent; she now had the opportunity. Casually dressed in slacks and a bright blouse, she sat in the living room of her home interviewing prospective leads. Within weeks, 250 hopefuls had auditioned. Sally Forrest, a dancer, read for the role of the unmarried girl who becomes pregnant. As

Forrest delivered her lines, Ida knew immediately she was perfect for the part.

A writer mentioned a struggling actor named Keefe Braselle, who was then selling trucks to make a living. Braselle was so nervous that Ida asked Collie to leave the room until he regained his composure. After his audition, he nervously looked at Ida. "You're in," she smiled. Leo Penn, a former bombardier, was the third unknown selected. Collie had spotted his photograph in a talent directory and called him to the house. Also cast was Rita Lupino, for a minor role.

The topic of illegitimate birth was still taboo in 1949. The Breen Office ripped into the script, rejecting Ida's title *Unwed Mothers*, indicating violations of the Code: "We pointed out to Miss Lupino that it was not good to indicate an actual precise 'point of contact' between Steve and Sally, a point at which the audience will have it brought home to them that here our two young people indulge in an illicit sex affair . . . the actual use of the word 'pregnancy' may be deleted by some political censor boards. We suggest that you find a somewhat less pointed substitute." Ida engaged in lengthy conversations with the Breen Office. "I found them amazingly helpful," she said. "We went over the script with them and they pointed out what it must do. They practically wrote the story for us."

For weeks, day and night, the Mouse House was the scene of intense script conferences, budget discussions, wardrobe fittings, rehearsals and crew meetings. Elmer Clifton, director of Emerald Productions' financially successful *The Judge*, was given the helm of *Not Wanted*. Maurice Vaccarino, assistant director, was a native of France who had disappointed his distinguished family of lawyers by announcing that he was emigrating to America to work in motion pictures. "You may as well join the circus," his father had said. But

Vaccarino felt his decision was rewarded ten times over by working alongside Lupino.

Fate had a hand in making *Not Wanted* a milestone in Ida's career. A few days before the cameras were to roll, Elmer Clifton suffered a mild heart attack. On February 28, 1949, the first day of filming, Ida Lupino became a director. The company assembled on Bunker Hill in downtown Los Angeles. Though Clifton had recovered enough from his seizure to be on the set, he was weak and confined to his director's chair.

Darr Smith, a reporter for the *Daily News*, came to watch. He was surprised to see Lupino giving instructions to the cast. Ida wasn't a member of the Directors Guild. "Heavens, no! I wouldn't think of directing," she hastily explained. "Elmer Clifton is the director and he's one of the best. He just asked me to take over the kids today. This is the first day of shooting and everybody's a little nervous." Ida told the reporter the production schedule was fourteen days, documentary style. "And it's going to be great," she insisted. "We're shooting it just like they used to shoot 'em back in 1915—on the streets of Los Angeles."

Smith was impressed by the fast and efficient method of Lupino's directorial skill. Scenes were rapidly completed in front of rooming houses, homes and stores. As he watched, an apartment was rapidly converted into a police station by mounting a sign on a wall, then adding iron bars to the windows. The scene called for Sally Forrest to descend the steps of the police station, spot Braselle, turn and run away.

Ida was dissatisfied with the first take: "Sally, when you come down those steps you're beat. You have no place to go. You have nobody to turn to, but the last person in the world you want to see is Keefe." The second take wasn't right either. "Turn your head slowly," Ida instructed. "Ask yourself where you're going. Then when you see Keefe, turn your whole body toward him quickly, hold it, then turn away from him and run. And Keefe, when I yell your name, take out after her."

"Places everybody!" yelled Maurice Vaccarino.

Ida repeated his call to assemble, then turned to the reporter. In a quiet voice, she said: "But remember, I'm not directing this. Wouldn't think of it."

The next day the *Daily News* carried an eyewitness account of Lupino in command. "Lupino isn't really directing this picture," wrote Darr Smith. "She says so herself. But it's difficult to tell just what she's doing if it isn't directing."

As the days went by, Maurice Vaccarino was astounded by the thirty-one-year-old Lupino's expertise. He had worked with many professionals, and he found it hard to believe that this was Ida's first try. The first week, she conferred with Clifton on how certain scenes should be played, then she became fully confident in her own judgment, and the ailing, elderly Clifton, sitting forlornly, became no more than a figurehead. Ida insisted on realism. As preparation she had visited homes where pregnant girls resided, observing that there was no discrimination, that women of all races and religions lived together. The original script had contained elements of such racial harmony, but word was passed to Anson Bond to eliminate such depictions.

He told Lupino that an investor was offended by a scene of the expectant heroine sharing a room with black, Oriental and Hispanic girls. Ida was astonished. She met with the investor and explained that situation existed in such homes. He answered that there would be trouble from "the race angle." Ida argued for an hour but was told to delete the scene or she "got no money." She finally gave in; she vowed that some day she wouldn't be obligated to men with such ideas.

Ida defiantly included an Oriental girl in the scene; later, she received a letter of complaint from the investor. Victory, however, was Lupino's. "It was too late then to reshoot and he had to stuff it down his pipe." Ida remembered her father's words: "We're in a tinsel business, Ida. We go from 8:30 to 11:00 and then they take us and the scenery away. And what's beneath us? The brick of the theater, and beneath that the earth." Stanley had told her that the earth mattered and so did the people who spring from it—"all the people, all kinds." He had cautioned her against phoniness and reminded her that the theater takes its life from people. He had warned: "If you ever lose touch with people your life will have lost its meaning."

Ida chose "Hitchcock's cutter," William Ziegler, to edit the film. She and Collie were about to screen a rough cut when they unexpectedly met Dorothy Arzner, a director whose work Ida admired. Arzner began in silents as a film editor. In 1926 she directed *Fashions for Women,* the beginning of a successful directorial career. Ida was especially taken with *Craig's Wife,* directed by Arzner in 1936, the story of a ruthless housewife that featured Rosalind Russell.

"Oh, Miss Arzner, I loved that picture. We're running the first cut of the first one I've directed."

"May I come and see it?" asked Arzner.

"I'd be delighted," said an enthralled Ida. "Oh, you're a talented lady. You're not looking at somebody like you."

"Oh, to hell with that. I'd love to see it."

At the end of the screening, Arzner turned in her seat. "Mr. Young, that lady sitting there is going to end up *directing* a picture starring Rosalind Russell. Congratulations."

Ida was deeply moved. "Miss Arzner, you've given me every birthday and Christmas present in the world."

Once under way, Ida asked her old friend Harry Mines to handle publicity. Money was so tight that she could offer him no salary. Mines offered to work without a fee, just to help her, but she insisted that he receive a portion of the profits, if any were forth-coming.

Striving to stay within the bounds of a small budget, Ida cut costs wherever she could. Mines watched as Ida cleverly found shortcuts: "The interior shots were filmed at California Studios. Ida used a set from an old Garfield picture, taking three walls and making each a different scene. She was amazing." Ida smoothly talked Dr. Maurice Bernstein, her personal physician, into appear-ing as a doctor in the delivery room. Even her houseman, John Franco, was brought to work. Franco contributed musical passages for the score. For Sally Forrest's wardrobe, Ida simply opened her own closet.

Forrest was grateful for Lupino's patience. As an actress, Ida had the ability to understand what the performer was experiencing. "She was a great communicator," says Forrest.

Ida and Collie devised the advertising strategy, promoting the film with stark realism. "A Frank Story As Bold As The Screen Has Ever Told! Here is a motion picture jammed with a lifetime of emotion . . . the story of one girl's mistake! The drama that is being lived by 100,000 girls! A movie you must not miss!" The Production Code prohibited use of *Unwed Mothers* as a title, but nothing stopped Ida in newspaper ads in which Sally Forrest, looking down-trodden and afraid, wore an oversize jacket and clutched an enormous suitcase. Bold type proclaimed: *UNWED MOTHER*. Ida never took credit for directing—she was credited only as the producer—but ads read, "Ida Lupino Presents *Not Wanted*."

With her increase in stature, Ida's image as a madcap vanished. Filmakers' publicity now presented her as a serious motion picture producer. Acutely conscious of her former image, both onscreen and off, Ida did nothing that would add to her reputation as an eccen-tric. "All of that was now forgotten," said Harry Mines. Mines scored a major publicity coup by informing Eleanor Roosevelt about the film.

Mrs. Roosevelt hosted a popular nationwide radio program and was always interested in the plight of the socially disadvantaged. Her daughter, Anna, hosted the show from the West Coast. On February 18, 1949, Ida was a featured guest, interviewed by Anna Roosevelt. Ida explained how she first became interested in the project.

"It was quite accidental," she said. "You see, I read a story that I somehow couldn't forget. So a group of us formed a producing company to make a picture of it."

Ida revealed that "several of the studios have turned down this story because they were afraid of it." She praised Breen and his staff for their "wonderfully constructive help" and added "they are much more than censors, by the way." She said she hoped to "show the public the heartbreak of the unwed mother" and believed that the picture would "show what can be done about this."

Ida was at her best when Roosevelt asked her about the unwed mothers she'd met. "They couldn't have better care," she said. "When the girls come there, frightened and ashamed—and all of them are—they are taken in and given sympathy and care. These homes are of all denominations and all races. The only thought is to help the mother recover from her mistake and to give her child a fair start in life." When asked if the majority of mothers were from poor homes, Ida responded, "Yes, some of them are, but not all. Some girls get into trouble from having too much money, too much indulgence, just as others do from having too little." Ida's solution to their plight was that "we should all work to alleviate the poverty and illness that really causes their plight. Love is a precious thing. All human beings need to love and be loved. Life doesn't give us the means of finding love without the bounds of our conventions and many of us will find it outside. And that is why we are making this picture. We feel that these girls are entitled to understanding."

Anna Roosevelt informed Mines that Ida's eloquence prompted an enormous response in listeners, who agreed with Ida's compassionate words. Reviews of the film, however, were mixed. The *Hollywood Reporter* found it "done with taste, dignity and compassion." The *New York Times* lauded it for avoiding cheap sensationalism and criticized only a "breach of good taste in an extended obstetrical sequence." But, though avoiding tawdry aspects of the subject, the film was called "dramatically limp."

Not Wanted was a greater success than anyone anticipated. It had cost a paltry $153,000. Only two weeks after its release, Emerald Productions had paid off the primary loan from the Chemical Bank of New York. By April 1950, the picture had grossed a phenomenal one million dollars. Lupino's first production electrified Hollywood. Harry Mines witnessed the wave of interest and adulation that came her way. "Everyone clamored to see *Not Wanted*. Joan Crawford called me and asked if I could bring a print to her house. Lupino was hot."

When Harry Mines received his first check he bought a new automobile. He drove to the Mouse House in his shiny new car. Ida watched as he came up the driveway and stopped before her. She eyed the car from end to end. "Well," she drawled, "thank God for knocked up girls, eh?"

Ida and Collie parted ways with Anson Bond when they were unable to agree on future business arrangements. They could now fulfill their dream of forming their own company. Ida insisted on including the writer who had hammered out the original story-Malvin Wald. The originality of Wald's idea had earned Lupino's admiration. When she first saw the story, she called Warner Bros. to ask Jerry Wald about his talented brother.

Malvin Wald, native New Yorker, was led by his immense curiosity to pursue an academic career before he took up writing. After military service he came to Hollywood, where his brother was a producer. But his mentor was Mark Hellinger. Wald had been inspired to write a story about real cops, and Hellinger had financed his trip to New York. Wald spent two months reading the unsolved cases in the New York Police Department files, and what emerged was *The Naked City* in 1948, a screenplay Hellinger handed to writer Albert Maltz for polishing. The outcome was a stunning film directed by Jules Dassin and featuring Barry Fitzgerald as a quiet, unassuming detective seeking the murderer of a beautiful model. Shot entirely on the streets of New York, it received acclaim for the accuracy of the homicide bureau Wald had created. The film resulted in his first Academy Award nomination for best original story. Ida and Collie were impressed with Wald's ability to infuse stories with intense social drama, and they selected him to round out the triumvirate known as the Filmakers. Collie was president, Ida was vice-president and Malvin Wald was treasurer.

The threesome had created a great challenge for themselves. Wald enunciated the essence of Filmakers: "We are trying to make pictures of a sociological nature to appeal to older people who usually stay away from theaters. We are out to tackle serious themes and problem dramas. We don't plan to make any melodramas, musicals or westerns."

In August, Ida and Collie announced that their new company would produce "documentary movies." The *New York Times* reported that Filmakers' first release would be *Never Fear*, a drama about polio victims, directed by Frank Cavett. Collie explained his marketing strategy to Hedda Hopper: "We're working on the theory that the ticket-buying public is more interested in *what's* in a picture than *who's* in it."

Though all partners seemed to share similar artistic goals, undercurrents of dissension swirled around their collaboration. Wald resented Young's pat answers and his assumptions that he was better educated and more informed when it came to business decisions. Ida always thought for herself and expressed her opinions freely but often deferred to her husband in the final vote. Wald was a full partner, but soon realized that his opinions meant nothing to Collie, who felt he knew better. For the moment, Wald was content to sit at his typewriter.

Collie reported to his partners that he had investors who would finance *Never Fear*, with one stipulation: that Lupino direct. Ida readily agreed but, even with investment capital, they were short of funds. To maintain control, Ida and Collie sank their personal savings into the project, the bulk of the funds from Lupino's bank account. Ida was so enthusiastic about directing that she made a startling revelation to Hedda Hopper: "I've never really liked acting. It's a tortuous profession, and it plays havoc with your private life. It's about time the screen got rid of the old faces, including mine. I intend to give up acting altogether eventually."

Ida busied herself with the script of *Never Fear*. She collaborated with Collie to develop the story of a young dancer who is stricken with polio. Ida's inspiration for the project was Jack Gregory, a respected physiotherapist at the famed Kabat-Kaiser Institute in Santa Monica. Since her terrifying bout with polio in 1934, Ida had donated money and assistance to fight the crippling disease. By July 1949, America was again in the grip of an epidemic; 7,539 cases were reported. Gregory, whom she had known since her own recovery, urged Ida to make a film about hope.

Ida was enthusiastic about the idea, and she recalled the courage in her own physician years earlier. She thought long and hard about a story line and jotted her thoughts on paper, constructing a narrative and inventing characters and dialogue. By that time she had been recognized as a professional writer. In May her short story "Exit Cue" had appeared in *Colliers*; scripts had also been sold to the radio show *Suspense*, one of her favorite programs

As Ida and Collie labored over the script, they realized that the production would require more capital. They asked Wald if he would like to invest in the picture, a project that had been launched before Filmakers was actually formed. Wald felt the concept was risky but decided to confer with industry friends before reaching a final decision. He consulted Bud Levin, whose family owned a hundred theaters in northern California.

"I know all about it," said Levin. "My fellow exhibitors say they're not going to touch that picture."

"Why?" asked Wald.

"Because it deals with polio." Wald protested that there were films which dealt with violence, war and crime. "Yes," agreed Levin. "The criminals and soldiers are somewhere in the distance, but polio can strike you and your family. It's a very personal thing. It will make audiences feel uneasy. I will not put that film in my theater. You can tell Ida Lupino."

Wald reported the conversation to his partners. Ida began to worry. Filmakers was a fledgling company that could not afford a failure. They had other scripts, dozens of them ready for filming. They could develop a screenplay that would excite exhibitors. Wald told them that he would not invest and that, in his opinion, they were making a mistake.

"Who is this man, Bud Levin?" snapped Collie. "I've never heard of him."

"They merely own a chain of theaters," responded Wald.

Ida spoke up. "Malvin's friend may be right," she said.

But Collier Young was insistent. "I know. I've been in this business for years. This fellow doesn't know."

Collie convinced Ida that the film would succeed. She pondered the gamble and considered the grave financial risk. Finally, she concurred with her husband that the project would continue. They were, however, at a dead end in their search for potential investors. The mention of polio scared away financiers. Ida told her agent to find a picture for her. They would gamble everything. Little did she know that the decision would change her life. As the days passed, John Franco grew close to Ida. He became more than a houseman; he was soon a trusted confidant. Franco immediately noticed her impulsive kindness. As he explains: "She used to give everything away. She never cared much for expensive jewelry. She was very down to earth." At first hand, he viewed both her brilliant and her eccentric sides. He saw an accomplished actress and budding producer who could use her intense concentration to oversee hundreds of details in a motion picture, but also a woman who was so forgetful in private that it was startling.

Sleepless nights were torture. Franco encouraged her to seek natural ways to relax. He discovered that a masseuse could ease her tension. They would go driving together in Ida's Cadillac for hours, as she wound down from the day's work. Franco met Ida's sister and noted the similarity. Both were outspoken and quite independent.

Ida had done all she could to advance Rita's career. When *The Corn Is Green* was announced in 1945, Ida went to Bette Davis and asked her to arrange a screen test for Rita. Davis agreed. Ida coached her sister and they viewed the footage together. "It was the only test of mine I'd glimpsed," Rita said, "that didn't make me shrink down in my seat." But the job fell through.

Rita eventually teamed with her instructor, Antonio Triana, and became a successful dancer. She was featured in three concerts at Carnegie Hall, with a full orchestra behind her.

Ida would listen to Franco's advice, and he could convince her to do things when others could not. He kept a close eye on her appointments and often had to search frantically for her. On one such occasion, she was expected for an interview on Sheilah Graham's radio show. Franco finally located her at Connie's apartment in Hollywood. She was engrossed in painting the living room.

"Oh, sweetie," she said, "tell her that I'm driving out of my driveway to see Dr. Bernstein because I twisted my polio hand. But I'll get her Ann Sheridan as a substitute." Franco had been flabbergasted. "She'd cancel things like that because she liked to housepaint!"

Franco would end his day preparing cocktails for the Youngs, then depart after dinner when they wanted to be alone. Franco observed that Collie could be a poor businessman. A tipoff that something had gone awry was when Collie encouraged Ida to have another drink "because he was going to lay a bomb on her."

Ida and Collie lacked capital, so plans for *Never Fear* came to a halt. Ida paced her home, anxiously waiting for Charles Feldman to find an acceptable script at the right price—seventy-five thousand dollars. In August, Filmakers announced a grandiose plan to produce six low-budget features. Ida said she wouldn't be appearing in any of these; as she joked: "I can't afford to pay my own salary." Finally, Feldman sent her *Woman in Hiding*, a murder mystery. Lupino gave her approval. The story was exciting, the money was right, and it would be easy working with her co-star, an old friend from Warners, Ronald Reagan. Or so she thought.

Distinguished actress, director, producer, and writer.

With Toby Wing and Buster Crabbe in *Search for Beauty* (1934).

With Gary Cooper in *Peter Ibbetson* (1935).

Artists and Models (1937) with Jack Benny and director Raoul Walsh.

With Ronald Colman in *The Light That Failed* (1939).

With Basil Rathbone and Nigel Bruce in *The Adventures of Sherlock Holmes* (1939).

Ida and her first husband, Louis Hayward, at their Westridge home.

Visiting the set of *Shining Victory* (1941). From left: Louis Hayward, James Stephenson, Geraldine Fitzgerald, Ida, and director Irving Rapper.

Above and opposite: Screen star of the forties.

With Humphrey Bogart in *They Drive by Night* (1940). "This was the film that put me over," said Ida.

Pard, Ida, and Humphrey Bogart in *High Sierra* (1941).

With Dennis Morgan and Joan Leslie in *The Hard Way* (1943).

Drying off after falling into a pool while on location for *The Sea Wolf* (1941).

On the set with Duchess.

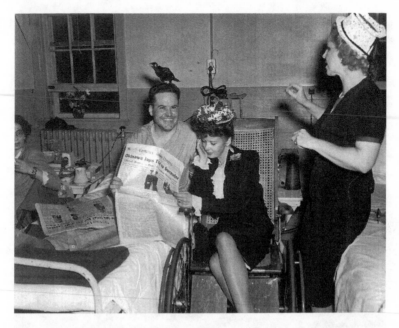

Cheering up wounded servicemen in Buffalo, New York, during WWII.

Wedding to Collier Young. From left: Reginald Gardiner, Harry Mines, Rev. George Culbertson, Harry Kurnitz, "Collie," Ida, Frances Robinson, Rita Lupino, and Connie Lupino.

With Richard Widmark and Cornel Wilde in *Road House* (1948).

Lining up a shot with Archie Stout on the set of *Outrage* (1950) starring Mala Powers.

Ida and third husband Howard Duff with Mary Comack, Bridget's nanny, on the set of *While the City Sleeps* (1956).

With Aldo Ray.

With Timmy at Old Oak Lane. Photo by William Donati.

"Lupi" the gardener.

Ida with author William Donati, Thanksgiving 1983.

11

HOWARD

She scared me. She struck me as being so alive and smart.
—HOWARD DUFF

We couldn't stand each other. —IDA LUPINO

As Ida memorized her lines for *Woman in Hiding*, a melodrama about a bride whose husband tries to kill her on her honeymoon night, she received word that Ronald Reagan was out of the picture. The news disappointed Ida. At Warners she had been friendly with Reagan and his wife, Jane Wyman, and occasionally visited them at their apartment at 1326 Londonderry in Beverly Hills. She found Reagan easygoing and down-to-earth; like Lupino, he was a liberal Democrat, and both had been avid supporters of President Roosevelt. She looked forward to playing opposite Reagan, who was to have been cast as the sympathetic stranger who befriends the terrorized bride. But the Saturday before the start of the picture, he severely injured his thigh in a charity baseball game. Newcomer Howard Duff was shifted from the role of the homicidal husband to play Reagan's role. Ida was disappointed. She didn't like Duff.

As a stalwart fan of radio dramas, Ida tuned in Sunday nights to enjoy *The Adventures of Sam Spade*. The show had debuted on September 29, 1946, and overnight it had topped the ratings.

Audiences were thrilled by the exploits of the wise-cracking detective. Women around the country sent Howard Duff hundreds of fan letters each week. One afternoon Mark Hellinger asked Ida if she had ever met the radio star. "No," she said, "but I just love his voice." They debated whether or not his looks matched his deep, sexy voice.

Shortly afterward, Ida met Sam Spade himself. He was Frances Robinson's date at a party aboard the *Bahia*. Ida was struck by his physical attributes. He was tall, with curly brown hair, light blue eyes and a rugged face. She was enchanted by the deep voice but thought he conveyed a conceited air. She told him he was "terribly egotistical."

"I could care less," he shot back.

When she arrived on the set at Universal, Ida found in her dressing room a bouquet of white orchids and a card that read, "From Howard Duff to Ida Lupino—whether you hate me or not." Once *Woman in Hiding* was under way, Duff's charm overcame Ida's icy disdain. "I melted," she admitted later.

Ida's acting was superb, emotionally on-target as a terrified woman whose greedy husband claims she is insane, then attempts to murder her. Director Michael Gordon was impressed with his star, especially when Ida, who was known to be fearful of heights, forced herself to climb the steep studio scaffolding for the film's chase sequence. Gordon found her such a creative actress that he simply "gave her a start, then let her go." Lupino and Duff had little trouble establishing a romantic rapport before the camera. Though reserved, Duff had a forceful personality, especially when pushed, and he was just the kind of man Ida craved.

Ida was drawn to Duff, and the distance between her and Collie widened. Artistic clashes had already eroded their marriage. Both were perfectionists who possessed tremendous vitality and energy. They put everything they had into the screenplay of *Never*

Fear. Ida would sometimes write for twenty-four hours straight, scribbling on anything at hand, from odd bits of paper to grocery bags. Ida and Collie had driven themselves relentlessly and had achieved financial triumph with *Not Wanted*, but they had argued bitterly. With their second production, the relationship deteriorated even further, as Collie publicly verified. "It's pretty hard to have an argument over a script at five-thirty, as all writers do, rather acidly, and be romantic and husband-and-wifely at six-thirty."

Ida arrived at Universal eager to see Howard Duff. But she immersed herself deeply in preproduction details for *Never Fear*, conferring with Michael Gordon on directorial technique, organization and plotting. The success or failure of the picture was largely in Ida's hands. The pressure was intense. She was traveling uncharted territory, risking her reputation. Only a small number of women had dared to direct. When word circulated that she was shifting from producer to director, none of her friends were surprised. They agreed that no one was better suited to direct. They knew her strong personality was infectious. An associate marveled that she was shy about entering a room filled with strangers, yet, once there, she dominated her surroundings. "If Ida feels good . . . her mood spreads all around. If Ida's got a headache, everybody in the place is sick."

Ida and Collie hammered out a script that was to star Sally Forrest and Keefe Braselle as a dance team on the verge of success when a polio attack cripples the young girl. While casting minor roles, Ida was taken with an unknown actor.

On a rainy morning, Hugh O'Brian had debated whether to buy breakfast or to use his last few dollars to make a donation in church. He went hungry. After a downpour, he walked several miles of wet, steep streets from Sunset Boulevard to Mulholland Drive. He had painstakingly copied the *Never Fear* screenplay by hand in his agent's office, then memorized the entire script. When he showed up to read for Ida, she offered the young actor breakfast, then led him to the living room and handed him the script. "Study it for a while," she told him.

O'Brian resisted an impulse to confess that he knew it backward and forward; instead, he pretended to absorb the pages before him.

When they finished reading, Ida was wide-eyed. "That's the best cold reading I've ever heard. You have the role."

Though he didn't confess immediately, O'Brian remembers Ida's reaction when he told her he'd copied the screenplay and memorized the part. "She got a big kick out of it. Ida admired anybody who took the business seriously."

Just as the film was launched, a financial crisis arose. While Ida was on the set, Collie sent word that the investors never came through; a sixty-five thousand dollar payroll was due within two weeks. Ida seethed, upset that her husband had failed. She feared an aborted production. She held her temper and coolly lined up takes until late afternoon, when she telephoned Charles Feldman and explained the predicament. Feldman asked to see the script. The following day, the money was in the bank. But it was only a loan.

Ida kept on track and maintained a tight shooting schedule. She earned the respect of the crew, many of whom were veteran technicians. Archie Stout, cinematographer, was especially impressed by the novice director's uncanny proficiency. Over a quarter of a century, Stout had filmed more than five hundred pictures, including Lupino's *Lust for Gold*. Ida proudly told everyone that she had John Ford's cameraman. The old pro was equally awed by Lupino. "Ida has more knowledge of camera angles and lenses than any director I've ever worked with, with the exception of Victor Fleming. She knows how a woman looks on the screen, and what light that woman should have, probably better than I do."

Lupino had worked with the greatest directors of her era, and she had learned from them. But Ida developed a directorial style of her own. She never bullied a performer but instead used her charm. She made the cast feel important, and they were inspired to give their best. Says Hugh O'Brian: "She was very, very patient but also demanding. If she felt that there was something better in you she would work until she got it. Though prone to bursts of anger in private, Ida never lost her temper on the set.

As a result of Ida's insistence on realism, a major portion of *Never Fear* was shot at the Kabat-Kaiser Rehabilitation Institute at 815 Ocean Front. Ida placed recovering polio victims alongside her cast. Before filming was under way, Hugh O'Brian borrowed a wheelchair and learned how to maneuver it, even playing basketball with the patients. "Ida knew that I had done my best to immerse myself in the role," O'Brian said.

Ida filmed an actual wheelchair dance, the first ever presented in a feature film. Harry Mines came to the set one morning and found Ida directing in a wheelchair, her foot in a cast. She had tripped over a cable and broken her ankle.

Collie never found additional investors. Ida was in debt to Feldman for sixty-five thousand dollars; in addition, her savings had been sunk into the project. Malvin Wald remembers her anger: "She told Collie she had worked very hard, ever since she was a little girl, and this should never have happened." In the midst of her dizzying rush to complete the film, Ida received an exciting message from W.R. "Billy" Wilkerson, publisher of the *Hollywood Reporter*. Howard Hughes was ready to do business. Hughes had recently acquired RKO studio, and he wanted to discuss future productions for his company. It was a welcome offer. Filmakers was in dire financial straits.

Ida had deeper problems. In the early days of their marriage, she and Collie had discussed adopting a daughter. A childhood disease had left Collie sterile, and Ida longed to start a family. In the shadows stood Howard Duff. He exuded confidence and masculinity. His square-jawed good looks brought Ida to Malibu for discreet lunches and long conversations. He offered a strong shoulder for support. Ida had practically carried the entire production of *Never Fear*. She had completed it in fifteen days for $150,000. Collie tried to interest theater chains in their film, but he found little interest, just as Malvin Wald had warned. Their dream of working outside the studio system vanished. Ida blamed Collie. She stormed out of their home and rented a beach house at 64 Malibu Colony. Howard Duff lived a few doors away. Ida shared the small residence with her aunt, Nell Beatty, Connie's older sister. Nell was a livewire who enjoyed kicking up her heels and having fun. Once a director in silents, Nell had traveled the world as a stage actress and invested sums in London theaters, allowing her a comfortable income. Ida introduced Nell to her circle of friends as an adored aunt. "She was just like Ida," says Harry Mines.

Filmakers was drawn into a web by a shrewd businessman. Explains Malvin Wald: "Howard Hughes had just bought RKO and didn't know what to do with it. He was worried about costs. He suddenly realized that Ida was a very brilliant young woman. Ida was able to bring out a low-budget picture like *Not Wanted* and make a ton of money. Hughes liked things dealing with sex. He liked things the public wanted. It was really Ida's ability as a director which brought about the RKO deal."

Filmakers was interested in seeing what RKO had to offer; a problem arose when no one could locate the eccentric Hughes. Billy Wilkerson referred them to attorney Greg Bautzer, a friend of Hughes. Bautzer agreed to negotiate any deal; if nothing transpired they owed him nothing. If they signed with RKO, his fee would be fifteen thousand dollars. Bautzer passed along Hughes's proposition: RKO would provide $750,000 for three films, production facilities and distribution, in exchange for half the profits.

Ida harbored an innate, suspicious streak, and she was especially suspicious of major studios and in particular the crafty Howard Hughes. She liked his personal charm but was wary of his business expertise. On the surface, the deal looked fine. As for approval on stories, they verbally agreed that Hughes would read a single-paragraph synopsis of proposed films. Malvin Wald was developing a screenplay about a rape victim. Hughes liked the idea and suggested signing a contract immediately. The threesome were full partners, but Collie was president and would negotiate the transaction. Ida described him as "the diplomat" and herself as "the bulldozer." Lupino and Wald cautioned Collie to be careful. Ida was still simmering over being in debt, but she felt that Collie was capable of concluding the RKO deal. On September 27, 1949, RKO announced that Filmakers had signed an agreement making it "an independent unit" with offices at the studio on North Gower.

Ida relaxed at the beach, resting and pondering her future. A month later, while production was under way for their first release, the detailed contract arrived with Collie's signature. It was a painful awakening. Recalls Malvin Wald: "We discovered that the voluminous contract gave Hughes complete control over everything. He had outfoxed us. He owned the pictures, the personalities developed by us, and we subsequently learned what hurt us most. The fine print stated that Hughes could use Filmakers' money to promote Filmakers' product. This drained all our profit." It was too late to back out. They had taken advances and spent too much money. Adds Wald: "In essence, we were not his partners but his slaves. This, of course, made matters worse between Ida and Collie."

John Franco tells a similar story. "The Howard Hughes thing is what really broke up Ida and Collie. She said, 'They're going to charge us. We're going to be the only company shooting at the studio and every secretary and everything will be charged.'"

Collie had tried to win her back with the RKO deal, but Ida was appalled, angry that he had bungled the contract. "Collie would cry on my shoulder," says Franco. "When Ida left for Malibu he didn't know what to do. He would invite a lot of ladies over, not for dinner, not for sexual affairs, just friends like Myrna Loy. I'd hate to leave him alone because I knew that he was wishing that Ida was back in the house. He was heart-broken."

Franco transferred more of Ida's belongings to Malibu. She and Collie worked together during the day, but their evenings were spent apart. Malvin Wald was in their office when Hedda Hopper called.

"Do you know where your wife was last night?" asked Hopper.

"It's none of your damned business!" replied Collie.

Ida's return to the Mulholland home brought more angry scenes, especially after she noticed blonde strands of hair on her pillow. Collie responded with bitterness, shouting that her affair with Duff was known to everyone. On December 28, Ida announced to the press that she was filing for divorce, complaining that their marriage never seemed to have a chance. Ida told newsmen that Collie had gone to Palm Springs to recover from a nervous collapse. They had lived together barely thirteen months. Ida later told friends that intense loneliness had been the reason for their marriage.

A month later, *Variety* praised Filmakers's new release. "As written by Ida Lupino and husband Collier Young, the screenplay is psychologically sound in dealing with the emotional ups-and-downs of the polio victims. And it's equally convincing as a documentary of treatment with effective shots of physical therapy."

Though reviews were favorable, the box office returns were poor. "She lost all that money," says Malvin Wald. "She said to

Collie, 'Remember what Malvin said? You should have listened to him.' She really chewed him out. He was trembling, stuttering, then he later turned to me, blaming *me* for the breakup of his marriage."

Ida began to appear in public with Duff. She was in love. Her new boyfriend had risen to unexpected heights in a short time. Raised in Seattle, where his father was a grocer, he had attended Roosevelt High School, then joined the Seattle Repertory Playhouse, whose alumnae included Frances Farmer and noted drama coach Sophie Rosenstein. During the war, he had been a sergeant and a correspondent for Armed Forces Radio. Upon his discharge in 1945, he joined the Actors Lab theater group in Los Angeles and attracted studio interest. He gained overnight acclaim as Sam Spade.

Duff was quiet, personable but distant. He readily admitted that when he wasn't reading he was sleeping. After the war, he shared a home with his close friend and manager, Mike Meshekoff. Jules Dassin, who had worked with Duff at the Actors Lab, brought him to the attention of Mark Hellinger for *Brute Force* in 1947. Duff gave a convincing performance as a convict involved in a failed prison break. Hellinger signed him to a personal contract and a larger role in *The Naked City*, where he registered strongly as a jewel thief. When Hellinger died of a heart attack in 1947, Universal bought Duff's contract.

Duff enjoyed the company of beautiful women. He was briefly engaged to Yvonne de Carlo and dated Piper Laurie and Swedish beauty Marta Toren, but his affair with Ava Gardner made news. When Ava left him, columnists wrote that he took it hard. "The torch he's carrying for Ava Gardner is so big they don't need lights on Sunset Boulevard," one wrote. Now Duff was being seen with Ida Lupino, a true star; his life had never been better.

Filmakers' first RKO release would be *Outrage*, Malvin Wald's story of a young woman who is raped and the emotional devastation that ensues. Wald had delved deeply into the subject and had conferred with welfare organizations and psychologists.

Ida began a search for the lead actress. Ida's philosophy was that acting was a gift; either you had the ability or you didn't. She knew exactly what she sought in a player. "Personality is the most important attribute an actor or actress may possess, far more in demand than good looks . . . second, is large eyes, particularly for actresses; I wouldn't even consider anybody, regardless of her other qualities . . . this is a must." In addition, she watched for an ability to learn quickly, move gracefully, and delve deeply into a character. Ida also wanted a performer with a sense of humor; she felt that laughter provided a sense of humanity. Ida interviewed over two hundred actresses before she met eighteen-year-old Mala Powers. As a child, Powers's father had taken her to see his favorite actress in *The Light That Failed*, a performance she never forgot. After she read a scene, Ida jumped up. She had found the girl.

According to the RKO contract, Howard Hughes had to approve both leads for the picture personally. The very day she selected Powers, Ida escorted her to the studio hairdresser and supervised a new coiffure to impress Hughes; then she called in a photographer and supervised the shooting of stills. Malvin Wald recalls the excitement at Filmakers' office when the eccentric studio owner reached a decision. A meeting had been arranged at the Polo Lounge. Howard Hughes met with Ida and her discovery. He asked the young girl if she could convey the trauma of rape. Powers said she could.

Bringing to the screen such a socially sensitive subject as rape brought Ida into numerous conferences with Jeffrey Shurlock of the Production Code Administration. Lupino and Shurlock would discuss ways to convey delicate scenes without violating the Code. Ida appreciated the suggestions and believed they "actually added value to the script."

Wald resented interference with his completed script. "I had written the screenplay, but Collie felt he needed to rewrite it. He wanted to be a writer. Collie, being a sophisticate, tended to write like people in his class spoke; so when he tried to write dialogue of small town people it seemed very stilted and awkward." In an interview, Wald made a thinly veiled reference to the simmering dispute. "Today the producer is in charge, but he is not a creative person. Where he should be primarily a businessman, he meddles in the artistic end," he said. Ida also had a hand in the screenplay; she contributed dialogue to the character of the rape victim.

RKO carpenters became accustomed to having Ida salvage dismantled sets. Once filming was under way, Lupino was a master of saving time and money. To simulate a large mill office, she filmed against the exterior of a soundstage. While on location at a park in North Hollywood, Ida tired of waiting for a wispy fog to clear; she filmed the park scene with natural haze visible in the background.

Outrage was Mala Powers's first film, and she felt insecure. Lupino gave her confidence. She didn't dictate but suggested. Ida encouraged her to take chances. Often, Ida would discuss an upcoming scene with the cameraman, speaking loudly enough that the cast could hear the instructions and grasp the idea.

Lupino's cinematic artistry is evident in the scene depicting the brutal rape. Graphic displays were prohibited by the Code, yet Ida was determined to convey the degradation of the experience. She rose to the challenge by creating a six-minute segment of suspense and terror that gives the audience the opportunity to identify with the victim's humiliation. The scene opens with a young woman leaving her office alone. A bright musical theme accompanies her departure, but the music abruptly changes to a somber melody as a leather-jacketed man stalks his prey. The frightened girl flees through deserted streets in an eerie silence, casting long shadows, running in terror. A high camera angle reduces the helpless girl to insignificance. She tries to hail a cab but fails. A close-up reveals tears streaming down her cheeks. She covers her mouth with her hand. She tries to hide in a truck cab but accidentally sounds the horn. The nerve-shattering blare splits the air and she flees up a flight of stairs, trips and falls on the pavement, weeping, as the rapist rapidly approaches. The camera suddenly pulls back to a high angle, again reducing the defeated victim to a helpless, forlorn figure who has been caught. She is mercifully hidden as the rapist advances on her like a hawk on a lamb. The spellbinding sequence had no dialogue. It was made powerful and moving by a skillful blend of music, silence, shadows, camera angles and Mala Powers's convincing emotions.

Always mindful of what Stanley had said about racial prejudice, Ida avoided stereotyping black citizens and chose them for roles the public might not expect them to play. It was her way of combating prejudice. One scene in *Outrage* called for a lineup of suspects at a police station. A black policeman stands guard. Conversely, she did not choose a black youth when the park scene needed a shoeshine boy—she selected a white youth for the part.

Malvin Wald, who was considered "front office" by his partners, seldom visited the set. He preferred to stay in his office. Connie would often stop by to chat while he was working. "Connie was a very lovely woman. She told me how the Lupinos had been in the theater hundreds of years. She desperately wanted a grandchild. I remember her telling Ida, 'You owe it to me. You have beauty and talent and must continue the family line.' She was overjoyed when Ida began seeing Howard. She said that her grandchildren, the offspring of these two beautiful people, would be beautiful."

Outrage was completed in March and released in late summer. Reviews were mixed. "This is one topic, no matter how skillfully handled, which would better have been left unfilmed," said *Variety*. But the *Los Angeles Examiner* praised it. "With courage and frankness, within the limits of good taste, *Outrage* points up the serious consequences to society . . . the story hits home to every family in that such an occurrence might happen anytime to any girl or woman."

Before the picture was released, Stanley Kramer had telephoned Filmakers. He was bringing *Cyrano de Bergerac* to the screen and was searching for an actress to play Roxanne. He asked to view a rough cut of *Outrage*. Ida agreed, eager to advance the career of Powers.

Lupino's three films sparked a frenzy of interest. She chose controversial subjects, adamant that Hollywood must produce "more experimentation in new film subjects." Ida had more stories she wanted to bring to the screen, but a major obstacle was Howard Hughes, who had final approval. To outwit Hughes, Ida would float stories in the press about her forthcoming projects, hoping for a fait accompli.

Ida announced that Filmakers planned to bring to the screen *The World Inside*, the story of a war veteran whose battlefield service rendered him sterile and who adopts a little girl to brighten his life. She also announced her interest in *Pachuko*, a story about the problems of Mexican-Americans, based on a novel by Irving Shulman. *The Atom Project* would detail the development of the atom bomb. None of these stories ever made it to the screen. "Hughes rejected them," explains Malvin Wald. "He liked stories dealing with sex in a positive way; sterility wasn't interesting for him, neither was a film about Mexicans. Hughes didn't want to do a film about the atom bomb since he had important defense contracts with the government."

Ida and Collie published a "Declaration of Independents" in trade publications: "We are deep in admiration of our fellow independent producers—men like Stanley Kramer, Robert Rossen and

Louis de Rochemont. They are bringing a new power and excitement to the screen. We like independence." The advertisement was a noble pronouncement but, as far as Filmakers was concerned, Howard Hughes gave the imprimatur for all stories, effectively depriving them of true creative independence.

Malvin Wald was an astute observer of Lupino's private life. He admired her artistry but recognized her as an eccentric. Connie had told him that her daughter was "an actress first." Her best husband, said Connie, had been Louis Hayward. Ida could be temperamental with Louis; they were both performers and enjoyed being dramatic. But Ida's peculiarities went deeper than temperament. Ida told Wald that she got many ideas from "communing with the spirits." Wald was startled one day when Ida burst into his office, anxiously telling him that she had lost touch with Stanley. According to Wald, "This communication was somehow or other tuned to a channel on television and it had to be a certain number." Collie and production designer Harry Horner were present. They offered a number.

"No, that's not the right number," said Ida. She asked Wald if he could suggest one. In jest, he said, "I've got the number but I'm not going to give it to you. Because I want to speak to Stanley. I've always heard about him and I'm going to speak to him today." Ida flew into a rage and screamed that Wald was preventing her from talking to her dead father.

"If you don't give me that number, I'll kill you!" she threatened. She eventually regained her composure when Wald convinced her that he had merely been teasing.

Ida became interested in Loving Cup, the story of a young tennis player and her scheming mother. Howard Hughes was an avid tennis fan, and he approved the production. The screenplay, by Martha Wilkerson, was based on John R. Tunis's novel Mother of a Champion. Claire Trevor was cast as the conniving mother and

Sally Forrest as her naive daughter. Eleanor "Teach" Tennant, the famous trainer of Bobby Riggs, Alice Marble, Pauline Betz and Maureen Connolly, coached Forrest on her form and traded shots with her before the camera. Ida cleverly interlaced footage shot at Wimbledon and Forest Hills with closeups of the cast filmed at the Brentwood Tennis Club. Ida made a cameo appearance, à la Hitchcock, with Robert Ryan beside her, both seen briefly as applauding spectators.

Ida had a good rapport with Hughes and was the only member of Filmakers who met with him; everyone else dealt with an underling. RKO executives marveled that Ida communicated with their boss so easily. Rumor had it that Hughes had visited RKO only once, in the middle of the night, and that he said but two words: "Paint it." Ida even had Hughes's personal telephone number, one of the best kept secrets in Hollywood. Strangely, Hughes seldom appeared on his own lot, but he kept an office nearby. Film editor George Shrader knew where to find the elusive studio boss. He worked for him day and night at the Goldwyn Studios, where Hughes rented an office and projection room. At night Shrader would run RKO footage. His boss was "very finicky about the way prints should be handled. He didn't like dirt. He wanted to see a nice clean print all the time."

When Shrader screened *Loving Cup*, he was impressed. "Ida did an excellent job with her version." Then Hughes began making suggestions. "He was a hard guy to please," says Shrader. "He was very nice but adamant about things he wanted done. I tried to please them both and it was a little bit of a struggle. Hughes didn't change too much but there was a lot of playing with it." When the editing was completed, Ida was proud of the film but dissatisfied with the title. Titles were bounced around in Filmakers' office for a while. Ida and Collie thought that *The Champion* might do. Explains Malvin Wald: "Hughes thought titles were the most important things for catching potential viewers. Next came the ads. He liked sex and action in the titles. He kept a former Time journalist at RKO just to work on titles. I thought of *The Money Game*, but Hughes felt it sounded like something from Wall Street." Ida asked Hughes for help. He said to call him the following day at a number in Arizona. He came through with *Hard, Fast and Beautiful*, a title she thought was perfect.

Hughes told Ida that the picture could make money if it were handled properly. He arranged an expensive publicity junket to San Francisco for seventy-five members of the press and eleven celebrities. The film opened at the Golden Gate Theater, accompanied by a live stage show presenting five performances a day. Harry Crocker introduced singer Tony Martin, who was followed onstage by Lupino, Robert Ryan, Mala Powers, Jane Greer, Sally Forrest, Jack Beutel, William Bendix, Tim Holt and Pat O'Brien. Hughes was rumored to be in the packed audience. Perry Lieber, RKO publicity chief, assembled the stars backstage and cautioned: "Children, father has his eye on you."

The lodgings, food and booze were the best. After a round of parties and nightclubs, the journalists and celebrities were driven to the airport and "poured on board . . . convinced that Howard Hughes is one of the finest gentlemen of our times." The extravaganza was repeated in New York and other major cities. Though Hughes was considered the gracious host, Filmakers paid the bills. *Outrage* was one of RKO's few profitable releases of 1950. But the profits from *Hard, Fast and Beautiful* disappeared in RKO's lavish promotion. As Malvin Wald put it: "We were fleeced. After we divided our profits, which was one-third each, it wasn't much. Hughes was very smart. He gave Filmakers a twenty-five-thousand-dollar bonus every time Ida brought in a picture under budget. She did it for each picture, but look at how much money he saved through Ida's hard work. He was very shrewd."

If the big money was missing, at least the artistic glory was abundant. Those close to Ida noticed in her a cocky self-assurance that occasionally bordered on haughtiness.

Despite the acclaim she was receiving, Ida had yet to pay off her loan to Charles Feldman. She was cast in RKO's *On Dangerous Ground*, a film about an embittered detective, portrayed by Robert Ryan. Ida was quite moving as the blind sister of the killer. She enjoyed working with director Nicholas Ray, whose artistry would reach its height five years later with *Rebel without a Cause*.

Ida paid her debts, then she and Collie agreed to a property divestment. She generously let him keep the home on Mulholland Drive. Collie was now romancing actress Joan Fontaine, who would soon occupy the Mouse House.

Ida had the man she wanted. She was in love with Howard Duff.

12

THE TURNING POINT

We're all crazy about Howard. —CONNIE LUPINO

Nineteen fifty was a phenomenal year for Lupino. With the release of *Not Wanted*, *Never Fear*, *Outrage*, and *Hard, Fast and Beautiful*, she became Hollywood's golden girl again, as she had been a decade before. As recognition of her new industry status, she was asked to present the Oscar for best director at the 22nd Academy Awards ceremony. Applause swept over her as she stepped to the podium. She announced Joseph Mankiewicz as the winner for *A Letter to Three Wives*. Said Mankiewicz: "Miss Lupino is the only woman in the Directors Guild, and the prettiest." The press hailed her extraordinary talent. *Holiday* magazine gave Ida a special award in recognition of her artistic courage: "To the woman in the motion picture industry who has done the most to improve standards and to honestly present American life, ideals and people to the rest of the world."

Not only was her professional life shining, but her personal life had taken an upswing as well. She was deeply in love with Howard Duff. He told a writer that Ida was the most fascinating woman he had ever known. When he vacationed in Hawaii, Ida followed. They returned on the same flight, decked in leis, unconcerned that Ida was still legally married to Young.

Knowing that Duff shared her fondness for pets, Ida surprised him with a kitten. One evening he returned to his rented Malibu beach house and tripped over the cat, tumbled down a flight of stairs, and shattered his right leg. He was hospitalized and his leg encased in a twenty-pound plaster cast; Ida visited along with rivals Piper Laurie and Marta Toren. Since Duff enjoyed reading, Ida brought him Budd Schulberg's *The Disenchanted* and *The Dream Factory*, Hortense Powdermaker's dissection of Hollywood. The latter disturbed Duff with its premise that actors are not men but commodities, bought and sold on the competitive market, like sardines. Scoffed Duff: "I know I can stay in Hollywood and be a whole man, my man."

Ida liked Duff's assertiveness. When she was on edge, sullen or angry, few dared to tangle with her. But Howard did. He could be demanding and had a mean side, especially when he was drinking. After Ida announced her divorce from Collie, Connie told a reporter, "We're all crazy about Howard." Later, echoing her daughter's thoughts, she commented to Malvin Wald that "Howard's a real man."

But Duff's friends said he was an elusive bachelor, too wrapped up in his career and easygoing life to give serious thought to marriage. Ida was a possessive woman. Howard loved her, but he wanted to chart his own course, to be his own man, to remain free. After an argument, they split up. Suitors just as swiftly appeared on Ida's doorstep. Errol Flynn—at that time divorced—and Ida became involved, but she declined an offer of marriage. The next man to enter her life was a lost soul.

It was past midnight when Ida drove her green Cadillac from Beverly Hills to the Roland V. Lee ranch in Northridge. Harry Mines greeted her, then they walked to where arc lights flooded a whirling carousel and carnival with an eerie, silver brightness. There stood Alfred Hitchcock, giving directions for the final scenes of *Strangers on a Train*. The portly director quietly spoke to the cast and lined up another take. Ida was thrilled to watch Hitchcock at work. When the arc lights finally dimmed, she embraced Robert Walker, the film's star, who was portraying an odd, boyish murderer in the best role of his career. Mines and Walker jumped into Ida's Cadillac for the long drive to Ida's rented home near Bel Air. A thick fog slowed their journey, but despite the gloom and the exhausting hours he'd spent before the camera, Walker was in high spirits.

Guests waited at Ida's residence, enjoying a party in full swing. With the thick fog menacing the roads, Ida invited her friends to stay the night. But there was little sleeping. "It was a mad night of roaming around," Harry Mines recalls. "Aunt Nell was there and she was whooping it up." Nell entertained the gathering with bawdy songs and her imitation of a French whore. "Come one, come all!" she bellowed to raucous laughter. As for Ida's new interest: "Bobby was a very sad guy," says Mines. "Lupino did a lot to help him."

Walker had been a troubled and unhappy man since his marriage to Jennifer Jones ended in 1945. Despite his $100,000 a year income, he described himself as "Hollywood's loneliest man." Walker had a drinking problem, which had been exacerbated by losing his beautiful actress-wife to powerful producer David O. Selznick. His unhappiness had led to a hasty marriage to Barbara Ford, daughter of director John Ford, a union that lasted only a few weeks. Walker had slipped into a state of chronic depression, often becoming violent, smashing windows with his fists; he had tried to straighten out his dismal existence by entering the Menninger Psychiatric Clinic. He readily admitted his personal problems in interviews. "Bobby was a very lovable fellow," says Harry Mines, "but his separation and divorce from Jennifer, and the fact the kids were pulled away from him, made him very morose."

The Selznicks had a separate house for the young boys, and they were provided with their own servants. Walker was angry that his sons were being raised in such lavish luxury at such an early age. He tried to keep them down-to-earth with simple outings. Ida often joined Walker and the boys for swimming at the beach.

Despite his desire to lead a normal life, Walker drank and became abusive. "Ida was the only one who could handle Bobby," says Mines. "One night he bashed his fist against a wall and Ida took a flying leap across the room to get him under control." Charming and kind when sober, Walker was a disaster when drinking, either full of furor or pathetically helpless. Lupino and Duff reunited.

Ida was pushing for marriage, but Duff still held out, to her annoyance. He didn't want to lose her, but he didn't want marriage either. They argued constantly over the future. But Howard Duff soon had more to worry about than romance.

The Red Scare was tightening its noose in Hollywood. Duff was a target. The House Un-American Activities Committee was purging the industry of "communist infiltration." In 1947 the committee, commonly referred to as HUAC, provoked a bitter controversy by citing "The Hollywood Ten" for refusing to cooperate with the investigating committee. The Ten were eight writers, one producer and a director who took the position that HUAC had no right to question them about their political beliefs, since freedom of expression was guaranteed by the First Amendment of the Constitution.

In September of 1949, scenarist Howard Koch had asked Duff to sign an amicus curiae petition in response to the contempt convictions of the Hollywood Ten. The legal brief, by the "cultural workers in motion pictures and other arts" stated: "Congress cannot impose a direct censorship upon the motion picture industry since motion pictures enjoy the same protection under the First Amendment as the press and radio. . . . Now the court is being asked, in this case, to vindicate these same guarantees against encroachment by the federal Congress in an abuse of the important power of investigation." Duff signed the petition along with numerous well-known figures such as Charles Chaplin, John Garfield, John Huston, Burt Lancaster, Ian Hunter and Dorothy Parker. His signature on the petition would come back to haunt him.

The specter of Communism and the accompanying HUAC investigation spread fear, anger and bitterness in Hollywood. Friends and colleagues of long standing found themselves pitted against each other as deadly political enemies. Political beliefs and past membership in suspected organizations were scrutinized. The Motion Picture Alliance for the Preservation of American Ideals, led by president John Wayne, called for the elimination of "Communist conspirators in our midst, treasonably obeying the dictates of a foreign tyranny."

Reputations and careers were ruined by whispers, innuendoes and outright blacklisting. Ida was shocked over the HUAC investigation. Several friends were now unwelcome at the studios. Howard Hughes refused to give Paul Jerrico, Ida's coauthor of *Not Wanted*, a script credit for *The Las Vegas Story*. Vincent Sherman suddenly learned that he was no longer welcome at Warner Bros. While directing Joan Crawford in *Goodbye, My Fancy*, he was summoned to Jack Warner's office. Warner angrily said he had heard rumors that Sherman was having an affair with Crawford.

Sherman responded that what he did on his own time was none of Warner's business. Warner told him not to make any more close-ups of Joan Crawford. Sherman stared in disbelief. He made the closeups and Warner was incensed. Sherman left the studio

where he had directed since 1937. He later discovered that Jack
Warner had purposely provoked the confrontation, fearful that
Sherman was a Communist sympathizer. And Sherman was only a
Democrat.

John Garfield had trouble finding film work, even though he
denied being a Communist. Ida saw her friend driven to despair.
"He was blacklisted by Warners after being hounded by society in
the form of righteous anti-Communist crusaders of HUAC."

When she saw Garfield drinking heavily at the Keys Club
across from the studio, she urged him to fight back. "Julie," she said
in a loud voice. Heads turned. "Are you letting those bastards crack
you up? I know you are not a commie!"

Columnist Jimmie Tarantino wrote that he was sickened by
"the active participation of top-flight Hollywood stars and
personalities in the Communist Party cause." Tarantino began a cru-
sade to inform movie fans of those he suspected of being subversives.
Among those denounced were John Garfield, Orson Welles, Charles
Chaplin, Lena Horne, Artie Shaw and "Howard Duff, radio and
screen star. Sam Spade Duff is a red fellow traveler and red sympathizer. He has also given comfort and his well-advertised name to
many commie fronts. . . . He signed a petition to the U.S. Supreme
Court to review the conviction of Lawson and Trumbo, two of the
Un-Friendly writers who were sent to jail."

Duff and the others denied the accusations. When *The Adventures of Sam Spade* was suddenly canceled, Duff received no explana-
tion. Later, he discovered that his name had been in *Red Channels*, a
publication sent to advertisers and radio and television networks
with the purpose of exposing those with subversive backgrounds.
For three years Duff couldn't get a broadcasting job. Between 1950
and 1951, though quite popular with fans, his work was limited to
three minor films. Years later, Duff looked back on his political

trouble. "It was crazy. I was never a Communist or anything like that. I was sort of a half-assed liberal. Everyone who knew me laughed at the idea that I was any kind of Red."

Lupino and Duff were both Democrats. Ida had idolized President Roosevelt, to whom she gave everlasting thanks for rebuilding an economically shattered Depression America. She was outraged by the Red Scare sweeping the motion picture industry. It was Ida who prevented Duff from being blacklisted completely. She went to see her "buddies at the FBI" to set the record straight about Duff and Garfield.

After his difficulty obtaining film work, Garfield returned to his roots, the New York stage. He was a smash in *The Big Knife*, *Peer Gynt* and *Golden Boy*. When Ida received assurance that Garfield had been "cleared," she flew to New York to deliver the news. Garfield had sent her tickets to see him onstage. She arrived at his apartment with a writer friend from the *New York Times* for a toast before the performance.

Garfield opened the door in his dressing gown. Ida was taken aback by his haggard appearance. "Hi, doll," she greeted him. "Oh, it's good to see you, Lupi." Ida introduced her escort, then Garfield prepared cocktails. "I have a little present for you, Lupi." He glanced at Ida's friend, then said: "I'm going to ask her to come into my bedroom but *not* for what you think." As Ida followed him, she felt uneasy. Garfield looked deathly ill, and he lacked energy and exuberance. He pointed to a basket of flowers, champagne and glasses. Ida read the note: "To my favorite sister. Sorry, I'm not going to make it tonight but I've always loved you, kid. Julie." Ida was perplexed.

"What do you mean?" she asked.

"I'm not going to make it tonight or any other night," answered Garfield. "I'm booked."

Ida was shocked. "I'm glad you gave me a good stiff drink. Now I have a present for you. All that junk about you being a Communist has been cleared up."

Ida and her friend declined to see the play, since Garfield wasn't appearing.

They dined at 21, then went window shopping. Ida, as she had promised, returned to Garfield's place to say goodnight. She was still worried about her friend. She tapped softly at the door and found it open. The living room was dark. In his bedroom a single lamp on a nightstand fell on Garfield, propped up on pillows sleeping.

"Goodnight, Johnny. We all love you," Ida whispered.

He opened his eyes and thanked her. She leaned down and hugged him. "Would you mind holding my hand till I drop off?" he asked. The words sent a chill through Ida.

"You bet," she told him. "I'll sit here till daylight if you want." She held his hand until he was sound asleep.

Ida returned to the coast determined to find a screen role for Garfield. Her next production was slated as *Day without End*. The thriller, originally titled *The Man*, had been a Broadway success with Dorothy Gish as a widow menaced by a psychotic handyman. Ida wanted to hire Garfield for her company but felt it was hopeless. Howard Hughes would never permit such a controversial actor to work at RKO. In fact, Hughes was continuing a merciless purge of those he suspected of being politically tainted, even deleting screen credits of his victims. John Garfield went before HUAC in April 1951 to testify publicly that he wasn't a Communist. Despite his denials, he had trouble revitalizing his screen career. The heart condition that had prevented him from performing the last evening Ida saw him soon took his life. The terrible strain of constantly living under a shadow of suspicion had been too much. He was thirty-nine years old.

Even though Ida hadn't been able to help Garfield, she did manage to assist those within her company. Viennese-born Harry Horner, a former actor with Max Reinhardt's famous company, was chosen to direct the forthcoming thriller. Horner had won an Academy Award for art direction in *The Heiress* in 1949. Ida had been impressed by his production design for *Outrage* and decided to give him a chance behind the camera.

John Franco was promoted from within Filmakers as well. Ida assigned him to the picture as an intern, and he became the first Mexican-American in the Script Supervisors Guild. She cast Robert Ryan as the maniacal handyman. Horner provided an uncredited production design for the film, and Ida lent her expertise to the novice director, unexpectedly contributing more than her acting. Recalls Horner: "My wife was in the hospital, so Ida stepped in and directed several scenes. She was very nice about this situation. She never complained about having to take over."

Production closed on August 3 after an eighteen-day shooting schedule. Ida was disappointed when RKO rejected the working title and also her second choice—*The Terror*—for *Beware My Lovely*. Reviewers generally liked the film as a suspenseful, well-acted drama but felt the ending was disappointing, when the near-victim awakes from unconsciousness only to discover that the murderous handyman has no recollection of his homicidal actions.

Horner had foreseen the script's inherent weakness. "I never liked the ending. It lacked an intense climax. In the stage play the woman is murdered, but Collie decided we couldn't use that." Filmakers wasn't allowed to handle its own ad campaign, and Ida was convinced that this contributed to the faltering box office receipts.

Despite their approaching divorce, Ida and Collie remained partners in Filmakers, even though rifts were frequent and stormy. As Collier Young told a journalist: "Things aren't normal unless

Ida resigns three times on every picture—once before it starts, and twice during production." Of course, Collie really had no place to go. Ida could have chosen anyone as her assistant, and this is what Collie truly was, but she genuinely liked him and felt a deep sense of loyalty, and perhaps guilt, so she kept Filmakers alive.

According to Malvin Wald, Connie preferred Ida's artistry to be before the camera. Ida assisted her mother financially and even gave her advice, but there were no secrets or distance between them. Ida told her mother the most intimate details of her marriages, and she listened to Connie as she did to no one else. First and foremost, thought Connie Lupino, her daughter was a great actress.

Directing, however, more than acting, writing or composing music, gave Ida a sense of fulfillment. As a director, she was in control. She and Collie were teeming with ideas for films. They submitted numerous stories to RKO. Ida was enthusiastic about *Something for Nothing*, her three-part gambling story, which would show how gambling could be as destructive as any drug. Collie had a script called *Bachelor Dinner*, a proposed film about a young man's party on the eve of his wedding; flashbacks would give the audience the opportunity to guess which of the women he had loved would become his bride.

Earlier in the year, Ida had gone to Palm Springs to receive an award from the Foreign Press Association as Woman of the Year. She had spent much of her time there interviewing Forrest Damron, one of two hunters who had been abducted and held prisoner by killer Billy Cook for eight harrowing days in Baja California. Cook had murdered five members of a family, including three children, and later had murdered a salesman. He was convicted in federal court and sentenced to three hundred years in Alcatraz. Filmakers released a press statement announcing plans to do a picture based on the frightening experience of the kidnapped hunters. The same day the news broke, Geoffrey Shurlock of the Motion Picture Association telephoned Lupino's office and voiced strong objections; the Production Code prohibited screen depiction of contemporary notorious criminals. But Filmakers went forward anyway, informing trade papers that film rights had been acquired to the project tentatively titled *I Spoke to God*. Not only had the kidnapped victims granted permission to Filmakers, but Cook had as well.

An intimate observer of Ida's hectic private and professional life was Diane Meredith. After several years in New York as an editorial assistant at Hearst Publications, Meredith returned to Los Angeles to work in the field of communications. She listened to the many story ideas Ida spun; one she found especially moving. Meredith recalls it as "a marvelous idea about a returning soldier who finds a deaf child on the streets of San Francisco." Ida encouraged Meredith to develop the idea into a screenplay.

But suddenly a halt came to Lupino's myriad projects. On a rainy night Harry Mines received a call from Ida: "Darling, you must come down right away!" she said dramatically. Mines sped to Malibu, practically bursting open the door. Ida sat near the fireplace, bathed in the reddish glow of the flames, smiling enigmatically: "I've got news for you," she said proudly. "I'm expecting."

The next day she breezed into Filmakers's RKO offices, ecstatically shouting the news. Malvin Wald found the situation startling, especially when Connie appeared, equally jubilant. "Connie was overjoyed," Wald said. "The fact that Ida and Howard weren't married didn't matter. The important thing was that the family heritage would not come to an end."

The sudden development brought Ida's romance with Howard Duff to a crucial point. Duff was feeling the heat from all directions. Rumors that he was a "commie sympathizer" threatened to bury his career. *Steeltown* would be his last Universal release, then he would be own his own. He balked at marriage, but he did love

Lupino, and marriage to a star of her magnitude would certainly boost his professional stature. Besides, Ida was pregnant with his child. Considering the circumstances, Duff proposed.

In the midst of the excitement, Ida learned from Harry Mines that Robert Walker was dead. Ida and Walker had remained close friends. Walker had found a girlfriend and his career had progressed. Ida listened in stunned silence as Mines recounted that on August 28 psychiatrists had been summoned to Walker's home on Sunset Boulevard. Their patient was emotionally upset. He was given a hypodermic sedative to calm him. He experienced a reaction to the drug and died of respiratory failure at age thirty-two.

"Ida and I were just heart-broken," says Mines, "we were so close to him, you know, like someone's breath gently passing on your cheek." A few months later the actor's closest friend, Jim Henaghan, wrote a memorial for *Photoplay*. He wrote of Ida's kindness to the troubled Walker, describing her as one who "always befriended the lost ones, the strays, the bewildered."

As the days passed, the emotional turmoil generated by Walker's death subsided. Ida and Diane Meredith packed their suitcases. "We both needed to be divorced," says Meredith, "so in a superbly practical arrangement, we went to Lake Tahoe to fulfill both plans—our divorces and our screenplay." On September 7 they arrived in Glenbrook, Nevada, on the shore of Lake Tahoe. Ida leased Sawmill Harbor, a rambling lakeside home that had been occupied the previous spring by Rita Hayworth, who had been in town to secure her divorce from prince Aly Khan. Clark Gable had a home nearby. Duff accompanied them on the trip to Glenbrook, then said farewell and returned to Los Angeles to complete his last picture.

Diane Meredith was introduced to the peculiar schedule of Lupino's life. "Ida did not wake up until noon or so, then she pursued an elaborate ritual of makeup which occupied her until the sun was sinking in the west, at which time she emerged with the vitality of three hundred years of performance, swooping upon the scene with energy and dedication."

In the evening they would work on their script, *The Magic World of Heidl.* Ida had now transposed the tale of the waif and the American soldier to Nuremberg, Germany, since she felt it would be more picturesque and cheaper to film abroad. "You do the balcony scene," Ida would order. "I'll do the street scene." The women used whatever writing materials were at hand, including grocery bags and tissues, and frantically set to work. Ida then read her scenes with full dramatic energy to the maid, who was delighted at such attention. Meredith realized that whatever Ida wrote, good or bad, was made brilliant by her acting. The dark-skinned woman became part of the trio, even offering comments on the screenplay. Ida insisted on bringing the housekeeper to dinner, often choosing a rough gambling casino on the lakefront. She became indignant at real or imagined slights regarding the maid.

"What country are we in?" she would bellow. Heads would turn. "Do we not believe in racial equality? Anyone who doesn't understand shouldn't be an American!" Lupino was a subject of fascination to those who recognized her. Fans would often blurt out, "I saw you in *High Sierra*—" before they hurried away. "Why don't they say whether they liked me or not?" Ida would growl.

One evening she was asked to visit the wife of a prominent casino owner. "It was dreadful," she recounted. "I was forced to look at every piece of tasteless jewelry and every slaughtered animal in her possession." Meredith observed that Ida relished scenes of horror that she could retell, imitating each of the participants. Since Ida hated to gamble, the casinos held small interest; she especially disliked the female hands scratching across the green baize of the gambling tables to collect the money.

They spent many evenings in the company of Clark Gable, a warm and friendly fellow, Meredith thought, and surprisingly devoid of pretentions. He invited them to attend a benefit in Reno. He was the master of ceremonies and, despite his he-man screen image, explained to the audience why he had given up hunting. "I shot a deer and it died in my arms. I vowed then—and I lived up to it—to never shoot another living thing." Ida admired such blunt honesty.

Despite efforts to finish the screenplay, the beauty of Lake Tahoe lured Lupino and Meredith from the $1,200-a-month lodge. Ida bought a fishing license and cast for rainbow trout. She swam in the chilly water.

Duff flew up for the weekends. Ida insisted that Meredith find a date. Ida met a *Life* magazine photographer who was doing a story on the wild mustangs of Nevada. When Meredith declined Ida's matchmaking, she exploded. "You're a schoolteacher, and I'm sick of it!" After the unexpected flare-up, the women bought bus tickets to Los Angeles. As the bus went from Reno to Tahoe, they sat in silence. Meredith gazed in admiration at the panorama. Suddenly she blurted, "Isn't the lake the supreme natural phenomenon?" Ida burst out laughing at Meredith's awe of nature; they patched things up, with Ida mimicking her friend's innocence. "Isn't that tree beautiful?" she would deadpan.

Shopping with Ida was an experience, as she bought anything she wished without regard to cost. She was gaining weight rapidly and searched for suitable maternity clothes. "I can't stand the way pregnant women look when they go to the market, dressing in baggy dresses and hair curlers," she sniffed. Ida chose expensive Chinese dinner coats and black slacks.

Ida paid for Meredith's divorce, calling it salary.

While Howard was visiting, the trio drove through a pine forest. "Howard, grab that cat!" shouted Ida. "It's a manx!" Duff caught it, to Ida's delight. "It's a performer. It will put on shows for us," she crooned with joy. Dubbed Rhubarb, the cat gave nightly shows, as Ida had predicted, racing, growling and climbing the walls.

One evening Ida answered the telephone, then called Meredith over. "Let me give you my secretary," she said. Meredith took the receiver. "I heard a string of the dirtiest language I'd ever encountered, all about what he was going to do to Ida when he got over here from the Wagon Wheel casino." They had about fifteen minutes, judging the distance. The police refused to come, claiming something more concrete than the threat was necessary. To Meredith's surprise, the target of the threat was enthralled by the high drama. "You take the andirons," she directed Meredith. The maid was handed a frying pan, and Ida grabbed a silver hairbrush. "Now we're ready," Ida said confidently.

The sex maniac never made it, but Aunt Nell did. Famous in musical comedy, Nell had a wicked sense of humor. After drinking and cards, Nell would perform a song and dance routine to "E's up Mother Brown." It was a fast-paced life, and Ida was unable to fully unwind. Her nights ended with sleeping pills, and her mornings began with pep pills, Meredith observed.

Ida became upset when C.J. Tevlin, chief of studio operations, rejected her gambling story as uncommercial. Ida was still fuming about RKO's advertising campaign for *Hard, Fast and Beautiful*, claiming it lacked punch and power. She telephoned her friend Barbara Reed, who lived in Lake Tahoe, and tried to interest her in *The Devil Is a Young Man*, the proposed story of murderer Billy Cook.

As Ida and Howard's wedding day approached, the household returned to a more sedate style. Ida and Diane spent afternoons collecting autumn boughs, flowers, leaves and pine cones, all of which they sprayed gold. At Lanz's in Reno they purchased expensive gowns. Meredith was given the once-over by Lupino, who suggested that her naturally brunette hair be lightened. She brought out a bottle of peroxide and went to work. She followed it by a large application of henna, then Meredith's head was wrapped in a towel. "You do the scene on the stairs, Ida directed, "and I'll do the scene at the boat." The night progressed, both women immersed in their writing. Ida suddenly yelled, "Oh, my God! Your hair!" When the towel was removed, Meredith's hair was a shocking bright orange.

On October 20 Ida officially ended her marriage to Collier Young. The next day she became the bride of Howard Duff in a simple ceremony conducted by Judge Guild, who, the day before, had granted her the divorce. For the quiet ceremony, the living room of Ida's home was decorated with the sprayed foliage. Neighbors sent food for a small reception.

Ida was lovely. She wore an elegant lavender and taffeta gown. An expensive diamond necklace graced her slender throat. Best man, Duff's agent Mike Meshekoff, and maid of honor, carrot-topped Diane Meredith, watched as Ida promised to "love, honor and obey" her new husband. Following the vows, photographers captured the couple embracing. They told the journalists that their marriage was going to be a successful one. During the reception, Clark Gable caused a stir when he stopped by to offer his congratulations. The couple took a train to San Francisco for a brief honeymoon. The pregnant bride was thirty-three years old, Duff was thirty-six. The following day, wire service photographs appeared in newspapers throughout the nation.

Later, at the beach house in Malibu, there were glimmers of things to come. At a post-wedding party, champagne flowed. In the midst of the festivity, Duff playfully goosed one of his buddies. Ida was furious. She called Howard outside, and on the sand before the house complained about his boorish behavior. He was never to humiliate her with such thoughtlessness again. "You are to behave, not like a jerk, but like a person. That is your role in life—to be a person." Diane Meredith watched as Ida and her third husband said goodbye to everyone. The huge gorgeous eyes were filled with love and hope. The Duffs lived for a while in Ida's Malibu home before they leased a partially furnished residence in the Hollywood Hills.

At that time, trouble was stirring for Filmakers. In March, James V. Bennett, an official with the U.S. Bureau of Prisons, sent an angry letter to Joseph Breen about Filmakers' "underhanded trick" of obtaining William Cook's release for the forthcoming picture. Bennett was incensed over the proposed picture and complained that it would glorify an atrocious murderer. He urged the Motion Picture Association to withhold approval. A month later, in a lengthy letter, Ida and Collier Young defended their actions. They explained to Bennett that they had paid Cook's attorney three thousand dollars for a "valid and legal release" and maintained that there would be no blood-letting whatsoever in the film. "We first became interested in this subject due to the compelling nature of the moral and religious experiences of their captivity," they explained. "We specialize in the documentary film and have found that in dealing with facts we can produce pictures of greater import and impact."

But neither the U.S. Bureau of Prisons nor the Motion Picture Association would allow a picture based on the murderous exploits of William Cook. In April the MPA issued its final ruling: "No picture shall be approved dealing with the life of a notorious criminal of current or recent times which used the name, nickname or alias of such." Filmakers had no choice but to fictionalize the story and delete all references to Cook.

In addition to the Cook conflict, the strained relationship between Collier Young and Malvin Wald threatened to sink the company. Ida and Collie had penned *On the Loose*, a story about wayward parents whose daughter becomes a delinquent and attempts suicide. Joan Evans starred as the unhappy daughter. In May, while production was still in the early planning stages, Ida had declined to direct. "It would have made five pictures in a row about women with problems and I didn't want to go stale," she said.

Malvin Wald was shocked to discover that distinguished actor Melvyn Douglas was being forced by RKO to appear in an obviously minor picture as political punishment meted out by Howard Hughes. Congresswoman Helen Gahagan Douglas, the actor's wife, was campaigning for the Senate against Richard Nixon, a prominent member of HUAC. Nixon claimed that Mrs. Douglas was a Communist sympathizer. Not only was she stigmatized as a "pinko," but her husband was as well. Both had long been liberal Democrats and publicly active in political causes and issues. Malvin Wald was appalled by RKO's treatment of a great actor, a star who had appeared opposite Garbo. But there was another devastating twist: "Howard Hughes made us—made Filmakers—pay his high salary. We could have gotten another actor for a fraction of the cost."

Not only was Wald surprised to find Melvyn Douglas in the cast, but he was stunned to discover that Collier Young had hired his friend Charles Lederer as the director. He was to receive 10 percent of the profits. Lederer was a noted writer but had never directed a film. Wald was a full partner but had not been consulted. He angrily disputed the arrangement. "Let me handle this!" snapped Collie.

Wald had seen Filmakers' hard-earned profits disappear because of a bad contract. Now, after Collier Young arbitrarily gave away 10 percent of this project, he felt he had no other choice but to sue. During production, Wald wanted a cast photograph with Melvyn Douglas. Crew members balked. "I'm not having my picture made with that Commie spy," grumbled assistant director Jim Anderson. "It was an insane time," laments Malvin Wald.

Ida was angry over Wald's lawsuit and very protective of her company; she was furious that Wald's attorney tied up the company funds. She remained loyal to Collie. On one occasion, Mala

Powers had come to the set of *Outrage* with a cold, feeling ill after a day on location. She playfully teased Ida that she would have to sue. Ida did not take her protégé's comment as a joke. Powers never forgot Lupino's withering stare. Now, with Wald's lawsuit threatening to bring the company down, Ida boiled with fury and worry. Wald and Filmakers reached a financial settlement, but bitter feelings lingered. Wald never again worked with his former partners. In later years, he suspected that Collie had sabotaged his career whenever possible. Wald's departure was a creative blow, for he provided an intellectual originality to the stories. Thereafter, pure emotion would predominate Filmakers' productions.

Ida awaited the birth of her child and tried to rest at home. She managed to pull off a clever directorial coup, witnessed by British actor Robert Douglas. He had met Ida through his first wife, Dorothy Hyson, when Ida was a young girl. In 1947 Douglas arrived at Warner Bros. to play the role of the Duke de Lorca in *The Adventures of Don Juan* starring Errol Flynn. He renewed his friendship with Ida. Now he learned that Ida could masterfully direct a scene off camera. To celebrate Duff's birthday, Ida told guests to arrive in pajamas around 10:00 P.M. Duff was awakened by singing and was thoroughly bewildered by the sight.

On April 23, 1952, as she dressed to attend a tennis match, Ida went into premature labor. She was rushed to Temple Hospital. Dr. Bernstein managed to pull her through the ordeal. Bridget Mirella Duff weighed only four pounds; she was placed in an incubator and given a fifty-fifty chance of survival. In June the baby was shown to the press by the proud parents. "After trying for twelve years, I'm very happy about it," said Ida. The baby was christened in an elaborate ceremony with Collier Young and Joan Fontaine as the godparents.

On November 12, 1952, Collie and Joan Fontaine wed. Howard exhibited no jealousy over his wife's professional relationship with her former husband. In fact, the two couples socialized and became close friends.

Ida was soon directing *The Hitch-Hiker*, a suspenseful screenplay she and Collie wrote with an adaptation by Robert Joseph, a publicist and writer. Based on the 1951 murder spree of Billy Cook, the story was the gripping account of two friends on a fishing trip who stop for a hitchhiker. Like Cook, actor William Talman was given a deformed right eyelid that eerily remained open, preventing the captives from knowing when the psychopath slept. Frank Lovejoy and Edmond O'Brien turned in memorable performances as the terrorized victims. It was seventy-one minutes of on-edge suspense. "A crisp little thriller," acknowledged *Time*.

Once again, Filmakers gathered critical acclaim while RKO reaped the profits. Collier Young decided they should risk total independence and leave RKO. They would distribute their own releases and reduce major studio costs by going to a rental lot. Collie designed a rather grandiose plan to shoot four films at once at $125,000 per picture. Filmakers had numerous stories, most written by Ida and Collie. A prospectus from this period, provided to investors, listed their proposed films. Among the titles: *Fire Bug*, the story of a arsonist who attempts to burn a city; *Sky High*, the story of helicopter pilots in Korea; *Dynamo*, the tale of murder on the assembly line; *The Chase*, a western about a sheriff tired of murder, from the Broadway play by Horton Foote; *I Bought a Gun*, the drama of a handgun in a home; *The Story of a Murder*, described as "The first serious scientific approach made by motion pictures to tell audiences *why* people kill and why murder can be prevented." But investors liked *The Bigamist*.

As 1952 drew to a close, Ida Lupino had everything she wanted: fame, fortune, beauty, a career, Howard Duff and a child. Christmas had always been the most important day of the year for Ida. In December, Duff packed his suitcase for England to make

Spaceways. Ida soon followed. "I simply couldn't bear the thought of spending Christmas alone, so I took off to join him about a week before the holidays and got trapped in that deadly fog that killed thousands."

Her stay in London became a nightmare. The foul air even brought a halt to Duff's picture. Ida lay in her hotel room gasping for breath. She told Howard she had to get home—and fast. He rushed her to a physician for medical treatment; then, though it was extremely dangerous to depart in the thick fog, they booked a flight. When they boarded the plane there were only six other brave passengers. When she landed in New York, she felt it was God's Christmas gift to her. She thanked her husband for caring for her.

She had everything she wanted. Or so she thought.

13

THE LONG GOODBYE

There is something obviously irking Howard a touch, for he is, according to witnesses, playing a scene that is on the heavy side. —LOS ANGELES EXAMINER

After fourteen months of marriage, Howard said goodbye. He was barely out the front door when Louella Parsons had the story in print: "The strangest separation of all time is that of Ida Lupino and Howard Duff . . . there had been no quarrel, no trouble of any kind, and Ida thought everything was going along smoothly when Howard walked out of the house. He said he was leaving and was through."

After hiding for a few days in Palm Springs, the wayward spouse suddenly reappeared. He telephoned Parsons, saying he had returned and everything was fine. His departure was the first of many such incidents. Like his wife, he could be unpredictable. Though forced somewhat by Ida's pregnancy, their marriage was fulfilling to both at the start. But soon, an undercurrent of strain surfaced. Both were forceful individuals with stubborn tempers, and both could be hostile when fueled by alcohol. Each liked to win, and violent arguments erupted.

Despite the clashes, something clicked between them. Emulating her parents, who had been a team, Ida wished to work with Howard, just as she had done with her previous husbands. She put Howard on a pedestal beside her. "It damaged her career," says John Franco. "She received so many great scripts, for her, but she insisted that Howard get the lead. Sam Goldwyn wanted her for several pictures, but he eventually lost interest."

In early 1953 the Duffs went to Santa Barbara for *Jennifer*, a mystery starring Ida as the frightened caretaker of a vast estate whose owner has vanished. Duff had a minor role as a grocer, second-billed after his wife. The film failed to capture audiences.

Shortly after their weeks on location, Howard Duff made headlines when he became the face on the barroom floor. The incident occurred at Howard and Ida's hangout, the Villa Nova restaurant at 9015 Sunset Boulevard. Witnesses told reporters that Duff became enraged, he threatened to dismember everyone in the place, and tossed a glass and an ashtray. He bellowed threats that sent patrons scurrying until, at the end of the bar, he confronted silver-haired Jack Buchtel, a prominent restaurateur, who tried to reason with Duff. Duff took a swing. Buchtel sidestepped Duff's punch and sent his attacker to the floor.

Ida ran up and tossed a glass of water in her husband's face. Howard struggled to his feet and threw a right punch. Buchtel blocked, then smashed Duff in the nose. He slumped to the floor again. Ida ran over with another glass of water, but this time she threw it in Buchtel's face. He made his way outside with the enraged Lupino following with another glass of water. The innocent bar patron began a fast walk down Sunset with Ida close behind. After several blocks she ran out of steam and returned to her half-conscious husband. The escapade was chronicled in newspapers throughout the nation: "Sunset Strip Row at Dawn Features Ida Lupino's Mate."

Ida had stolen the spotlight from her brawling husband. As time passed, Duff came to realize that he lived in the shadow of his famous wife. He was "Mr. Lupino," and he didn't like it.

In June *The Bigamist*, which had been described in Ida and Collie's prospectus as "not the sordid story of a sex maniac, but the strangest story ever told with detection by the law coming closer every minute," went before the cameras and into the newspapers. The daring theme raised eyebrows in 1953, especially since there was a curious relationship among the principals. Collie shrewdly cast Joan Fontaine, his wife, in a film directed by his former wife. Edmond O'Brien played the bigamist, and Lupino and Fontaine were his film wives. The Youngs were coolly blasé about the situation, reporters noted. "We want to be grown up about it all," said Collie. "I don't know how people in Kansas feel about this . . . but after our divorce, Ida and I decided to stay in business because our company was a good thing. Since the divorce, the quality of our movies has actually improved." Added Fontaine, "Ida and I are old friends. . . . I knew her before Collier did. . . . I'm his third wife and Ida is his second. In fact, when I go to New York I always visit the first Mrs. Collier Young. We're all good friends." Fontaine said they had even tried to get Louis Hayward to do a bit as a bus driver, but he had declined.

Collie talked his mother-in-law, Lillian Fontaine, into making a screen appearance. Collie's script, based on a story by Larry Marcus and Lou Shor, was a social drama of a man who makes a tragic mistake. Both lead actresses created vivid characters, different personalities that appeal to their shared husband. Fontaine plays a distant, career-oriented wife, while Lupino is a waitress in a Chinese restaurant. Though a small-budget release, the cast boasted three Oscar winners: Joan Fontaine had won for her work in *Suspicion*, Edmund Gwenn for the Christmas classic *Miracle on 34th Street* and Jane Darwell for *The Grapes of Wrath*.

While essentially a serious film, *The Bigamist* had light moments and inside jokes; Gwenn's character, an adoption officer, "looks just like Santa Claus," a reference to his role in *Miracle on 34th Street*. In another scene, Ida and Edmond O'Brien meet on a tour bus as it cruises through Beverly Hills. The driver points out the homes of Jack Benny, Jane Wyman, Barbara Stanwyck and Edmund Gwenn. Says O'Brien: "I like movies, but I really don't care where Clark Gable lives."

Ever conscious of budget, Collie talked the cast into accepting "a participation deal," with profits from the first grosses, after the costs of advertising and prints had been paid. He made a cameo appearance, sitting at the bar of the Chinese restaurant where Lupino waits tables, wearing a fake scar on his cheek, undoubtedly giving his friends a laugh when they saw his uncredited presence.

With *The Bigamist*, Ida Lupino became the first woman to direct herself in a major motion picture. It was difficult for her to determine the quality of her performance, so she depended on Collie's judgment. She later revealed: "I'd always sworn I'd never do this . . . it was a new experience telling myself what to do. . . . I'm one who wants and needs direction but I never in the world expected to be doing it myself. I think it's the toughest thing I've ever attempted in my career."

To defray production costs, Collier Young featured Coke, United Airlines and Cadillac for remunerations. Scenes were also shot in public sites such as MacArthur Park and Chinatown, rather than on rental lots. Ida was acutely conscious of budget considerations. She carefully planned each scene, to avoid technical mistakes.

Ida worked closely with editor Stanford Tischler. She knew just what she wanted. "She wasn't the kind of director who would shoot something, then hope any flaws could be fixed in the cutting room," says Tischler. "The acting was always there, to her credit."

Collie convinced Ida they should distribute their own pictures; the greater the risk, the higher the profits. *The Bigamist* opened to mixed reviews. The ending was considered weak and lacking resolution. But Ida liked the end, as a judge suspends his verdict until a later time. She preferred to give the audience the opportunity to resolve the issue in their own minds. The *New York Times* hailed Ida. "This fragile director keels the action with such mounting tension, muted compassion and sharklike alacrity for behavior the average spectator may feel he is eavesdropping on the excellent dialogue."

Though Lupino again received critical acclaim, the financial rewards were meager because of the costs of self-distribution. But Collie insisted that the profits would eventually grow.

Only weeks after *The Bigamist* was completed, Filmakers announced that Lupino would direct her husband in *The Story of a Cop.* Shortly afterward, Duff dropped a bomb. He told Ida that he wanted a legal separation. Stunned, she expressed her bewilderment to Hedda Hopper. Louella Parsons reported that she interviewed "a very unhappy Ida," who lamented, "This time he means it. I don't want to get a divorce because I love Howard and he's really a fine person. Right now he's surrounded by people who give him the wrong advice. It's just that I don't believe Howard likes being married." Ida realized that her husband felt trapped and was unable to even tell her of his unhappiness. When pressure increased, he would simply disappear.

By this time the Duffs' marital problems were evident, and gossip had it that the end was near, but to everyone's surprise, they reconciled. With fervent optimism, they found a rambling ranch-style home in a secluded area of Brentwood just off Sunset Boulevard. The neighborhood was the picture of upper-class living, not ostentatious but comfortable. Their new residence was at 13211 Old Oak Lane, just a few minutes from the Westridge home where Ida had lived as Mrs. Hayward. The Duffs' new home was

spacious, with a swimming pool, lush foliage and tall trees sur-
rounding it. Ida paid sixty thousand dollars for the residence, out
of her funds, and the title was in her name. Duff left again. She was
close to giving up.

While pondering a divorce, she was offered an acting assignment that would alter the course of her career. She received a
telephone call from George Diskant, cinematographer for *The Bigamist*. He explained that he was with Four Star Productions, a
company owned by David Niven, Dick Powell and Charles Boyer.
Diskant suggested that she move into the television field.

"Television," Ida cried, "really, George, you're out of your
mind."

Not long afterward, David Niven telephoned, asking her to
do a guest spot on the show.

Like most in the movie industry, Ida regarded early television
with curiosity, then, when it became popular, as a deadly enemy that
robbed movie theaters of audiences. But she was always one to take
a chance; Ida decided to make her television debut in the highly acclaimed *Four Star Playhouse*, the 1951 brainchild of agent Don
Sharpe. Dick Powell and Charles Boyer had been the original duo,
with Joel McCrea nearly the third star. But McCrea lost interest,
and David Niven took his place. The fabulously successful company was already turning out other series, such as *The Zane Grey
Theater* and the *Alcoa-Goodyear Theater*. Four Star took over the RKO-
Pathe lot in Culver City, formerly Selznick Studios, where such
famous pictures as *Gone with the Wind* had been made. Ida was impressed by the quality of Four Star productions and, on the last day
of 1953, she made her debut on the small screen in "House For
Sale," playing a woman who encounters a psychopathic killer. She
immediately saw the opportunities.

After a three-month separation, Ida and Howard met to discuss terminating their marriage. The outcome of the meeting was a

decision to give it another try. They finally moved into their new home, which Ida filled with Early American furniture, selecting blue as the predominant color. Walls, upholstery and even chair pads were in her favorite color, never to change. The living room, with its raised hearth, was a gathering place when guests arrived. Above the brick fireplace was a painting by Edgar O. Kiechele, depicting a street scene of a rather sad young woman sitting forlornly on a stairway.

Managing the household was Mary Comack, a cheerful Scottish woman known to the family as Nanny. Hired as Bridget's nursemaid, she came to Ida one day and said, "She can look for herself, but you and Mr. Duff need someone to look after you." Nanny was a second mother to Bridget. The jovial woman had a knack for keeping the peace and tactfully cooling tempers. Over the years, Mary Comack learned to keep telephone numbers handy and to contact the Duffs' close friends when arguments got out of hand.

In February, Ida returned to television, starring opposite Jack Lemmon in "Marriageable Male" for *Ford Theater*. Ted Post leaped at the chance to direct Lupino, an actress he had admired for years. By April, the Duffs were again estranged and were no longer speaking to each other. Ted Post had an idea, a rather risky one. He asked Ida if she would like to appear in a romantic episode called *Season to Love*. Then Post called Howard and asked if he'd like to play the lover. He told neither of them who they would play opposite, so when they came to the rehearsal, they were quite surprised. But Post's gamble paid off; not only did they do a superb show, but the Duffs patched up their marriage.

Ted Post enjoyed working with Ida but couldn't understand her preoccupation with the lighting. "Darling, don't shoot me as if I were an eighteen year old," she pleaded. "We need some soft lenses. Or maybe a horse blanket," she would joke. Though only thirty-six years old, Ida was, as always, insecure about her looks.

With the Duffs again reunited, Filmakers proceeded with its crime drama, now titled *Private Hell 36*. Ida and Collie had collaborated on a script about cops and greed. She didn't dare direct the picture, for fear of a marital rift. Instead, she chose Don Siegel, having admired his low-budget *Riot in Cell Block 11*.

Before production began, Siegel asked Ida if there was money in the budget to assist a struggling writer. Ida hired the unknown as dialogue coach. On Stage 12 of Republic Studios, script supervisor John Franco met Siegel's friend. "He was Sam Peckinpah," says Franco. "This was the first time he had ever set foot on a stage. He was living in a shack in Malibu; half of it was covered with cardboard boxes and aluminum. Ida gave him his start."

The script had Duff and Steve Cochran as detectives investigating counterfeit cash. Lupino plays the nightclub singer who receives a fake bill as a tip. According to Siegel, he encountered difficulty from the beginning. First, the script wasn't ready. Once production was under way, he felt he was battling for every decision. As Siegel described his problems: "There was too much alcohol in the air and I thought the people I was working for were pretentious—talented but pretentious. They'd talk, talk, talk, but they wouldn't sit down and give me enough time. They wouldn't rehearse. Perhaps it was my fault." Steve Cochran was a good actor, acknowledged Siegel, but not when he was drunk, "and I had a hard time catching him even slightly sober." Don Siegel felt that he simply could not communicate with his cast and that the picture showed it.

Filmakers also completed *Mad at the World*, a low-budget melodrama about juvenile delinquency. Keefe Braselle played a distraught father whose life is shattered when teens attack his family, killing his baby with a whiskey bottle. Ida and Collie scored a coup by traveling to Washington and convincing Senator Estes Kefauver, chairman of the Senate committee investigating juvenile delinquency, of the value of their story. Kefauver endorsed the picture and even made a brief appearance in the opening.

But their efforts were in vain. Filmakers went under, never to surface again. "We made one fatal mistake," lamented Ida. "We got talked into going into the distribution business. I opposed the move every step of the way. 'We're creative people, we're picture makers. We know nothing about distribution. Let's stay away from it.' But I was out-voted and pretty soon we were out of business." Ida's dream of working independently turned to ashes.

With the demise of her company, Ida was forced to find acting jobs. Producer Bryan Foy starred her as a sadistic warden in *Women's Prison*. Duff tagged along, sixth-billed as a prison doctor. Actress Audrey Totter played a pregnant inmate mistreated by the gorgeous but brutal warden. Totter observed that Ida enjoyed playing the vicious warden, cleverly insisting on stylish dresses, earrings and jewelry. "It was Ida's idea," says Totter. The prisoners were forbidden to dress like women; only the warden could look elegantly feminine. "This makes my character crueler," smiled Ida.

Totter was married to a prominent university medical professor, and *Women's Prison* was her last film before she retired to raise a family. Despite the somber atmosphere, she found Ida great fun. Ida was curious about who had delivered her child.

"The head of UCLA's medical department," answered Totter.

"Do you know him personally?" asked Ida.

"Yes," she said. "I'm friends with all the doctors over there."

"How odd," remarked Ida, "one day, there you are at a cocktail party, with your arms up having a drink, and a little later on you're meeting this *obstetrician* in an entirely different *position*." Ida acted out the scene, which Totter found wildly amusing.

With their constant cycle of breakup and reunion, the Duffs were a common item of talk in Hollywood. The home on Old

Oak Lane was known as "the place where peace breaks out." When the fourth big split came, the columnists pointed to Howard's public appearances with tennis ace Gussie Moran. The pair had been spotted at the Mocambo nightclub and the swank Macayo restaurant in Santa Monica. Most often, they were observed playing tennis on the courts of the Beverly Wilshire Hotel. One version in print claimed that Ida had become jealous of Howard's attentions to Miss Moran at a party, and during an argument, she heatedly told him to get out. Connie was given as the source of this version and also of the rumor that Ida had a change of heart while Howard remained adamant, still seeing "Gorgeous Gussie." Duff gave the press his side of the feud: "I did not leave my wife for another woman. Miss Moran, with whom I've been rumored, is engaged."

In his years as Lupino's husband, Howard's facade of calmness had melted. Ida's vibrant personality was like a sunburst, blinding and dazzling but also fiery. Her many years in the movie industry provided her with unsurpassed film knowledge. Her brilliance had blossomed to the point where she was lauded as an actress, director, writer and producer. She could do it all. Yet she had refrained from directing her husband in *Private Hell 36,* her own company's release. Perhaps she felt it would have made Howard feel doubly insignificant to take acting direction from his wife. He was wed to a brilliant woman, and he was jealous.

They planned a divorce. Ida engaged Greg Bautzer as her attorney and instructed him to go ahead with the property settlement. "What's there to argue about?" asked Duff. "About all I have is a cat and a car." Friends felt a divorce was inevitable, but the cycle continued. Duff returned to Lupino.

While Duff found employment in forgettable B-pictures, Ida was selected for better films. She now embarked on the most psychologically tortuous role she would ever play.

Robert Aldrich telephoned. "Ida, I'm going to make a picture called *The Big Knife.*

"Oh, you just ran it through me!" exclaimed Ida, thinking of John Garfield and the play he had made famous.

Aldrich wanted Lupino to play the wife. He said they would fight it through to make a success. Aldrich had worked a small miracle in bringing Clifford Odets' controversial play to the screen. The stage success had been a personal triumph for the playwright and had kept alive Garfield's career. But the play, the story of an anguished film star blackmailed by his studio boss, had raised a furor in Hollywood. The play was attacked as a gross distortion of the motion picture industry. Gossip circulated that the blackmailer was a thinly disguised portrait of Louis B. Mayer. Odets penned a defense in the *New York Times*, writing, "the picture is not an indictment of Hollywood but an indictment of ruthlessness and evil."

Aldrich chose Jack Palance for the lead. Aldrich rewrote dialogue, handing Ida a taut script that pleased her. "My God, Bob, you're a strange person. You have written for me words as if I'm talking to John, who has passed on."

"That's *exactly* what I want," said the director. After nine days of intense rehearsals, the picture was made at the Sutherland Studios on Occidental Boulevard utilizing one basic set. It was completed in fifteen shooting days, a feat Lupino applauded. Aldrich produced the film on a tight budget of $423,000 with $260,000 for the cast. Ida's forceful performance was recognized with praise, especially the ending, where she responds to her husband's suicide with a shattering scream. Every scene for her was a heart-rending experience; the similarity between the blackmailed actor's downfall and Garfield's persecuted end was emotionally upsetting to her. Ida told Aldrich the last scene gave her an eerie chill.

"Well, you felt that way when you got the news," remarked the director.

Ida gasped. "Yes, you're psychic. I asked God to help me. I'd lost one of my dear friends and I had such hopes that I had found a way up a clean path for him."

"That's life, isn't it?" Aldrich said. "But there others beyond the forest."

"Oh sir, you are one of them and I love you for it," Ida said.

14

MR. ADAMS AND EVE

We are getting along so well it's almost boring. —EVE/IDA

In December 1955, Ida announced she was joining *Four Star Play-house.* Since her first appearance two years earlier, she had eagerly returned for ten episodes. Director Roy Kellino praised Four Star's newest addition: "She is a trouper. She is never late. She always knows her lines. She knows how to improvise. And she will stand all day on a recently broken ankle because she knows that if the picture goes into another day of shooting, it will cost more money. I admire Miss Lupino tremendously."

Ida adored her charming partner, David Niven. Like Ida, he was high spirited and loved a laugh. In *Bring on the Empty Horses,* Niven recounts a lively evening that began at Old Oak Lane and ended at Ciros nightclub. Niven and his Swedish wife, Hjordis, had come to the Duffs' house for dinner. They decided to have fun with columnists Hedda Hopper and Louella Parsons and arranged a scene at Ciros. After Niven strolled into the nightclub with Ida on his arm, someone tipped off the press and photographers gathered in the bar. When Howard and Hjordis walked in the reporters sensed trouble and made ready with their cameras. Duff suddenly pushed his table over with a crash, pointing across the room with a dramatic gesture. "He'll kill you!" screamed Ida to Niven.

At the edge of the dance floor, Niven and Duff confronted each other. They removed their jackets and rolled up their sleeves. The room was still, spectators ready for a deadly fight. They sprang at each other, kissed on the lips, and waltzed around the dance floor. The next day the gossip queens chastised the pranksters.

Since Ida was thoroughly captivated by television, Collier Young convinced the Duffs he had a concept for a series. It was *Mr. Adams and Eve*. They agreed to shoot a thirty-minute pilot for Four Star. Ida's romance with television was heightened by her directorial debut in January 1956. As part of the motion picture industry's mass exodus into the new medium, NBC presented *Screen Directors Playhouse*, a half-hour weekly drama with each episode selected and filmed by a major director. Ida wrote a story about a woman living alone in a mountain cabin, her quiet life disrupted by bank robbers who were being pursued by police. For the cast of "No. 5 Checked Out," Ida chose Teresa Wright, Peter Lorre and William Talman. She would have forsaken films altogether, but she had two remaining commitments.

While the City Sleeps was a murder yarn brought to the screen by director Fritz Lang. Producer Bert Friedlob promoted the picture as "a weapon in the growing battle against the corrupting force of comic books on young minds." The "lipstick murderer," played by John Barrymore, Jr., reads comic books, then murders women. Lupino nearly steals the film as a sharp-tongued gossip columnist who attempts to seduce a seemingly virtuous anchorman.

Lang had established his reputation with memorable films depicting an individual in conflict with society. *M* in 1931 dealt with a child murderer, hunted and nearly lynched by a mob; *Fury* in 1936 conveyed the ruin of an innocent man, unjustly accused of a crime; *While the City Sleeps* became in his capable hands an engrossing film noir, subtly exposing the ambition and hypocrisy of the media, out to catch, at any cost, a deranged killer.

Lang was brilliant but rather eccentric, harboring a suspicious streak that was noticed by assistant director Ronnie Rondell. "I worked with him on several pictures. He was firm with the cast, but not overbearing. I noticed he would always wear dark glasses; he put them down one afternoon and I saw that he had mirrors built in the sunglasses which allowed him to see what was going on behind his back."

In April, Ida was honored by the Masquers, a prestigious theatrical organization. She was warmly praised before three hundred guests and given the George Spelvin Award for excellence in her craft. Ida listened nervously, ill at ease before the large audience, as Edmond O'Brien joked that she was "the nicest smelling director I've ever worked with." His wife, Olga San Juan, sang, "I Love to Look at You." Kind words were expressed by Alan Dwan, Hedda Hopper, Mala Powers and Howard Duff. When Ida rose to speak, she thanked the gathering, then quoted her father's advice on speeches: "Ida, if you ever write a play, kill off the actors in the last act so they can't make a speech." With this brief comment she sat down.

Strange Intruder was the last feature film she would make for sixteen years. "It was a quickie," says director Irving Rapper. The drama starred Edmond Purdom as a former POW returning home from Korea, mentally unbalanced and obsessed with punishing the wife of a dead comrade. At Warner Bros., Rapper had gained fame by directing Bette Davis in *Now, Voyager* in 1942 and *The Corn Is Green* in 1945. He was used to fireworks. He approached Lupino about starring in the picture, and he was quite pleased with her attitude. "Over lunch she said, 'Irving, I'd love to work with you and I'm going to do it. I want you to know that *you* are the director and

I shall do everything you tell me.' And she did. She was absolutely wonderful."

Lupino's acting career shifted to the realm of television with frequent appearances on *Four Star Playhouse*. She was hailed for "The Stand-In," a script she wrote for herself, the story of a washed-up actress, bitterly hated by the woman who lives in her shadow. Collie, also active in television, asked her to direct an episode of *On Trial*, a series he created and guided as executive producer, for it dealt with her political idol, Abraham Lincoln. "The Trial of Mary Surratt" was a gripping courtroom drama of the woman hanged as an accomplice in the Lincoln assassination. For years, Ida wanted to bring to the screen a picture about Mary Todd Lincoln, the unhappy First lady. Ida saw her as a villainess who was cold and cruel to her husband.

Ida would have preferred full-time directing, but CBS had other ideas. The network television series starring Lupino and Duff, *Mr. Adams and Eve*, would soon be seen by millions. Comedy specialist Sol Saks was chosen as the show's writer. Saks liked Collie's premise about a movie star couple but immediately eliminated their characterization as "always feuding." He became a familiar face at Old Oak Lane, sitting in the den with Ida and Howard outlining the basic structure of the show and discussing stories. They developed a smooth rapport. Saks grew especially close to Ida, who took an avid interest in every aspect of the production. When CBS wanted Fred de Cordova assigned as producer, she responded: "You'll have to check it out with Sol." The cast included Hayden Rorke as their agent, Alan Reed as a studio boss and Olive Carey, widow of actor Harry Carey, in the role of the housekeeper. Ida selected Frances Robinson to play Eve's bitchy friend, the wife of a studio executive. *Mr. Adams and Eve* debuted on January 4, 1957, with the premiere episode featuring Gloria Talbot as a starlet who talks Howard Adams into giving her a bit part in a film, then proceeds to steal all of Eve's scenes. The show was an instant hit, as Lupino proved her flair for comedy. Subsequent episodes featured guest stars David Niven, Joan Fontaine, Sir Cedric Hardwicke and Francis X. Bushman. Johnny Carson, a neighbor of the Duffs and the host of the popular game show *Who Do You Trust?* made a cameo appearance.

But it was the comedy antics of Ida and Howard that brought the high ratings. Viewers wondered if they were watching a thinly disguised documentary about the Duffs, and often they were. Actress Lee Patrick was added to the cast as Eve's eccentric mother, "Connie," who would do such odd things as boil jewelry for a good shine. One show had Eve and Howard placed on studio suspension with no paychecks, lamenting how they were going to support "my sister, mother, your brother. . . ." The Adams home was a replica of the interior of the Duff's residence on Old Oak Lane. Each day, Ida and Howard hauled a set of heavy brass candlesticks from their den to the set as props. These were also Ida's good luck charms. Duff credited Collier Young for the show's success. "I guess he just watched us in action," Howard said.

Sol Saks told reporters that his stories were actually based on the Duffs' private life. Ida admitted they were "sixty percent true." Saks found Ida a joy to work with and was grateful for her trust in his ability. "I wrote the script and the next time they saw it was when they were sitting around in their den reading it with the cast." Only once did CBS try to tamper with a script. Ida made it clear that if Saks left the show over the incident, she would too. Often Saks came to Old Oak Lane to discuss ideas. On one occasion, Mary Comack came in to ask if they wanted to place any bets at the race tracks. "She was booking bets for them, so I did a story on this. Any rewrites were between the three of us. That was all."

Ida and Howard became nationally famous as a couple. Their marital squabbles of earlier years were ignored by the press. So solid

were they as a married team that American Express chose them to
endorse its credit card.

At the beginning, Ida had attempted to direct the series,
but fireworks had erupted. As she explained, "When I directed
Howard, it wasn't good. Now we have another director and we are
getting along so well."

Richard Kinon, the director of the series, had been surprised
to discover that, unbeknownst to him, Ida had gone to CBS executives and insisted that he be included in the package. In 1955 he
had started on *Four Star Playhouse* as a script supervisor. Kinon had
impressed Lupino with his ability to get the best from actors. At
age twenty-eight he found himself at the helm of a hit comedy
series starring one of the most famous actresses in the world. It was
a rewarding experience, says Kinon. "*Mr. Adams and Eve* was ahead of
its time. We got away with murder. The bright dialogue was right
up to the edge of being censored." Though Kinon was inexperi-
enced, Lupino never tried to take over. "The situation was right for
me to be massacred. Ida was the star, married to her co-star, but she
never tried to use her clout." But Ida always had suggestions and
"some of her ideas were outrageous." He observed that Ida had the
technique of acting before the camera honed to a scientific edge, but
she modestly described her talent as "just a matter of making the
right faces at the right time."

Before each scene, Ida would ask the makeup man to hand
her a mirror, then she would take a powderpuff and touch up her
nose. It was a simple subterfuge. "Actually," says Kinon, "she was
looking in the mirror to see if the lighting was right." If it did
not meet her satisfaction, cameraman George Diskant was summoned. "George, darling," she would say, "don't you think the
lights should be a little higher for dear old Mum? I'm not twenty-
two anymore."

After thirty-five shows, Kinon was exhausted and needed a rest. He begged for time off. But Ida was worried. "Who will we get?" she asked.

"Well, what are you doing, Ida?"

"Oh, no, Dick, I can't do it," she protested. "It's enough for me to get here and put the face on in the morning."

One of the cleverest episodes came when "Ida Lupino the Director" was called on to direct Eve Adams. Split screen effects were used, and Ida played both roles brilliantly. The story's big joke was that Howard Adams disliked "Lupino the Director." Actor Jerry Hausner, home after working abroad for Radio Free Europe, sought out his friends for a reunion. They apologetically told him, "this is like being in jail." To find time for a reunion, Hausner was written into an episode as an acidulous drama critic. Ida made sure he received more than the standard pay and had a special cake sent over during lunch.

Each episode was filmed in three grueling days. After the final scene, cast and crew would relax with a drink and the name of a good restaurant would be tossed out. But, to Sol Saks' amusement, they never made it. "We'd always end up at her home and Ida would prepare something for us. She did not like to go out. At the height of her fame and beauty she was somewhat of a recluse."

Saks was surprised when Ida told him she had always felt unattractive. She understood that people regarded her as beautiful, but she saw herself differently. "I have an unusual, striking sort of face but I'm not good looking. My forehead, my eyes . . ." She shook her head, pointing out what was wrong with her features. Saks came to understand that Ida was a very complex woman. She was a movie star who was playing a movie star on television, seen by millions every week; yet, in real life, she disdained the glamor and the hoopla. She preferred to stay at home and hoped to remain unrecognized in public. Occasionally, she could be talked into leaving her refuge.

Howard liked to unwind in nightclubs, and one evening the Duffs joined Sol Saks and his wife at Ciros. They were having an enjoyable evening until a roving fortune teller stopped at their table. She failed to recognize the famous couple but stared at Ida and said she looked familiar. Ida became uncomfortable. The stranger made the comment a few more times, then Saks playfully added, "People tell her she looks like Ida Lupino." "Oh, yes," said the woman, "but you're much prettier. She's older looking." Ida's face tightened and the fun vanished.

On another occasion, Saks witnessed Lupino's wit. He, Ida and Duff were sitting in his car discussing strategy for an important conference with CBS big shots. The audience from a studio taping exited a nearby building, and two women stopped; one pointed to Ida, then came over to the car.

"Pardon me for interrupting," she said, "but aren't you Marge Champion?"

"No, I'm not," said Ida brusquely.

They resumed the discussion, but the woman returned. "I know you're her. I talked to my friend and she said *you are* Marge Champion."

"NO," said Ida, "I'm not, and will you please leave us alone? We're busy." Lupino cursed the woman.

"Ida," chided Saks, "you shouldn't have talked to her that way."

Ida raised an eyebrow. "So she'll hate Marge Champion."

CBS asked the Duffs to make a personal appearance on *The Ed Sullivan Show.* Ida informed executives that she couldn't go to New York "unless my writer and his wife come along." Saks and his wife got a free vacation. During their train's stopover in Chicago, Ida made a startling suggestion. "She offered to meet my family," says Saks. "Ida liked me a lot. She was grateful to me and, in her own precious way, she was willing to give her most valuable possession—herself." In New York the Duffs got into a fierce argument and never made it to the Sullivan show.

At the height of their fame, the Duffs were a subject of interest. The semi-autobiographical episodes of *Mr. Adams and Eve* prompted intense curiosity about their private life.

One evening Ida and Howard sat in a real estate office. Ralph Edwards, host of the popular *This Is Your Life*, suddenly appeared with a cheerful greeting. Ida squirmed nervously and glanced around with shock. Edwards pulled her to her feet and dramatically proclaimed, "All America is watching. That's a television camera right out there. Tonight, Ida Lupino, this is your life."

"Oh, no," she gasped.

Edwards explained to Ida, and the millions watching, that the real estate office was merely a lure; a television studio was nearby and a police escort was ready to whisk her away. Ida stared at the camera in apparent disbelief. *This Is Your Life*, "the program you dare not miss"—had snared "beautiful, tempestuous star Ida Lupino." While the Duffs were being rushed to the studio, viewers were shown a scene from *Mr. Adams and Eve*, an episode that satirized *This Is Your Life*. Ida's comical reactions as Eve Drake were similar to what had happened when Ralph Edwards surprised her. Edwards launched into the history of the Lupinos as Ida, looking ill at ease, removed one glove; she absent-mindedly wore the other for the remainder of the show.

Suddenly, a booming voice is heard from off stage. Ida listens wide-eyed. Uncle Barry emerges, hugs his niece and playfully spanks her. He merrily recounts how young Ida broke "a good many rules as a child," but, he says, "I admired your pluck." His daughter, Tonie, is heard next: "That imagination! It's a wonder we survived it. You scared the wits out of all the children in the family." Tonie, her brother Barry and Rita surround Ida, relating tales of their youth.

Connie, quite elegant in a fur and jewelry, sits beside her daughter and dramatically tells the audience of Ida's polio attack. Ida listens, obviously uncomfortable. A grimace comes over her face as she relives the terrible night when she collapsed and feared her career had ended. William Wellman, the man who gave Ida a chance to play Bessie Broke, is introduced. He energetically relives the moment Ida stormed into his office and convinced him of her talent.

"Mother Lupino" is then greeted by her protégés, Mala Powers, Sally Forrest and Keefe Braselle. Powers, in a voice choking with emotion says: "You not only gave me the greatest chance of my life but you gave me something more, the greatest thing a performer can have, you believed in me and I just had to succeed for you."

Howard comes onstage. He says that their romance took hold on the beach in Malibu, a case of "love they neighbor."

"You're not scared to be married to both brains and beauty?" asks Edwards.

"Man, I count on it," responds Duff.

He thanks Ida for the greatest gift she had given him— "our child." Five-year-old Bridget runs to her mother. The closing shows family and friends gathered around Ida. Ralph Edwards bestowed several gifts, including a party in her honor, a gold bracelet and a one-thousand dollar check donated to the National Foundation for Infantile Paralysis in Lupino's name since, says Edwards, "You put your heart into bringing hope and courage to polio victims." Then comes another surprise, a new "hi-fi" and a special record. For the first time, Ida's face registers joy as she hears her father's high-pitched voice singing his famous novelty tune "Tweet! Tweet!"

Finally, the agonizing event ended. Ida jumped up. "Which way is the bathroom?" she asked. Shortly afterward, a party was in full swing at the Hollywood Roosevelt when Howard Duff approached Harry Mines and asked anxiously, "Did you hear it?" Mines, who had been present, was perplexed by the question. Duff wanted to know if Ida's cursing under her breath could be heard. Ida had been inwardly seething over being ambushed by Edwards. She intensely disliked surprises and especially hated having her life scrutinized before millions of prying eyes. As her relatives had told stories about her, she had mumbled throughout. When Duff emerged, he heard his wife curse under her breath. When the show aired, no curses were audible, to the Duffs' great relief.

With *Mr. Adams and Eve*, Ida and Howard became familiar faces around the globe. Each week millions of fans laughed at Ida's comedy routines. Ida proved herself a clown, just like her father. Her fine acting led to an Emmy nomination as best leading actress in a comedy series. At the Eleventh Annual Emmy Awards, Lupino lost to Jane Wyatt of *Father Knows Best*. The loss really didn't really matter since the series had brought Ida such professional acclaim and personal joy. Most important, the show's success had improved her marriage. She and Howard shared the limelight, both basking equally in the glow of fame and fortune. After sixty-six episodes, the show was canceled in 1958. According to Sol Saks, rumors at the time attributed the show's demise to the wives of CBS executives, who disliked the snooty executive wife played by Frances Robinson. Ida loved the character and told Saks that the bitchy portrayal was a true comment on "this type of woman." Ida would recall the momentous years of *Mr. Adams and Eve* as the happiest of her life.

The Duffs stayed busy with television appearances. They were guests on *I Love Lucy*, playing themselves in a humorous encounter with Lucy and Ricky Ricardo. Ida had a grudging respect for the show's star, whom she found talented but demanding. Ida referred to her as "Old Ball," "Big Ball," or just plain "Ball." Ida was taken aback by Desi Arnaz, who whispered that they should go sailing together. She declined the invitation.

Shortly afterward, the Duffs again tried to repeat their television success. Ida directed Howard in a pilot titled *The Green Peacock*, an adventure mystery about an ex-cop living in Mexico. They also proposed a series based on *Tom Sawyer*, Mark Twain's famous novel. None of the programs ever made it to the airwaves.

In October 1959, Ida gave one of her most memorable television performances in "The Sixteen-Millimeter Shrine," an episode of *The Twilight Zone*, written by Rod Serling and directed by her old friend Mitch Leisen. She gave a moving performance as aging actress "Barbara Jean Trenton, whose world is a projection room, whose dreams are made of celluloid," whose wish to return to the happier days of the past come true. Ida played the former movie queen with convincing poignancy and impact.

Ironically, the theme of aging film stars entered Ida's own life, the very week the haunting *Twilight Zone* episode was broadcast. On October 19, 1959, Ida and Howard made the sad journey to Forest Lawn Cemetery in Glendale to attend the funeral of Errol Flynn, her deeply loved friend. At age fifty, Flynn had succumbed to a heart attack in Vancouver. He had lived high and fast during his quarter-century as filmdom's heroic swashbuckler. Flynn had never wanted to grow old. Toward the end, he told friends that he had done everything twice. Shortly before his death, he had telephoned Ida and related that he had cancer, heart trouble and other ailments. Ida grieved over his passing, telling the crowd of reporters: "He was one of the most loyal and honest friends a person could have. He was a wonderful guy."

In the Church of the Recessional, Ida was distraught at seeing Flynn's remains on view. She told Patrice Wymore that

Flynn wouldn't like for his friends to see him that way, and the casket was closed for the service. More than once, Flynn had told Ida that he wished to be cremated and have his ashes scattered at sea. But Wymore felt that he should be buried in the famous cemetery where his peers lay. Ida sat beside Flynn's close friend and stunt double, Buster Wiles. She wept as Dennis Morgan sang a requiem with the lines, "Glad did I live, and gladly die . . ."

Flynn's death was a personal tragedy, but for Ida there was a worse one ahead. On Christmas Eve the Duffs were guests at a party hosted by Richard and Tinx Whorf. Harry Mines noticed that Ida seemed nervous. She explained that she was uneasy because of a strange foreboding. "She told me several times," says Mines, "that she had the strangest feeling that something had happened to her mother." Ida sensed Flynn's presence beside her, and he was saying that Connie was in danger.

On their return to Old Oak Lane, a ringing telephone greeted them. Duff answered. The news was terrible, just as Ida sensed. Connie had been injured in a car crash.

Connie's last years had been spent in Las Vegas. Refusing to be a burdensome mother-in-law and a nuisance to her daughters, she moved to the gambling mecca close to her friends, Colonel and Dottie Marks. Ida purchased an apartment building for her mother. Connie was happy playing bridge and relaxing with her boyfriend Alfred Quoback, a professional gambler.

On Christmas Eve, Connie was a passenger in an automobile driven by Quoback; they were on their way to Los Angeles for the holidays. As they sped along rain-slick Highway 91. Quoback tried to pass another car but lost control of the vehicle. The Duffs rushed to Barstow Community Hospital where Connie was conscious and seemed to be recovering. Ida sat with her mother around the clock. But Connie took a turn for the worse and died on December 26 at the age of sixty-eight.

Ida was beyond herself with grief. She decided that her mother would be buried next to Errol Flynn, whom Connie had loved like a son. On December 31, a private service was held at Forest Lawn's Wee Kirk of the Heather. Ida's songs "Is This a Dream?" and "Close Your Eyes" filled the flower-decked chapel. In a final tribute, Connie's theme, "Tea For Two," was played and, one by one, Collier Young, Joan Fontaine, Harry Mines and other mourners each placed a single white carnation on the casket in a farewell gesture.

Friends of Lupino say that Ida never really recovered from her mother's death. She and Connie had been very close and had depended on one another. In later years, Ida had listened to her mother's advice. Now she was gone. Ida's grief was made worse by the thought that Connie had been coming to see her for the holidays. Ida kept the gift she had bought for her mother, wrapped gaily in decorative paper, for decades.

15

MOTHER

I love being called mother. —IDA

It was Richard Boone who encouraged Ida to become a television director. Boone, who had a gravel voice and a face to match, began a screen career playing thugs and killers. Fame had come with the top-rated *Have Gun Will Travel*. As Paladin, the cowboy trouble-shooter dressed in black, Boone delighted audiences with his blazing action series. Lupino's superb direction in *The Hitch-hiker* had caught his eye, and he invited her to direct an episode of his show. Ida much preferred being behind the camera. "Directing is much easier than acting. The actor deals in false emotions, produced on cue. The director has his problems but they're all normal. He doesn't have to smile into a camera while suffering an early morning grouch."

For "The Trial" Ida had only one day of rehearsals, then three days of filming. "Terrified" is how she described herself, but Richard Boone had complete trust in her judgment. "I don't care what you do," he told her, "just don't ask me to rehearse." Ida came to the set dressed in a white scarf, pink sweater, black velvet slacks and the cowboy boots that "Dicky Bird" had given her. The scarf saved her the trouble of morning hair styling and soon became her trademark.

On her second episode, she tangled with the star. She made a suggestion, and Boone refused. "Darling, the reason I ask you," she explained, "here, get behind the camera and see how lousy it is for you. You don't want me to shoot right up your nose do you?"

Ida earned the reputation of being an action director. She began freelancing for other series. In October 1960, *Dante* premiered. It was a Four Star production, in which Duff starred as a nightclub owner who is also a detective. Ida directed the pilot, but Duff didn't ask her to stay with the show. "Not that she isn't a good director," he said, "she's really great. We didn't have any problems, but I want to keep it that way."

But there were problems. Like oil and water, the Duffs were hopelessly incompatible. It seemed that everyone knew it but them. After their series ended and the excitement subsided, they returned to their former pattern of constant bickering. There was a competitiveness between them and a contest of wills. Despite the public claims of his wife's talent, Howard's words had a hollow ring. Certainly Ida was a good director, said Duff, but not good enough for him.

Their drinking made matters worse. Alcohol was an integral part of the fabric of Hollywood life, and while drinking, the Duffs found temporary solutions to their problems. Ida drank English vodka. Howard liked his scotch. Whenever parties were held at their home, liquor flowed freely, and they would encourage guests to refill their glasses.

The peaceful days of *Mr. Adams and Eve* were in the past. There were fights, splits and reconciliation. Duff made it clear who ruled the roost, and Ida learned to accept his domineering behavior. John Franco was appalled. "The things he did to her and to

Connie, too, they were just awful. I have no respect for Howard."
Eventually, in conflicts, Ida backed off, allowing Howard to win;
the man was supposed to be the head of the house. So she stayed
with him.

Bridget grew up privileged, attending exclusive schools in
Brentwood with Mary Comack and Eleanor Davis looking after
her. It was a household filled with constant bickering.

By the fall of 1960, the Duffs were again living apart. Duff
had packed his bags and continued with *Dante*. Ida stayed busy directing an episode of *Alfred Hitchcock Presents*. "The Master," as Ida
dubbed Hitchcock, had offered her the lead in "Sybilla." She
didn't care for the role but told Hitchcock that she would love to
direct it. The star's salary was $5,000. Ida directed "Sybilla" for a
mere $1,250.

During her separation from Duff, Ida received a telephone
call from Dick Powell. Once a boyish crooner in the thirties, Powell
had matured into a shrewd businessman, still handsome and quite
wealthy. He and his wife, June Allyson, lived close to the Duffs in
Mandeville Canyon. Allyson had begun a romance with Alan Ladd.
Powell telephoned Ida one evening, despondent over the collapse
of his marriage. He suggested that they meet, but Ida hesitated.

A few years later, both were again in marital difficulties. In
fact, June Allyson had gone to court to divorce Powell. He again
telephoned Lupino and asked her to come to his Four Star office,
ostensibly to discuss Ida's outline for a television series called *A
Matter of Minutes*. But the conversation soon turned personal. He
asked how she and Duff were getting along. Ida said they were
separated. He said he and June were fighting like mountain lions.

"We're a fine pair, aren't we?" Ida asked.

"Yes, I think we'd make a damn fine pair," Powell replied.

Powell explained that his health was poor and he wished to
spend the remaining days with someone he liked.

As a loyal and devoted friend, Ida went sailing with him. He asked if she would spend what little time he had left as his companion. She agreed she would. Powell made an attempt to beat the cancer that was spreading through his body. His health declined, and he died several months after his lonely plea not to be alone at the end. But June Allyson returned and cared for him in the final days, to Ida's joy. Lupino's friends hoped she wouldn't return to Duff. She was still a desirable woman and could try another marriage. But their pleas were to no avail.

The final curtain fell for Uncle Barry in September 1962. He died at the age of eighty in a Brighton Hospital, leaving numerous children from his marriages and romances. Wallace Lupino and Lupino Lane were also gone; their offspring had never measured up to the great entertainers of previous years. Aunt Nell had gone to live in France; unfortunately, she went broke and became ill. Ida paid for her aunt's transfer to England where she soon passed away.

Though the British branch of the family faded, Ida's star continued to rise. She and Howard had great plans for their daughter. Both wanted Bridget to become an actress. As a child they had placed her before the camera in *Private Hell 36*. As Ida said at the time, "Bridget goes to nursery school, and one day the teacher asked her how she felt. 'Terrible,' my daughter said. 'My feet are killing me right up to my eyebrows. I've had *such* a day under those hot lights.' Then one day I came home and found her in front of a mirror, impersonating Howard Duff . . . and there's not a television commercial she doesn't know."

By the early sixties, Lupino's acclaim as a director was at its zenith. She had a wonderful time directing episodes of *Thriller*, a mystery-horror show, bringing to life such tales as "Trio For Terror," "Lethal Ladies," "Guillotine" and "The Bride Died Twice."

Ida and Richard Lupino, her third cousin and an aspiring actor, co-wrote *The Last of the Sommervilles*. Ida directed Boris Karloff in this *Thriller* story of two cousins who wish to kill off their aunt for the family inheritance. Because of her "cool hand with terror," Ida earned critical accolades and a reference as "the female Hitchcock." She had long exhibited a fascination with the macabre, poring over mystery and murder novels. Ida pitched an idea to the television networks for a rather unusual series that she would host. It was to be titled *Ida Lupino Presents This Is Murder* or *Theatre of Crime Classics*. "It's about when people love too much. Or hate too much. Or lust too much. It's about murder. All kind of murders. In every land. From every time. And the difference is: they are all true." Ida intended to act in the stories also. Though the proposed series was rejected, friends began calling her "Winnie Judd," after an infamous murderess.

For one who was enthralled with tales of murder, Ida had a rather mild nickname emblazoned on her director's chair—*Mother*. She regarded her production company as a special family, and she treated them as such. "I love being called Mother," she said. "I would never shout orders at anyone. I hate women who order men around, professionally or personally. I wouldn't dare do that with my old man . . . and I don't do it with guys on the set. I say, 'Darlings, mother has a problem. I'd love to do this. Can you do it? It sounds kooky but I want to do it.' And they do it."

Ida realized that, as a woman, she was eyed curiously by her male crew. She vowed to always stay on top of the situation by carefully preparing in advance and never appearing indecisive. "I would never think of indulging in what has come to be known as the woman's right to change her mind. As soon as I get a script I go to work on it. I study and I prepare and when the time comes to shoot, my mind is usually made up and I go ahead, right or wrong."

Ida enjoyed people on the set relating to her maternally. She affectionately called those she liked "my son" or "my daughter." A reporter for *Time* studied Lupino as she directed performances in a meat cooler on the set of *The Untouchables*. "Peter, darling, hold the knife this way. And make sure we see that sweet meathook," she'd say. Unlike many directors, Lupino preferred to be in the thick of the action rather than sitting comfortably at a distance.

Reviewers lauded her style, especially her ability to link scenes together cleverly, as when the distorted image of a gangster in a funhouse mirror fades to reveal a beautiful woman admiring her new fur coat. Mother Lupino was right at home on *The Untouchables* set, adjusting the plastic welder's mask she wore to protect her from flying chips and plaster.

Lupino was in demand. Rod Serling asked her to direct "The Masks," a script he had written for *The Twilight Zone*. Ida was taken with the tale of a wealthy man dying at Mardi Gras time in New Orleans. His parasitic relatives come to his deathbed solely for the inheritance. He makes them don grotesque masks that reflect their inner greed. At his death, they remove the masks, but their faces have been molded into replicas of what they wore. It was a powerful ending, a "twist finish" that Ida admired. With "The Masks" Lupino became the only woman ever to direct an episode of the famous *Twilight Zone*.

With her fabulous success as a director, Ida liked to quote her mother's comments about her preference for high drama. "Ida, darling," Connie had said, "you are the roughest, toughest director. I wonder if they'll ever give you a love story. I don't think so." Despite Connie's prediction, she was hired to direct "Deadeye Dick" for *The Virginian*, a romantic episode about love between a teenage girl and a weather-beaten cowboy. Ida found herself at the helm of a tough assignment, vigorously trying to maintain order in the middle of dusty acres in sweltering heat. On the last day at the

Iverson Ranch, Ida was several pages behind in her shooting schedule. An actress fell from her horse and cracked a vertebra, a wild chase sequence went astray, then the sky clouded over with drops of rain and brought the production to a halt. The cast, crew, wranglers, stuntmen and publicists waited for the director's next move. Despite the setbacks, Ida remained calm. She viewed the situation with patient understanding, though the pressure was enormous. "I sometimes wonder how anything ever gets on film," she mused.

Ida had offers to direct abroad, but she declined. As she explained at the time: "I have my old boy and daughter and I love them and life is too short for me to leave them and go flipping off for five or six months or seven months. I just won't go." Ida preferred to do all of her directing close to home, preferably as a guest director in television.

Her old friend Sol Saks asked a favor and once again witnessed her kindness and professionalism. Saks supervised all comedy shows at CBS and was faced with a major problem trying to patch together one of the network's new programs. Rehearsals had floundered, to Saks' dismay. "It was *Gilligan's Island*. It wasn't even on the air yet. I asked Ida to come down and direct the pilot. It wasn't her kind of show, but she came as a favor to me." When Saks walked on the set with Lupino, the cast stared in amazement. Where they had grumbled, Ida's presence quieted them. "She revived that show," says Saks. "She made them think that if Ida Lupino is here, *we* must be something. Ida's appearance had a lot to do with that show going on and becoming a success."

At the height of her directorial fame, she began writing a script she considered her "dream project." It was a feature-length animation idea about two cats named Sam and Socrates. Ida was enchanted by their love and respect for each other and their ability to communicate "things too many of us long-legged creatures lack."

To her profound regret, Walt Disney released *The Incredible Journey* in 1963, the film adventures of two dogs and a Siamese cat. Her dream of animating the lives of Sam and Socrates never reached fruition, another unfilmed script among many. But Lupino stayed busy behind the camera, directing episodes of *The Fugitive, Bewitched, The Rogues, Dundee and the Culhane, Hong Kong, Sam Benedict, Mr. Novak, Dr. Kildare, Kraft Suspense Theatre, Hotel de Paree, The Ghost and Mrs. Muir* and many others.

Ida never varied her directorial style, which she termed "a feminine approach." Despite her hair trigger temper, she always exercised extreme self-restraint on the set. As she explained, "I try never to blow—they're just waiting for you to do it. As long as you keep your temper the crew will go along with you."

The social upheaval of the sixties brought changes to the cinema world. By mid-decade the sexual revolution was permeating motion pictures. Though certainly no prude, Ida was startled by sexually explicit films. "I'll go and enjoy a picture like *Room at the Top*," she said. "But if you want filth, I'd sooner starve."

Producer William Frye chose Ida to direct *The Trouble With Angels*, the story of high-spirited girls in a religious boarding school. Frye had tried to obtain Greta Garbo for the role of Mother Superior, without success.

Rosalind Russell was hired for two hundred thousand dollars. Hayley Mills was cast as the mischievous student ringleader. The exteriors were filmed in Ambler, Pennsylvania, at St. Mary's Home for Children.

The Sisters of Nazareth watched curiously as crewmen made the seasons change on their front lawn, scattering fall leaves and, later, truckloads of plastic snow. Ida became fast friends with the religious order. When production came to a halt because strong winds were whipping the nun's veils, the sisters redesigned the costumes, to Ida's gratitude.

Ida worked closely with Lionel "Curley" Lindon, a British cinematographer who had won an Oscar for *Around the World in 80 Days*. She kept both her poise and pace, and the production sailed along.

Rosalind Russell's respect for the director increased. She and Ida became close friends and thoroughly enjoyed themselves. Ida found Russell "the most wonderful, patient woman I've ever come across, always good humored." Russell, famous for her portrayal of the free-spirited *Auntie Mame*, was a devout Catholic. She studiously avoided being photographed in her nun's habit with cigarettes or cocktail in hand, but she was an earthy soul, just like Lupino. Ida broke into fits of laughter every time Russell uttered a naughty word while dressed as Mother Superior.

Ida's task was a difficult one, treading between comedy and religion. She and Russell wondered how much controversy they would generate with the film, especially with stripper Gypsy Rose Lee in the cast as an "interpretive movement instructor." Russell had final approval of the film's director and, after the uncertainty of the first weeks had vanished, was happy to have Lupino in charge. As she told the press: "The sex of a director doesn't mean a hoot. The one all-important thing is talent. Somehow it has evolved that directing is a man's profession. A woman has a tough, almost impossible time breaking down this caste barrier. Miss Arzner managed it. Ida is doing it now."

Russell especially admired Ida for her decisiveness and for coming to the set prepared. Ida added risqué touches, such as having Mother Superior hold a brassiere to her bosom. Lupino and Russell laughed heartily over such spice, wondering if the film would create controversy. Gypsy Rose Lee brought mirth to the set as she demonstrated to the curious nuns how she removed her clothes onstage. Ida lacked creative control, and after she submitted her edited version Twentieth Century-Fox deleted several scenes, to her dissatisfaction. She received thirty-five thousand dollars for directing what would be her last feature film.

Throughout her adventures behind the camera, Ida had continued to act, appearing in one television show per season. In *I Love a Mystery*, a Universal television film, Ida enjoyed herself playing the eccentric billionaire owner of an island estate, quite flamboyant as a crackpot who conducts bizarre experiments on detectives Les Crane and David Hartman.

Duff was now a familiar face on television, playing tough investigator Sam Stone in the series *Felony Squad*. Though years had passed since Duff's political brush with the Red Scare, he was still a subject of interest to the FBI. When J. Edgar Hoover got wind that Howard was playing a police investigator, he sent out agents to probe his background again to make certain that nothing would embarrass law enforcement officials whom he depicted.

Both Ida and Howard had achieved success in their careers. On the surface, their marriage seemed successful, too. They had by then been wed for sixteen years, and by Hollywood standards their marriage was a long one. Although the Duffs were together, there was still considerable tension in their tempestuous union. They were featured in a *Photoplay* article titled "If the Neighbors Couldn't Hear Them Fighting, They Knew Nobody Was Home." Boasted Ida: "People are still saying, 'How do these two stay together?' because, you know, I have certainly not tamed him, if I wanted to. You don't marry a man to change him. There isn't a day that goes by that Bridget and I don't call him 'God's Angry Man.' And we love him for it. He is a demon about the little things. He will suddenly charge into the room, roaring, 'Where is the book section from the *New York Times*?' And I will immediately start to shake and say, 'Wh-which section?' . . . and we hop to, Bridget and I."

Close friends were truly amazed that the marriage had lasted so long. As a woman Ida was strong-willed and outspoken. But as a wife, she often humbled herself to smooth things along. When approached about any type of business project, she always tried to include her husband. She wanted to keep her man, at any cost. Time was rushing inexorably on, and Ida was aware that middle age suited Duff, while she felt the erosion of her loveliness. As she bluntly revealed at the time: "The other night I said to him, 'Darling, so many men are suddenly flipping for twenty-year-olds. Do you think you'll go for some young girl?' He looked at me and saw I was rather serious . . . and then he started to laugh. . . . 'What's the matter with you, darling? What a perfectly ridiculous question. Don't you know that old chickens make the best soup?'"

Ida and Howard professed love for each other and, more often than not, they had shared good times. Howard thought Ida one of the wittiest and funniest women he had ever met. But their fights were searing battles that left emotional, if not physical, scars. After a hard day at work they would unwind with cocktails; jangled nerves would suddenly ignite stubborn tempers and they would argue violently. But the public simply saw them as a veteran Hollywood couple. Such identification led to many television appearances together. In March 1968, Ida and Howard were guests on *Batman*. Lupino played the evil Dr. Cassandra, who could turn invisible. Duff was, surprisingly, her bumbling stooge.

Though they were often at odds, they were in complete agreement politically, as staunch Democrats. President Kennedy was one of Ida's revered heroes. She was ecstatic to learn that Kennedy, while a young senator from Massachusetts, was a devoted fan of *Mr. Adams and Eve*. On the other hand, Ida found it incredible that her old friend and former fellow Democrat was now Governor Reagan, a conservative Republican. In the fifties the two families had been close. The Reagans had occasionally left their children with the Duffs while they retired to the country for a quiet weekend. But those days were over. Ida was angry that Reagan had deserted the Democrats.

The Duffs were asked to attend a reception for Premier Sato of Japan. Although contributors to the Democratic Party, they were still perplexed about the prestigious invitation. Ida rushed out and bought a long, formal ball gown of alençon lace with matching coat and gloves. Both were "frightfully nervous" when their taxi arrived at the White House. They were met by a young officer who explained state protocol. Afterward, they were escorted to the East Room for cocktails. Forty minutes later, President Johnson and Premier Sato arrived. The guests then gathered for the receiving line. Protocol dictated that the gentlemen be introduced first, a Japanese custom that intrigued Ida. In the state dining room she was seated next to cabinet member Robert McNamara while Howard sat next to Mrs. Hubert Humphrey. Twelve strolling Air Force violinists played songs from *Camelot* and *Hello, Dolly*. Later, the Duffs learned why they had been invited to the diplomatic soiree. A decade after its demise, *Mr. Adams and Eve* was then being broadcast in Japan, and Premier Sato liked the show.

As the sizzling sixties came to an end, fifty-one-year-old Lupino was interviewed by reporter Judy Stone of the *New York Times*. Ida spoke while she clipped her hedges. Her thoughts were on the heavy winter storms that had sent trees crashing in Mandeville Canyon. She wondered if the storms were the result of underground nuclear testing in Nevada. The previous night she had been staring at the moon with her binoculars, amazed that an American flag had been planted on its surface. Reminiscing about the old days of Hollywood jolted Ida into an angry comparison. She paced and said contemptuously: "I was sent a perfectly filthy script. . . . *I Am Curious—Yellow* must be a virtuous film compared to this." Ida denounced film nudity, saying it embarrassed teenagers out on a date, though she did have praise for the way David Lean handled bedroom scenes in *Doctor Zhivago*.

She defended television and maintained that it wasn't responsible for teenage unrest, campus riots and crime. "If you really want to be shocked, turn the knob and see the boys dying in Vietnam. I mean, violence for the sake of violence I don't like at all. But there's violence in all of us." As for racial turmoil in America, she harkened back to the font of wisdom, Stanley Lupino, who denounced racial intolerance. "Man has always wanted to persecute man in any shape or form," she noted sadly. "It worries me all the time, all the time."

As the sixties faded, so did Lupino's career as a director. In 1969 she directed an episode of *The Bill Cosby Show*. She later said, "I was more like a visitor on that show, since Bill is a genius of a performer and, you know, does his own thing."

The demise of Lupino's directing career was startling and quite unexpected, especially considering how much pleasure it gave her. Even her intimate circle of friends was bewildered that she resumed acting while her directing career languished. "She was always very modest whenever anyone singled her out for distinction," says Harry Mines. "Even though she was one of the most famous women directors, she shrugged off such compliments, especially the feminist tag. Ida could easily have directed more features but I don't think she promoted herself enough."

Ida had always been in demand as one of Hollywood's most distinguished actresses. She kept busy with guest spots on *Mod Squad*, *Columbo*, *It Takes a Thief*, *The Name of the Game*, *Family Affair*, *Nanny and the Professor* and other popular shows. As time passed, Ida's circle of friends grew smaller.

On a hot day in August, Frances Robinson went for a swim in her pool on Ozeta Terrace. She took a nap and never awoke. Ida

went to the funeral to say a last goodbye to Frannie. Ann Sheridan
had succumbed to cancer in 1967. Barbara Reed died a suicide.
Death's beckoning left Ida upset. Deep within, she felt that Duff
might leave, too. Ida prayed her marriage would improve and
endure, just as the nation survived the crisis of the sixties.

"Touch wood," she told Judy Stone, with fervent hope. "We
have nineteen years coming up in October, dear, and so you weather
the storms."

16

ALONE

No, this time he's not coming back. This time it's for good.

—IDA

In January 1972, Ida headlined *Women in Chains*, a suspenseful television drama depicting brutality in a women's prison. Ida was chilling as the sadistic matron. Next she acted in her first theatrical film in sixteen years. She and Robert Preston were cast as the parents of Steve McQueen in *Junior Bonner*, a contemporary western. Sam Peckinpah had achieved acclaim with *The Wild Bunch* and *The Ballad of Cable Hogue*. His directorial skill brought success as well as criticism of his use of graphic violence. Ida boarded a plane for Prescott, Arizona, though she did not want to leave her family and her black Persian cat, Dolly Bird. She was excited over the picture, eager to please and especially delighted that her old friend John Franco was script supervisor. As always, she carefully marked her script, underlining key words and instructions to herself as she prepared for the first scenes. At the age of fifty-four, she was playing McQueen's mother, though there was only a fifteen-year difference in their ages.

While Ida used charm as a director, Peckinpah had his own technique. John Franco was shocked by Peckinpah's lack of deference to Ida's stature. On the first day of shooting, just before the cameras rolled, Peckinpah made a sarcastic comment about her lipstick, which embarrassed Ida before two hundred cast and crew members. She angrily confronted the director, threatening to quit. Only roses, champagne, and an apology brought her back.

Ever the professional, Ida strove for realism in her portrayal and was unconcerned about her looks. She wore a red wig and no makeup; there were no diffusion filters or special lighting. She knew she didn't look pretty with sweat on her face, but she tried to play the role as honestly as possible. McQueen was in awe of Lupino and kept his distance. "Hi Mom, give me a kiss," he said when he walked on the set, then he was silent. Despite the apology, Peckinpah maintained an arrogant attitude throughout the remainder of the production. "It hurt her," says Franco. "He got Ida so confused with his directions . . . and just made a nervous wreck out of her. It just embarrassed her. And here was the lady who gave him his chance."

In spite of Peckinpah's boorishness, Ida created a vivid character, playing Elvira Bonner with force as she clashed with her estranged cowboy husband and refused to be a submissive wife. The performance brought glowing reviews. Paul Gardner interviewed Lupino and discovered a woman who was strangely oblivious to her accomplishments. "I don't know why the critics have been so nice to me. I can't judge my acting. I can't stand to see myself on the screen. Why? Because I don't care for myself." Ida proclaimed she was not "one of the ladies who go in for women's lib. Any woman who wishes to smash into the world of men isn't very feminine. . . . Baby, we can't go smashing. I believe women should be struck regularly like a gong."

Lupino's comment must have sparked shudders in female fans, especially those who admired her as a director and for breaking ground in a traditionally male territory. But a career was secondary anyway, she said: "If a woman has a man who loves her, she better stick close to home. I've turned down jobs in Europe because I'd have to leave my husband and daughter and cats." Just as she had stated decades earlier, the man in her life came first.

She had raised Duff onto the pedestal beside her, and he expected it.

Scripts and offers to direct poured into Old Oak Lane. Ida discussed directing several features but each time either lost out to someone else or the proposed film never got out of the planning stage. She was enthusiastic about the autobiography of Frances Farmer, *Will There Really Be a Morning?* Ida had known Farmer from the time the Seattle-born actress was at the height of her fame until the time she suffered a nervous collapse and disappeared into a mental institution. Ida carefully studied the autobiography, underlining shocking sections that could be spun into scenes: "I was raped by orderlies, gnawed on by rats, and poisoned by tainted food. . . . I was chained in padded cells, strapped into straitjackets, and half-drowned in ice baths." Ida believed Farmer's tragic story held the essence of what could be a remarkable film.

She was especially taken with Emily Dickinson's poem from which the title was drawn, feeling that it could be sung softly as a theme for the opening. Ida believed that the essence of Farmer's story was her insecurity about her parents' love for her. Ida never found the opportunity to develop this project.

In the summer Howard packed his bags and flew to Connecticut. He was to star in *The Price* for a four-week run at the famous Ivoryton Playhouse. Ida was to join him, but Howard telephoned and persuasively suggested that she remain at home. He was

241

gone for several weeks. The night before he was to return, Ida received an anonymous telephone call. "You'd better be careful," the voice said. "Your husband is not coming home to stay; just to get some clean clothes."

Ida was stunned by the message and tossed in her bed all night. The following day, Duff returned. He told his wife that he was in love with Judy Jenkinson, a young woman in her late twenties who worked at the playhouse. Howard packed his suitcase and disappeared. He later sent word to Ida that he had checked into a motel on Sunset Boulevard and would send a man for additional belongings. Ida was in a state of shock. They had played this scene innumerable times, but now, there was a finality in his voice. She knew he meant what he said.

In September, Ida said she planned to file for divorce. "Old chickens make the best soup," Duff had once told her. Now the rooster had flown the coop. This was what she had always feared. Even in his late fifties, Howard still looked quite distinguished with his silver hair and mustache. His deep voice never failed to turn female heads.

Not long after the breakup Sol Saks spoke with Ida when she came to visit his wife, who was hospitalized. They knew how much Ida disliked attracting attention in public, so the couple was grateful for the effort she made. Eventually, the conversation turned to Howard.

"You've had fights before," counseled Saks.

"No," responded Ida morosely, "this time he's not coming back. This time it's for good."

Each day with Duff had been a challenge. Ida existed on high drama, but Howard retreated. Now he had chosen a plain woman, someone younger and less experienced than Ida, a partner who would never tower over him or challenge him. Howard's departure was a blow to Ida's self-esteem.

Strangely, though, the Duffs did not file for divorce. They would remain married for more than another decade. Initially, Ida did anything she could to win Howard back, including loaning him money, but the blow to her ego left wounds that never healed. Friends urged her to busy herself with work to keep Howard out of her thoughts. She spent the night of her twenty-second wedding anniversary alone in a San Francisco motel room.

Her thoughts were still on Howard, and her loneliness grew. Occasionally, an anguished Ida would telephone Rena Lundigan, married to actor William Lundigan. "He's making no money. I'm trying to get Bridget educated," she tearfully told her old friends. She publicly admitted that adjusting to life alone at the age of fifty-seven was difficult. "My personal life knocked me for a loop . . . suddenly nothing . . . it's a rotten feeling."

Ida tried to stay busy with guest appearances on television shows and with industry events. She buried the hatchet with Jack Warner, at least for one evening, and joined "A Fifty Year Salute to Warner Bros." The black-tie audience cheered Ida and Paul Henreid. Television executive Marvin Paige, a longtime Lupino admirer, kept Ida busy with acting assignments. Paige would laugh heartily at Lupino's mordant wit. "Lupi telephoned me one night," recalls Paige. "She said, 'I was just watching *Susan and God* with that Joan Crawford and, do you know something? She gets billing over Frederic March *and God.'*" Her recognizable voice also was heard throughout the country in a radio spot soliciting funds for the Crippled Children's Campaign. Ida was a presenter at the Emmy Awards and also at the Golden Globe Ceremony, where she was photographed with James Stewart, an actor she had admired for years. She made a brief appearance in "The Swan Song," an episode of *Columbo*. Singer Johnny Cash made his television acting debut as a murderer who parachutes from an airplane. In an episode of *Manhunter*, she played the machine-gun toting Ma Gantry.

Actress Anna Navarro invited Ida to dinner, where she met Tom Foley, a forty-five-year-old car dealer. Their names were linked by columnists. The dates seemed spurred by her loneliness and were, most probably, an attempt to match Howard's success in finding a new romance. Duff and his girlfriend found a home on Sea Level Drive in Malibu, to Ida's dismay. Foley soon disappeared from Ida's life.

In February 1975, Ida was in Durango, Mexico, for *The Devil's Rain*. A journalist interviewed her as she nibbled a chicken leg through heavy horror makeup. She peered out of black, hollow eye sockets. Her wig was too tight, and she had a terrible headache. Her uncomfortable costume made her long for home and her cat Dolly Bird. "If someone would leave me an oil well, I'd only do this as a hobby." This was Ida's first horror film and she was not enthusiastic. But she refused to appear in R-rated motion pictures and carefully inquired beforehand if scripts were sexually explicit.

After Howard left, Ida's relationship with Bridget deteriorated. She had disappointed both parents by failing to become an actress. Ida was especially hurt that her daughter found the glamorous life unappealing. Bridget moved out of the house on Old Oak Lane and settled down to a quiet life far from Hollywood. Ida remarked with bitter irony how she had refused directing jobs abroad. "I didn't want to leave my family. Ha Ha. Okay? Turnabout. They left me."

Mary Comack died. Howard and Bridget were gone. Only a housekeeper remained with Ida. Publicist Joe Hoenig, who had represented both Lupino and Duff, found Ida to be one of the most delightful women he had ever worked with in all his years in publicity, but after Howard left, Ida began to distance herself from him and other friends, who wanted nothing more than to help her. Ida did see more of her sister, but both had strong personalities, and Ida preferred giving advice to receiving it. Ida wanted to be left alone.

In November 1975, Ida and Glenn Ford were honored by the Screen Smart Set, an organization that raised funds for the Motion Picture Country Home and Hospital. At the ceremony, Edie Adams accepted Lupino's award. Ida sent a telegram from Canada, commending the Smart Set for their charity work and thanking them "with pride and humility" for the recognition.

Ida had been unable to attend the event because she was on location for *Food of the Gods*, a low-budget horror film loosely based on the famous novel by H.G. Wells and filmed in Vancouver on Bowen Island. Ida had a character role as a country woman who finds a strange liquid oozing on her property and valiantly fights off monster worms before being devoured by a giant rat.

A few months later, Ida appeared in what was to be her final feature film, *My Boys Are Good Boys*. Ralph Meeker produced and starred in the drama about teenagers who break out of a maximum security prison, rob an armored car and return to their jail cells without being detected. Veteran actor Lloyd Nolan played an investigator who cracks the boys' alibi. Lupino played Meeker's wife, who masterminds the heist. The film wasn't much, but Ida gave her usual, fine performance.

By this time, Bridget had married, and Ida disapproved. Bridget was still searching for a meaningful way of life, as were many youngsters of the sixties generation. But Ida felt that Bridget was too young to marry.

As her personal life unraveled, Ida sought spiritual comfort. She would slip inside St. Martin of Tours church to pray when it was empty. But the path before her became more difficult. She drank more. Family and friends pleaded with her to stop, fearful she would damage her health and injure her career.

In August Ida and Joel McCrea were inducted into the Hollywood Hall of Fame. While the honors bestowed upon her were numerous, she still sought a good role to boost her sagging career.

For years, Ida had been known as an inexhaustible source of energy who seldom slept yet pushed herself to perfection as an actress and a director. And she had long been an insomniac. Matters were complicated by her basic high-strung temperament.

Ida managed to land the lead in *The Thoroughbreds*. In October, she flew to Kentucky. It became apparent that Ida could not retain her lines. An assistant was assigned to get her through the scenes. At first, cue cards were tried, without success. Next the young woman crouched below Ida and whispered the dialogue. This failed, too. When informed that she was being replaced, Ida was crushed. She had never been dismissed from a production. After sleeping pills were found in her dressing room, crew members took turns watching as she slept, worried she would harm herself. *Variety* reported that Ida had been replaced by Vera Miles, owing to "artistic differences." But the circumstances became known in the industry. "She was fired in Kentucky," says Paula Stone. Stone's daughter had worked on the production, growing fond of Ida, and did her best to help her make it through the scenes, without success. Harry Mines and John Franco also heard of the incident and worried about their old friend.

At home she brooded about the dismissal. The words Stanley had spoken to her back in the Little Theatre when she hid at the sound of her entrance cue must have come back to her. *If you ever let your fellow actors down, dry up in a scene, or fail to be a good trouper, I shall disown you.* She reached a drastic decision. Then the unexpected happened.

While she hurriedly dressed for a dinner engagement, Ida collapsed. Eleanor Davis reached for her emergency telephone numbers. At the top of the list was John Franco's name. He notified friends and sped to the hospital.

Ida underwent extensive tests. Friends heard the seizure had been triggered by the sudden withdrawal of pills and alcohol without medical supervision. She halfheartedly agreed to participate in counseling sessions. After two weeks, she was dismissed. To be on the safe side, she was warned to stop driving. Since Connie's tragic death, Ida had never felt comfortable in an automobile. Her top cruising speed at the wheel of her station wagon was usually thirty miles per hour. She agreed to stop driving, even though it meant a loss of independence. But her drinking resumed.

In January 1977, just a few weeks after her hospitalization, Ida starred in "I Will Be Remembered," an episode of *Charlie's Angels*. She portrayed a former actress who believes that someone is trying to drive her insane. It was a demanding role and a measure of her artistic courage that she accepted such a difficult role so soon after her hospitalization. Ida wanted to prove to herself that she could still act, but it was a terrific struggle. On the set Ida was nervous and tense, according to assistant director Nat Holt. "She was very unhappy because she just couldn't remember her words," says Holt.

Fortunately, Ida managed to get through her scenes. She gave a magnificent performance, expressing terror and bewilderment as only a great actress can. After forty-five years of hard work, her energy had dissipated, her self-discipline had waned, and her desire to achieve stardom had been satisfied. The spotlight dimmed.

Sometimes Ida argued with her neighbors, often hurling insults over minor issues. Friends who telephoned the house might find Ida her usual self or might get an earful of angry words. On one occasion Harry Mines sat with her at Old Oak Lane. Her friend of forty years tried to comfort Ida. She was in a foul mood and drinking. She suddenly balled her hand into a fist and shook it threateningly in his face. "See this?" she asked angrily. "*This* is what makes the world go round."

There was no question among her lifelong friends that Lupino was terribly unhappy. To make matters worse, Eleanor Davis left her employ after years of service. Ida was alone.

Though her career faded, her fame remained. She was in demand at parties and motion picture industry events. In May 1979, Ida attended the National Film Society Banquet to receive their Artistry in Cinema Award. George Raft came to the podium to laud Ida for her outstanding career. She appreciated such honors, and there were many, but the glamor of parties, tributes, and banquets held no real interest for her. But the fiery personality remained.

The Duffs' old friend, Jerry Hausner, met Ida during the intermission of *The Little Foxes*, starring Elizabeth Taylor. Hausner asked her opinion of the play. "Well," Ida boomed in her distinctive voice, as heads turned, "Taylor is no Tallulah Bankhead!"

At a party, Hausner met Duff. Howard introduced Judy to the guests as Mrs. Duff. Hausner was perplexed and took his old friend to the side. "Are you guys married or aren't you?" he asked. "How in the hell can I be married when I'm not even divorced?" answered Duff. "Ida won't divorce me."

Ida cherished her quiet life more than ever. During her marriage to Duff, she was basically a homebody, and she had remained so. Ida drifted into deeper isolation, both physical and emotional. The house seemed larger than ever with only Ida and her cats to occupy it.

Ida delighted in growing roses and watering the plants and trees around her home. Strangers, usually fans lurking on the street, made her nervous. Motorists who parked too close to the driveway alarmed her. Growing fearful of crime and prowlers, Ida erected an iron gate to discourage intruders. She laced the gate with a thick chain and padlock. Inside her home, she spent most of her time in the den, where she could keep an eye on the front premises. Ida discouraged visitors. John Franco tried his best to keep her spirits high, offering to repair things around the home or to assist in any manner. After a while, though, Lupino became even more reclusive. "She told me not to call her. She would call me," says Franco. "When she really needed the people who loved her, she turned them away. It just broke my heart."

Lupino still made a vivid impression—ashen anger, gentle affection, raucous laughter, or biting sarcasm. Ida had always seemed larger than life. But for her the glitter of fame no longer sparkled.

17

MADAME DIRECTOR

We'll laugh like hell at all the people who really tried to screw us up. —IDA

The eighties were a decade of further loss and isolation for Ida. Illness and death robbed her of her close friends. In July 1980, Reginald Gardiner passed away. His marriage had been one of the happiest in Hollywood. As Ida had told Nadia Gardiner: "Yours is the only marriage I was ever in that stayed together."

Collier Young remained a trusted confidant. Since the demise of Filmakers, he had achieved a prominent career as a television producer, responsible for *The Rogues, One Step Beyond,* and *Ironside.* His marriage to Joan Fontaine had ended in 1961. In divorce court Fontaine complained Collie drank a great deal. But his former wife held fond memories of him. Always looking for a laugh, Collier sent friends a unique greeting card one Christmas; it was a color photo of "the Mouse House" with the message, "When next in California be sure to visit the former home of Ida Lupino and Joan Fontaine. Merry Christmas. Collier Young." In 1965, he entered a blissful union with his fourth wife, Marjory. Collier Young said that his marriage to Lupino was an adventure in celluloid, often unpredictable. "I complained to my director one night that she had gone terribly over budget. By way of reply, she hurled a siphon bottle at my head. When she married Howard Duff we went on working together and she could hurl things at him." Young's death came as a great shock to Ida. The circumstances were eerily similar to Connie's tragic end; he died as a result of injuries he suffered in an auto accident on Christmas Day 1980. A bright light had gone from her life.

Though Ida only saw those she wished to see, she attended parties if she knew old friends would be there. When she received an invitation to honor Hayden Rorke, a former cast member of *Mr. Adams and Eve*, she promptly responded. "For Hayden, I'd do anything," she told the host of the party. Among the guests who were surprised to see Ida were Barbara Eden, Cesar Romero, June Lockhart, Rock Hudson and Larry Hagman.

"I was just flabbergasted," says Rorke. "She came up and threw her arms around me. I couldn't believe it because I knew she was something of a recluse. I was so touched by her presence. She stole the show."

Ida's loyalty to old friends was steadfast. She was upset by the controversy over Charles Higham's *Errol Flynn: The Untold Story*, which claimed that the actor had been a Nazi spy. Like many readers, I was curious. I obtained the declassified government files the author used as the basis of his accusations against Flynn. I interviewed many who knew the actor, including Hermann F. Erben, the physician who was the true source of the controversy. In Vienna Dr. Erben told me of his own work as a German spy but said that Flynn was not involved.

I sent a letter to Lupino and inquired if she had any comments. She certainly did, and she telephoned me one evening to defend Flynn. I read to her the official FBI statement, which exonerated Flynn from allegations that he had been a German espionage agent. Ida was elated by the news. A few days later we spoke again. She listened attentively about my research. She gave me her private telephone number, which she regarded as a top secret, and insisted that I call her anytime for information about Flynn, her own career or just to chat. Ida explained that there was a special code: three rings, hang up, then another three rings and she would answer, a system designed to screen unwanted callers.

In October 1983, at Ida's invitation, I drove down Sunset Boulevard on a warm afternoon and turned off at Riviera Ranch Road. Buster Wiles and I were writing a book about Errol Flynn and Ida agreed to an interview. I parked in front of a rustic, ranch-styled home nestled in a quiet neighborhood. A fence and dense shrubbery encircled the property. Ida had told me that the entrance on the left would be open, but it was secured by a thick, rusty chain and padlock. The place looked deserted except for an orange cat that sat beside the large swimming pool. Thick oaks, pines, and acacias swayed slowly in a gentle breeze above me. An air of tranquility permeated the home. I returned to my car, wondering if my Sunday afternoon would be wasted. I drove to a service station, used the code and spoke with my hostess, who apologized. She explained that since I was late, the gate had been relocked.

On my return the gate was ajar. I slipped inside and walked down the quiet driveway. In the backyard under an ancient tree was a blue and white director's chair emblazoned with "Lupino." On the back porch was a stuffed gorilla at least five feet high, surrounded by Christmas cards and festive bows tacked on the wall behind it. I knocked and a young woman welcomed me inside. Behind her stood Ida. She was casually dressed in blue slacks and matching sweater, a blue scarf tied about her head. A St. Jude medal was pinned to her red blouse. She posed, clenched fists placed firmly at her waist, elbows jutting. Her blue eyes were luminous.

Ida glared. Her smooth pale face was cold. Her eyes seemed to bore a hole through me. In a sharp, sinister voice, she said, "Was I tough enough in my films, baby? I still am!" Images of the women I'd seen Ida play flashed through my mind. Then she smiled and her laughter had a raucous quality. "Oh, yes," she said. "Bogie and I called ourselves the gruesome twosome. We swore that tough characters were all we would play. They're more fun, darling." A mischievous glint came into her blue eyes. Her voice took on a dramatic seriousness.

"Don't I look good for eighty-seven?" Then she laughed, explaining how a tabloid had mistaken her age. Ida turned to the smiling young woman and introduced me to Mary Ann Anderson. Ida suggested that we chat in the den. She led the way through a large living room past her piano and fireplace. At the far end of the room stood a silver Christmas tree and multicolored bows and cards.

"Is Santa coming early?" I asked.

"Darling," laughed Ida, "every day is Christmas here."

Ida settled onto a blue sofa lined with pink pillows. Behind her was a painting of a deserted beach with black clouds rolling over the surf. Across the room, atop the television, was a photograph of her parents and another of her with Bogart. She reached toward a coffee table, stocked with cigarettes and lighters. The orange cat jumped into her lap. "This is Timmy," said Ida. "He's the naughty boy of the neighborhood." I commented on the stuffed gorilla in the backyard. Her eyes lit up. Ida pointed out more stuffed animals fans had sent her over the years.

As I set up my tape recorder, a large sheepdog began licking my face. "That's Chuggles," said Ida. She offered me a cigarette, which I declined. Ida praised Buster Wiles for his stuntwork at Warner Bros. and for being a loyal friend of Flynn. She had recently been the subject of an article in the *Hollywood Studio Magazine* and was very proud of her defense of her friends. "How courageous they are to attack the dead. Tyrone Power, there was a really wonderful person. Like Errol, you could always feel at peace and talk about anything with that man. For those people who write anything about a man like Tyrone Power, and I say a man, M-A-N! He was not a bisexual or homosexual. Errol Flynn was definitely not pro-Nazi. John Garfield, he was not a Communist—*ever!* It was the most terrible thing for him because word went to every studio head. John was a wonderful human being who cared about others. If they had worries or if they looked ill, he'd want to do something to help them. At one time I said to him, 'You and I like to do something for people who we can tell need help.' If we Democrats, today, could be called liberals, that does not mean we are Communists."

Ida knew a great deal about Hollywood politics. "I was never unfriendly with the FBI. Whenever I could turn in information and, I was not one of their operators, but I did know some of those gentlemen there, and oh, they were intelligent, great people. I knew a lot about the Nazi bund in Los Angeles. I'm sorry to say they still exist today. Just put the swastika on black shirts on them at night and they're around." At sixty-five, Lupino in the flesh was just as assertive as the gutsy dames she had played onscreen.

Ida thoughtfully discussed the media and life as a celebrity. She had only praise for Hedda Hopper and Louella Parsons.

When it came to voicing her opinion, she wasn't the least bit reticent, especially concerning political comments. Ida explained why she was a lifelong Democrat. "I came to the U.S. at the end of 1933, and I thank God for President Roosevelt. He pulled this country out of what it was going into, which was the gutter. On Wall Street there were suicides and bank closings. He was fantastic. There was a president who, when he died in his fourth term, my God, my mother and I, who were both born in England, really cried." On the paneled wall of her den was a portrait of John Kennedy, surrounded by bows of many colors. She singled out Dwight Eisenhower and Abraham Lincoln for praise. And Ronald Reagan? Her eyes lit up. She told of directing him in an episode of *General Electric Theater*. There was talk that he would run for governor as a Republican, an idea that Ida, a staunch Democrat, found implausible. She described waiting on the set impatiently while Reagan studied his dialogue. "Finally he came out," she said, "then muffed his lines. He put his glasses on and grabbed a script. 'Uh, what do I say here?' I said, 'Rotten Ronnie, go back to your dressing room and learn your lines.' I turned to the cameraman and said, rather sarcastically, 'God help us if *he* ever becomes governor!' Well, the big joke is on Ida—he became *president!*" She laughed so hard she had to pause to catch her breath.

Ida was utterly charming. She delighted me with her stories of her years in Hollywood and even quoted snatches of dialogue from her films. She laughed deeply and remarked that she was thoroughly enjoying herself. While telling the story of the death of Primmie Niven, she remarked, "I had one of my funny psychic feelings," adding, "it's amazing how some psychic, strange things are in people." Ida had no doubt that she would see her dear friends on the other side. "In this other world where I'm going to meet them some day, again, we will laugh like hell at all the people who tried to really screw us up."

When I glanced at my watch I was startled. Ida had entertained me for several hours. She insisted on escorting Mary Ann, her business manager, and me to our cars. She carried a flashlight in one hand and a hammer in the other. In the darkness she bid us goodnight, then secured the iron gate with the thick chain and made certain that it was fastened.

Lupino's life had been brightened by Mary Ann Anderson, the adopted daughter of "Queen of the Soaps," Emily Mclaughlin, who played nurse Jessie Brewer on television's *General Hospital*. Anderson had first gone to Old Oak Lane with a gift of flowers.

Though Ida was suspicious, they began talking as if they had known each other for years. Usually distrustful of strangers, Ida liked Anderson. Ida's home had fallen into poor condition. Ida was greatly relieved when Anderson had the home's plumbing and heating repaired. The business management firm shared by Lupino and Duff received a letter stating that Anderson now represented her. Ida requested that all monies, stocks and bonds belonging to her were to be returned. In 1983 Ida filed for divorce. Duff sent a detective to investigate Anderson. A bitter divorce battle loomed on the horizon.

Ida petitioned the court to appoint Anderson as her conservator or guardian. She related that she was estranged from her family and gave a statement: "I am informed that there has been a considerable diminution in the size and deterioration in the quality of my estate over the last ten years. During the last five I have not maintained my home, and it deteriorated substantially until I engaged nominee Mary Ann Anderson as my business manager. Miss Anderson has, in the ten months she has been my business manager, arranged for repair of the plumbing, heating, and sprinkling systems, each of which had become completely inoperative before her engagement. I am no longer licensed to drive an automobile in the State of California and am entirely dependent upon Mary Ann Anderson for transportation to and from medical care, and the purchase of food, clothing, and other necessities of life. Mary Ann Anderson enjoys my complete trust, confidence and affection. There is no other person, either relative or otherwise, in whom I have such confidence." The court determined that Ida was unable to care for herself.

Without fireworks the Duffs' divorce became final on June 7, 1984. Duff had been earning a high income as an actor, but Ida did not seek alimony, even though her assets were only about

$70,000. The home remained her possession. On July 6 Mary Ann Anderson was appointed conservator of Lupino's estate.

In February 1985, Louis Hayward died at the age of seventy-five. His last year had been spent battling lung cancer, after having smoked three packs of cigarettes a day for half a century. Hayward's second marriage had been a disaster, but in 1951 he had wed model June Blanchard in a successful union that produced a son. In Lupino's eyes, Louis Hayward remained a true hero, a devoted soldier who risked his life for his adopted country.

After enduring a difficult and stormy marriage at Old Oak Lane, where in later years she had been lonely and unhappy, Ida desired to move to a new residence. In May, a judge authorized the sale of Ida's home for $750,000. She was ready to leave Old Oak Lane. With the money from the sale of her home she could live comfortably in her senior years.

Life at her new residence was pleasant. She loved her vast English Tudor home, surrounded by a high fence and a protective iron gate. Warnings of constant surveillance were posted. Others later appeared: "No trespassing," "Don't Even Think of Parking Here," "Don't Mind The Lion—Beware of Owner." Ida constructed a pool in the front yard, where she spent most of the day stretched in the sun in a deck chair.

As for her personal pleasures, Lupino's tastes were simple. She enjoyed television and outings to restaurants as well as trips to stables where Mary Ann Anderson kept her horses. Ida was enchanted by the horses, feeding them apples and carrots. Ida preferred Anderson's young circle to the older crowd.

In 1987 Lupino's health declined. The more intense aspects of her bipolar personality became evident. Deep within her remained a seething cauldron, the "little black devil" she had mentioned so long before. Outbursts of temper required Anderson to be on call at unexpected times to work out problems with neighbors, workers and utility meter readers. Anderson reported to the court Ida's "changing mental and physical states." Medical ills led to stays in various hospitals, with around-the-clock nursing. At one point, Ida spent several months in the Motion Picture, Television Country House. William Blakewell, a board member and old friend, visited Ida and found her feisty despite her illnesses. In June of 1988 the *Globe* tabloid published a confidential report from the conservatorship file and described Ida as "in her lonely last days." While Ida was indeed quite ill, she endured. The drinking stopped. She relocated to a high-class apartment building, residing quietly with her cats. As befitting a star of her stature, old friends from the past came to visit, offering cheer, paying homage to a Hollywood queen. She took an avid interest in animal rights issues and child welfare abroad, adopting foster children.

On July 9, 1990, Howard Duff died of a massive heart attack at his Santa Barbara home. He had finally married his longtime girlfriend and remained an actor to the end. Throughout his life Duff was a tight-lipped private man. In later years, he seldom spoke of his first wife in interviews. During their long separation, if anyone asked about Ida, he feigned ignorance of her whereabouts. He remained a drinker to the end. Obituary notices were inaccurate regarding his marital history. There was mention he left a wife, Judy, "of seventeen years." If true, Duff had been a notorious bigamist. The error was a supremely cruel footnote in their marriage.

For, in truth, Lupino had been abandoned once again and could not accept the rejection. Consequently, her decline began, and she herself rejected even her closest friends. Though she had been one of the most talented women to stand before or behind a motion picture camera, her fabulous career came to an end at age fifty-nine.

Friends could understand the unhappiness caused by her failed marriage, but Howard Duff was no prize, they thought. Duff had been a domineering and jealous husband, but Ida was unable to let him go. She allowed their financial affairs to be entangled for years, though that was clearly not in her best interest. She would not divorce him even when he began to live openly with another woman, whom many believed was his wife. What was it about Howard Duff, Ida's friends wondered, that so obsessed her? Or was her inability to put him out of her mind the symptom of a deeper wound?

Like the masks of comedy and tragedy, there existed within Ida intense and divergent moods. From her public and private statements about herself it was clear that Lupino was aware that she had a unique personality. Like lightning, her moods could flash in startling and magnificent displays, hiding her vulnerability. But what was the essence of Ida Lupino? And what is the key to understanding her rise and fall?

For all her bravado, her childhood abandonments and losses haunted her and influenced her behavior for life. Lupino meets the classic criteria for a borderline personality—stress related characteristics such as frequent mood shifts, impulsivity, inappropriate and intense anger, and uncertainty over identity are common. Borderlines are extremists for whom the world is sharply defined. Their emotions are intense, never vague. They love and hate deeply, for the world appears black and white. Most significant, they are oversensitive to perceived abandonment, which manifests itself as rage and manipulation. Intense and unstable relationships are a key feature of borderline personality disorder, and the condition often runs in families as parents pass on their fears and sustain throughout their adult lives the patterns of instability learned in childhood.

Her father acknowledged that "Ida never had a normal childlife" and that she was often left behind by her performing parents. She was at school at four years of age, and when she came home, wrote Stanley Lupino, "she never saw much of Mommy and Daddy." Ida was an actress for as long as she could remember. Her grandmother kept her occupied by creating a small theater where Ida became "spectator and actor." Her parents often returned home to discover their little daughter in her mother's costumes, "asleep on the floor just as she had fallen, out of sheer exhaustion from the weight of the dresses that, needless to say, were miles too long for her."

Ida wanted desperately to emulate her parents and to please them. Family was everything. The weight of her mother's dresses was transformed into a psychic weight as Ida learned to do her duty as part of the great Lupino family. As a child she was placed in a boarding school when her parents left for America. "But you will come back, promise!" she had pleaded. She had been deeply hurt by what she perceived as abandonment on the part of her parents and was scarred for life by the pain. As any child would be, Ida was unable to fully put family tradition ahead of her desire for love. Deep within her, anger and fear grew. Ida developed an ambivalence: wishing to be seen as good by her parents, accompanied by a resistance to obeying them, created in her a mixed feeling of anxiety and depression leading to the need for constant reassurance. Consequently, she became hypersensitive to anticipated rejection. As she said in 1936: "I'll tell you what real love is . . . when you love a man you love him when he is cruel to you, as well as when he's kind, you love him even though he knocks you down—you get up and you go on loving him because there is no help for it . . . . I never expect anything to last . . . neither success nor love . . . . I can't be hurt. . . . I suffer so much in anticipation of suffering."

Her parents encouraged Ida to go to America when her chance came. Career, as always, came first, and she traveled with her mother to Hollywood. She suffered additional inner turmoil when Stanley Lupino, alone in England, fell in love with a younger woman and her parents became estranged, living separate lives for a decade. While her father risked his life as an air raid warden, she was far away. And when he died, she felt personal failure accompanied by guilt. She had transferred the strong attachment she felt to Stanley Lupino as her caregiver to all of the men in her life, all of whom failed to support her emotionally. The sudden death of her first boyfriend was another abandonment, as was Louis Hayward's rejection of her in his time of deep emotional pain and Collier Young's inability to offer her professional support. Her concept of love was "blind devotion." This was her great strength but also her weakness. She gave all she had to give, both in her career and her personal relationships, yet the men she loved never returned her depth of devotion. She made her husbands her professional partners; as a spouse she stepped back and allowed the men to lead. She made sacrifices for her family, then she was left alone.

For many years Ida was able to keep her intense personality somewhat in check by the use of tranquilizers and alcohol. Duff's abandonment led to increased inner disharmony and self-damaging use of stimulants. Alcohol is a notorious enemy of good sense and good health, and, ultimately, Ida paid the price of such abuse with cerebral circulatory problems and resulting mental deterioration.

Lupino's life has the elements of a Shakespearean tragedy: heroic accomplishments and the fatal flaw that produces tragic consequences. In her artistic life the creative factor was a matter of temperament—the expressions of passions such as anger, revenge, love, madness, jealousy, ambition and hate. The fire must always have a source, and without the inner turmoil, the depth of passion she projected onscreen would not have existed. Lupino displayed true professionalism from an early age and achieved great success. She held true to family tradition, though she later realized she had become imprisoned by the spotlight. Ida once lamented to her close friend Harry Mines that she wished she could have been a doctor but was hindered by her lack of formal education. She even admitted publicly that she never really liked acting but that she never abandoned the profession because it was "in her blood." She heroically tried to be a good trouper until personal unhappiness overwhelmed her.

Ida Lupino died in August 1995 at the age of seventy-seven, but the glory of her fine screen performances will never fade. Lupino was one of the greatest dramatic actresses of her era. On film, she will always have the ability to captivate audiences with her fiery edge and unpredictable energy. Her performances from behind the camera continue to teach and inspire.

Reminiscing about her father, the man she idolized, Ida succinctly said it all: "'You're a strange one,' said Dad. 'I think you're going to end up doing what my son would have done. You will write, direct and produce.' I said, 'Well, that sounds lovely but . . . it scares me. You think I will?' He said, 'I'm funny. I have that psychic feeling.' And that" Ida added, "is what I ended up doing."

And she became the greatest Lupino of them all.

18

A Critical Appraisal

I was just a director who tried my best.

—MADAME DIRECTOR

A film attains immortality because it retains a deathless audience through time. If successive generations can watch and be drawn into the story, it will survive; if not, it will disappear into the shadowy vaults of obscurity. A director also achieves timeless acclaim by the enduring success of his motion pictures. Or *her* motion pictures. And what about Ida Lupino?

New themes and new faces was Filmakers' creed in 1949. Lupino chose to make films with socially controversial themes. As a woman director she received enormous publicity. But she never sought to exploit her sex. Having been born into show business, Lupino never saw herself as anything other than a performer. She never singled herself out as a symbol of female advancement, though she certainly blazed a trail for those who followed. Lupino's fame as an actress drew attention to her directing; she was lovely and popular rather than a faceless director, like most. Lupino stood out. She did not direct to prove that a woman could do it but simply for the creative pleasure it provided. Her salary as an actress dwarfed her director's pay.

Fiercely independent, Ida Lupino wanted to create without the restraints of studio interference. She always viewed herself as a humanist, a working director out to present the human condition, and she sought stories about "poor, bewildered people."

Lupino's early productions were sympathetic accounts of the human condition, directed in a style she called "documentary." She employed a straightforward unfolding of events; her films do not contain elaborate sets or famous faces.

In *Not Wanted*, for example, the story of a young girl who becomes involved with a pianist and finds herself pregnant, the harsh realism of the characters' lives is presented without sentimentalism. The message conveyed is that an unwanted pregnancy has dire consequences but that solutions exist. Because of changes in our society, the impact of being single and pregnant is often lost on today's viewers.

Modern audience identification with the expectant girl is difficult. The terminology of reviewers reveals the depth of controversy that surrounded *Not Wanted* at the time. The lover of the young girl is a "debaucher" and "seducer;" the pregnant girl has experienced "degradation." The film has a "sordid theme" and lacks "moral indignation." These critical terms are almost as outdated as the concept of "illegitimacy." Nearly half a century after the release of *Not Wanted*, the shame and agony once associated with unwed motherhood has vanished, and single mothers are a fact of life in modern society. Although the film thus fails to interest modern moviegoers, it was an artistic and commercial success at the time of its release. It produced public discussion and launched the acting careers of Sally Forrest and Keefe Braselle. It also led Lupino to a directing career.

Never Fear, Lupino's official directorial debut, is also dated. The fear of polio no longer exists, but at the time it frightened audiences away. The psychological devastation of a dancer crippled by a forgotten disease is lost on the modern viewer. At the time, the very word *polio* was enough to shock and frighten, very like the current scourge of AIDS. But *Never Fear* is a respectable production, in which Lupino conveyed a message of hope, indicating that with therapy recovery was possible. A highlight of the film is a wheelchair dance, expertly captured by the director, a joyous moment that provides insight into the world of the disabled, a positive view recognizing that paralysis victims are no different from the rest of humanity.

Outrage explored the destructive nature of rape, a topic that was quite controversial for a film in 1951. An exceptional performance by Mala Powers as the victim combined with the powerful theme to create a dramatic comment on society. The subject of rape was deemed unfit for the screen by many reviewers in a period when the word itself was never used in newspapers and the act was described in print as "criminal attack." *Outrage* raised the consciousness of audiences and drew attention to the vulnerability of women in society and the horrific aftermath of sexual violence.

With *Hard, Fast and Beautiful* Lupino turned toward the type of film in which she would excel, the essence of which is pure drama. The clash of human beings is what she understood. As an actress, she was a master at creating high-powered tension onscreen. Director Lupino brought to life the story of a manipulated daughter pushed by her domineering mother to become a tennis star. Claire Trevor was superb as the conniving mother and Sally Forrest excellent as a naive but increasingly enlightened adolescent. The documentary style of the earlier films is evident, but there is more of a typical unfolding of events. Lupino builds the mother-daughter conflict and adds small touches that are stylistically representative of her later skill. The coldness of the mother is manifest in her rejection of her husband's affection; she is more intent on polishing her nails, an exterior adornment of self. Later, as her daughter becomes aware of being manipulated, the guilty mother bites her nails in worry; she has destroyed her own loveliness, just as she destroys her relationship with her daughter. The ending is powerful as the rejected mother sits alone in a deserted stadium. The wind whisks yesterday's crumpled newspapers through the silent stadium as the sound of a pounding tennis ball echoes plaintively.

Lupino might have gone further—with themes of racial prejudice, infertility, and atomic disaster—had not Howard Hughes vetoed such ideas. Her "new themes" became less societal and increasingly dramatic. She made plans for pictures dealing with pyromania, murder, helicopter combat, and western shootouts.

With *The Hitch-Hiker*, Lupino reached the apex of her directorial career in feature films. Originally titled *The Persuader*, the film was pure drama. Edmond O'Brien and Frank Lovejoy are kindhearted fishermen who give murderer William Talman a lift. It is a fast-paced hellish ride through Mexican wilderness toward apparent death. Lupino made the most of a simple kidnapping of two innocent men. Small touches underscore larger themes. Forced to break into a service station to steal gas, one of the victims leaves a wedding ring behind; a symbolic token of eternal love, which will become all that remains of the murdered victim, or a clue to identification and escape.

With *The Bigamist*, Ida again chose a controversial theme. Edmond O'Brien portrayed a guilt-ridden lonely salesman in love with an attractive but infertile wife and with a vivacious waitress. Lupino was especially masterful in conveying the levels of emotion and distance between the salesman and his business-oriented wife. Joan Fontaine as the wife is stylish, elegant and remote, except when adoption is mentioned. The toy soldier she purchases becomes the symbol of the wished-for child; though only an object, the toy provides a completeness to the family and a contrast to O'Brien's

266

second family, with a real child and a wife who cares for his happiness. The unity of the couple is understood to be mechanical and limited. Another powerful moment is the discovery of the bigamist, exposed to an adoption investigator not by his second wife but by the unexpected cry of their baby. The child is the symbol of completeness, but its cry destroys the false life the bigamist has created. The film's ending of suspended judgment was purposely ambiguous, artistically daring with a denouement left to the audience's imagination.

As for Lupino's characters in her early productions, they are not superhumans; they are people with limitations who cannot exist without both societal and individual assistance. Institutions and personal relationships are inextricably intertwined: the home for unwed mothers, the polio institute, the court and the police offer solutions. The victims find respite in men who love them rather than solutions they discover outside of conventional wisdom.

Great directors make great films, and good directors make good films. Those whose work transcends time and changing values earn undying recognition. Within the confines of low-budget, modest films, Lupino's features were commendable for the period but fall short of being great films. Lupino took chances within a confined realism, away from the studio sets and typical subjects, but the stories remained within the realm of the predictable. Modern critics would prefer modern solutions—the unwed mother should have defiantly raised her own child rather than allow it to be adopted, the polio victim could have chosen suicide to loss of freedom, the rape victim should have maimed her attacker, and the bigamist should have flaunted his loves in a polygamous union. But those would not be Lupino's films, nor would they be true to the times in which they were made.

After her feature films, Lupino continued her career as a director in television. It is unfortunate that so much of her work was in this transient medium. Access to various episodes she directed for television shows is difficult, as series gather dust in warehouses. However, the prestigious Film Center of Chicago did sponsor a unique retrospective, "The Unseen Lupino," in 1987. Film scholar Barbara Scharres organized the event to demonstrate Lupino's proficiency as a television director. According to Scharres, "The range of her television work makes it clear that Lupino could handle almost any subject with great technical skill and highly imaginative use of the camera, as well as define what it was that interested her most in terms of a power struggle in any script."

In 1966 Lupino directed her last motion picture—*The Trouble With Angels.* The story of life in a convent school was a far cry from themes of unwed mothers and bigamy. At a time when the youth of the sixties were rebelling against the conformity of society, searching for self-fulfillment outside societal guidelines, the story of a high-spirited girl who decides to become a nun was hardly on the wave of controversy. Indeed, Lupino seemed purposely to disassociate herself from filmmakers making waves. As she said a few years later, "You name it, and we did it, but it was in good taste. That's the way movies and television stories should be—stories about people done in good taste."

The fiery edge of the younger director was gone; the mature Lupino was content to demonstrate her expert craftsmanship in television, providing gems in various series. Unfortunately, there is more glory in feature films than in the small screen.

To celebrate its Golden Jubilee, the Directors Guild offered special screenings to honor illustrious colleagues. The Guild's tribute to Lupino was a double bill of *Hard, Fast and Beautiful* and *The Bigamist.* Mala Powers and Sally Forrest fielded questions and praised their mentor. Mala Powers eloquently hailed Lupino: "What Ida has given us most of all in her films is courage. . . . Ida took a chance. She risked her reputation and her fledgling company for her values. With her brilliance and courage, she succeeded."

Ida Lupino's greatest directorial skill was her ability to reach her cast. The performers gave their best for her, secure under her guidance, aware she would not allow them to give a bad performance. They took chances for her, and like a good mother she coaxed the best from them. This was her real family.

Filmakers' policy of providing opportunity to its family led to acting careers for Sally Forrest, Mala Powers, Keefe Braselle, and Hugh O'Brian. Robert Eggenweiler became a producer; John Franco rose to become one of the highest paid script supervisors in the industry; Harry Horner became a director. John Franco sums up the feelings of those whose careers were boosted by Ida Lupino: "If it wasn't for her, I wouldn't have anything."

APPENDIX
Ida Lupino's Career

FILMOGRAPHY

Her First Affaire (1932)
A St. George's Production (Sterling Film Co. release); producer, Frank Richardson; director, Allan Dwan; screenplay, Brock Williams, Dion Titheradge, based on the play by Frederick Jackson, Merrill Rogers; photography, Geoffrey Faithful; film editor, Dr. Seabourne; continuity, Dilian G. Day; art director, James Elder Willis; costumes, Gilbert Clark. 71 minutes. Cast: Ida Lupino, Arnold Riches, George Curzon, Diana Napier.

Money for Speed (1933)
Hall Mark Films (United Artists release); director, Bernard Vorhaus; screenplay, Vera Allenson, Lionel Hale, Monica Ewer, based on a story by Bernard Vorhaus; photography, Eric Cross, Fred Ford; film editor, David Lean; sound, G. Burgess. 72 minutes. Cast: Ida Lupino, Cyril McLaglen, John Loder, Moore Marriott.

High Finance (1933)
First National-British; producer, Irving Asher; director, George King. 67 minutes. Cast: Gibb McLaughlin, Ida Lupino, John Batten, John Roberts. Note: *High Finance* seems to have disappeared. Warner's Teddington studio in England was bombed in July 1944. Most British studios donated prints of pre-1940 films to the National Film Archive. A worldwide search failed to turn up either stills or prints.

The Ghost Camera (1933)
A Julius Hagen-Twickenham Production; producer, Julius Hagen; director,

Bernard Vorhaus; screenplay, H. Fowler Mears; story, J. Jefferson Farjeon; art director, James A. Carter; music, W.L. Trytel. 68 minutes. Cast: Ida Lupino, Henry Kendall, John Mills.

I Lived with You (1933)
Twickenham Films (Gaumont-British release); producer, Julius Hagen; director, Maurice Elvey; screenplay, H. Fowler Mears, from the play by Ivor Novello; photography, Sidney Blythe; sound, Baynham Honri; art director, James A Carter; musical director, William Trytel. 100 minutes. Cast: Ivor Novello, Ursula Jeans, Ida Lupino, Minnie Raynor.

Prince of Arcadia (1933)
A Nettlefold-Fogwell Production (Gaumont-British release); producers, Archibald Nettlefold, Reginald Fogwell; director, Hans Schwarz; screenplay, Reginald Fogwell, based on "Der Prinz Von Arkadien" by Walter Reisch; photography, Geoffrey Faithful; sound, Michael Rose; music, Robert Stolz. 80 minutes. Cast: Carl Brisson, Margot Grahame, Ida Lupino, Annie Esmond.

Search for Beauty (1934)
Paramount; producer, E. Lloyd Sheldon; director, Erle C. Kenton; screenplay, Frank Butler, Claude Binyon; story, David Boehm, Maurine Watkins, based on the play *Love Your Body* by Schuyler E. Grey, Paul R. Milton; dialogue, Sam Hellerman; director of photography, Harry Fishbeck; film editor, James Smith; sound, Joel Butler; music, Ralph Rainger; lyrics, Leo Robin; dances, LeRoy Prinz. 77 minutes. Cast: Larry "Buster" Crabbe, Ida Lupino, Robert Armstrong, James Gleason.

Come on Marines (1934)
Paramount; producer, Albert Lewis; director, Henry Hathaway; screenplay, Joel Sayre, Byron Morgan, from the story "The Pink Chemise" by Philip Wylie; director of photography, Ben Reynolds; film editor, James Smith; sound, Jack Goodrich; art directors, Hans Dreir, Earl Hendrick; music, Ralph Rainger; songs, Ralph Rainger, Leo Robin. 68 minutes. Cast: Richard Arlen, Ida Lupino, Roscoe Karns, Grace Bradley.

Ready for Love (1934)
Paramount; producer, Albert Lewis; director, Marion Gering; screenplay,

J.P. McEvoy, William Slavens McNutt, from the play *The Whipping* by Eulalie
Spence, based on the the novel by Roy Flanagan; director of photography, Leon
Shamroy. 62 minutes. Cast: Richard Arlen, Ida Lupino, Marjorie Rambeau,
Trent Durkin.

Paris in Spring (1935)

Paramount; producer, Benjamin Glazer; director, Lewis Milestone; screenplay,
Samuel Hoffenstein, Frank Schultz, from a play by Dwight Taylor; director of
photography, Ted Tetzlaff; film editor, Eda Warren; sound, Harry Mills; music,
Harry Revel; lyrics, Mack Gordon. 80 minutes. Cast: Mary Ellis, Tullio
Carminati, Lynne Overman.

Smart Girl (1935)

Paramount; producer, Walter Wanger; director, Aubrey Scotto; assistant director,
George Blair; screenplay, Francis Highland; additional dialogue, Wilson Collison;
director of photgraphy, John Mescall; art director, Alexander Toluboff; musical
direction, S.K. Wineland; film editor, Tom Persons; sound, Charles Althouse. 69
minutes. Cast: Ida Lupino, Kent Taylor, Gail Patrick, Joseph Cawthorn.

Peter Ibbetson (1935)

Paramount; producer, Louis D. Lighton; director, Henry Hathaway; screenplay,
Vincent Lawrence, Waldemar Young, additional scenes, John Meehan, Edwin
Justus Mayer, based on the novel by George du Maurier, adapted by Constance
Collier; director of photography, Charles Lang; film editor, Stuart Heisler; sound,
Harry Mills, Don Johnson, Frank Goodwin; special effects, Gordon Jennings; art
directors, Hans Dreier, Robert Usher; music, Ernst Toch; musical director, Nat
W. Finston. 88 minutes. Cast: Gary Cooper, Ann Harding, John Halliday, Ida
Lupino.

Anything Goes (1936)

Paramount; producer, Benjamin Glazer; director, Lewis Milestone; based on the
play by Howard Lindsay, Russel Crouse (no screenplay credits); director of photography, Karl Struss; film editor, Eda Warren; sound, Jack Goodrich; art
directors, Hans Dreier, Ernst Fegte; set decorator, A.E. Freudeman; special effects, Farciot Edouart; dances, Leroy Prinz; music and lyrics, Cole Porter;
additional songs, Leo Robin, Richard A. Whiting, Frederick Hollander, Hoagy
Carmichael, Edward Heyman; costumes, Travis Banton; production adviser,

Vinton Freedley. 93 minutes. Cast: Bing Crosby, Ethel Merman, Charles Ruggles, Grace Bradley.

One Rainy Afternoon (1936)
A Pickford-Lasky Production (UA release); producers, Mary Pickford, Jesse Lasky; director, Rowland V. Lee; assistant director, Percy Ikerd; screenplay, Stephen Morehouse Avery, adapted from "Monsieur Sans Gene" by Arnold Pressburger, Rene Pujal; additional dialogue, Maurice Hanline; directors of photography, Peverell Marley, Meritt Gerstad; film editor, Margaret Clancy; sound, Paul Neal; art director, Richard Day; musical director, Alfred Newman; music, Ralph Irwin, lyrics for "One Rainy Afternoon," Jack Stern, Harry Tobias, lyrics for "Secret Rendezvous," Preston Sturges; costume, Omar Kiam. 80 minutes. Cast: Francis Lederer, Ida Lupino, Hugh Herbert, Roland Young.

Yours for the Asking (1936)
Paramount; producer, Lewis E. Gensler; director, Alexander Hall; assistant director, James Dugan; screenplay, Eve Green, Harlan Ware, Phiilip MacDonald, based on the story "The Duchess" by William R. Lipman and William H. Wright; director of photography, Theodore Sparkuhl; film editor, James Smith; sound, Harry M. Lindgren, John Cope; art directors, Hans Dreier, Roland Anderson; interior decorator, A.E. Freudeman; musical director, Boris Morros; costumes, Travis Banton. 68 minutes. Cast: George Raft, Delores Costello Barrymore, Ida Lupino, Reginald Owen.

The Gay Desperado (1936)
Pickford-Lasky (UA release); producers, Mary Pickford, Jesse L. Lasky; director, Rouben Mamoulian; assistant director, Robert Lee; screenplay, Wallace Smith, story by Leo Birinski; director of photography, Lucien Andriot; film editor, Margaret Clancy; sound, Paul Neal; art director, Richard Day; music director, Alfred Newman; songs, Giuseppe Verdi, George Posford, Miguel Sandoval; costumes, Omar Kiam. 85 minutes. Cast: Nino Martini, Ida Lupino, Leo Carrillo, Harold Huber.

Sea Devils (1937)
RKO; executive producer, Samuel J. Briskin; producer, Edward Small; director, Ben Stoloff; assistant director, Kenneth Holmes; screenplay, Frank Wead, John Twist, P.J. Wolfson; photography, J. Roy Hunt, Joseph August; film editor,

Arthur Roberts; sound, John L. Cass; special effects, Vernon Walter; art director, Van Nest Polglase; set decorator, Darrell Silvera; musical director, Roy Webb; costumes, Edward Stevenson; technical advisor, Lieutenant H.C. Moore. 85 minutes. Cast: Victor McLaglen, Preston Foster, Ida Lupino, Donald Woods.

Let's Get Married (1937)
Columbia; associate producer, Everett Riskin; director, Alfred E. Green; assistant director, Sam Nelson; screenplay, Ethel Hill, based on a story by A.H.Z. Carr; director of photography, Henry Freulich; film editor, Al Clark; sound, Lodge Cunningham; art director, Stephen Goosson; gowns, Kalloch. 68 minutes. Cast: Ida Lupino, Walter Connolly, Ralph Bellamy, Raymond Walburn.

Artists and Models (1937)
Paramount; producer, Lewis E. Gensler; director, Raoul Walsh; assistant director, John Burch; screenplay, Walter Deleon, Francis Martin, based on adaptation by Eve Green, Harlan Ware, story by Sig Herzig, Gene Thackrey; director of photography, Victor Milner; film editor, Alma Ruth MacCrorie; sound, Harold Lewis, Louis Mesenkop; art directors, Hans Dreier, Robert Usher; interior decorator, A.E. Freudeman; musical director, Boris Morros; musical numbers staged by Leroy Prinz; costumes, Travis Banton. 95 minutes. Cast: Jack Benny, Ida Lupino, Richard Arlen, Gail Patrick.

Fight for Your Lady (1937)
RKO; producer, Albert Lewis; director, Ben Stoloff; screenplay, Ernest Pagano, Harry Segall, Harold Kusell, story by Jean Negulesco, Isabel Leighton; director of photography, Jack MacKenzie; film editor, George Crone; sound, Hugh McDowell; art director, Van Nest Polglase; musical director, Frank Tours; music and lyrics, Harry Akst, Frank Loesser. 67 minutes. Cast: John Boles, Jack Oakie, Ida Lupino, Margot Grahame.

The Lone Wolf Spy Hunt (1939)
Columbia; associate producer, Joseph Sistrom; director, Peter Godfrey; assistant director, Cliff Broughton; screenplay, Jonathan Latimer, based on Louis Joseph Vance's novel *The Lone Wolf's Daughter*; director of photography, Allen G. Siegler; film editor, Otto Meyer; sound, Lodge Cunningham; art director, Lionel Banks;

musical director, Morris W. Stoloff; gowns, Kalloch. 67 minutes. Cast: Warren William, Ida Lupino, Rita Hayworth, Virginia Weidler.

The Lady and the Mob (1939)
Columbia; producer, Fred Kohlmar; director, Ben Stoloff; assistant director, Wilbur McGaugh; screenplay, Richard Malbaum, Price Day; director of photography, John Sturmar; film editor, Otto Meyer; art director, Lionel Banks; musical director, Morris W. Stoloff; gowns, Kalloch. 65 minutes. Cast: Fay Bainter, Ida Lupino, Lee Bowman, Henry Armetta.

The Adventures of Sherlock Holmes (1939)
Twentieth Century-Fox; associate producer, Gene Markey; director, Alfred Werker; assistant director, William Eckhar; screenplay, Edwin Blum, William Drake, based on the play *Sherlock Holmes* by William Gillette from Sir Arthur Conan Doyle's novel; director of photography, Leon Shamroy; film editor, Robert Bischoff; art directors, Richard Day, Hans Peters; music, Cyril J. Mockridge; costumes, Gwen Wakeling. 85 minutes. Cast: Basil Rathbone, Nigel Bruce, Ida Lupino, Alan Marshall, George Zucco.

The Light That Failed (1939)
Paramount; producer and director, William Wellman; assistant director, Fritz Collings; second unit director, Joseph Youngerman; screenplay, Robert Carson, based on the novel by Rudyard Kipling; director of photography, Theodore Sparkuhl; film editor, Thomas Scott; sound, Hugo Grenzbach, Walter Oberst; art directors, Hans Dreier, Robert Odell; set decorator, A.E. Freudeman; technical director, Capt. Jack R. Dunham-Matthews; music, Victor Young. 97 minutes. Cast: Ronald Colman, Walter Huston, Muriel Angelus, Ida Lupino.

They Drive by Night (1940)
Warner Bros.-First National; executive producer, Hal B. Wallis; associate producer, Mark Hellinger; director, Raoul Walsh; assistant director, Elmer Decker; screenplay, Jerry Wald, Richard Macaulay, based on the novel *The Long Haul* by A.I. Bezzerides; director of photography, Arthur Edeson; film editor, Thomas Richards; sound, Oliver S. Garretson; dialogue director, Hugh MacMullen; art director, John Hughes; special effects, Byron Haskin, H.F. Koenekamp; music, Adolph Deutsch; musical director, Leo F. Forbstein; orchestrator, Arthur Lange;

montages, Don Siegel, Robert Burks; makeup, Perc Westmore; gowns, Milo Anderson; unit manager, Lou Baum. 93 minutes. Cast: George Raft, Ann Sheridan, Ida Lupino, Humphrey Bogart.

High Sierra (1941)

Warner Bros.-First National; executive producer, Hal B. Wallis; associate producer, Mark Hellinger; director, Raoul Walsh; assistant director, Russ Saunders; screenplay, John Huston, W.R. Burnett, from the novel by W.R. Burnett; director of photography, Tony Gaudio; film editor, Jack Killifer; sound, Dolph Thomas; art director, Ted Smith; dialogue director, Irving Rapper; special effects, Byron Haskin, H.F. Koenekamp; music, Adolph Deutsch; musical director, Leo F. Forbstein; gowns, Milo Anderson; makeup, Perc Westmore; unit manager, Al Alleborn. 100 minutes (1941 release); 96 minutes (1948 re-release). Cast: Ida Lupino, Humphrey Bogart, Alan Curtis, Arthur Kennedy, Joan Leslie.

The Sea Wolf (1941)

Warner Bros.-First National; executive producer, Hal B. Wallis; associate producer, Henry Blanke; director, Michael Curtiz; assistant director, Sherry Shourds; screenplay, Robert Rossen, from the novel by Jack London; director of photography, Sol Polito; film editor, George Amy; sound, Oliver S. Garretson; art director, Anton Grot; dialogue director, Jo Graham; special effects, Byron Haskin, H.F. Koenekamp; music, Erich Wolfgang Korngold; orchestral arrangements, Hugo Friedhofer, Ray Heindorf; musical director, Leo F. Forbstein; costumes, Howard Shoup; makeup, Perc Westmore; unit manager, Jack Saper. 87 minutes. Cast: Edward G. Robinson, John Garfield, Ida Lupino, Alexander Knox.

Out of the Fog (1941)

Warner Bros.-First National; executive producer, Hal B. Wallis; associate producer, Henry Blanke; director, Anatole Litvak; screenplay, Robert Rossen, Jerry Wald, Richard Macaulay, from the play The Gentle People by Irwin Shaw; director of photography, James Wong Howe; film editor, Warren Low; sound, Everett A. Brown; art director, Carl Jules Weyl; dialogue director, Jo Graham; special effects, Rex Wimpy; musical director, Leo F. Forbstein; gowns, Howard Shoup; makeup, Perc Westmore. 93 minutes. Cast: Ida Lupino, John Garfield, Thomas Mitchell, Eddie Albert.

Ladies in Retirement (1941)

Columbia; producers, Lester Cowan, Gilbert Miller; director, Charles Vidor; assistant director, George Rhein; screenplay, Reginald Denham, Garrett Fort, based on the play by Reginald Denham, Edward Percy; director of photography, George Barnes; film editor, Al Clark; art director, Lionel Banks; production designer, David Hall; musical score, Ernst Toch; musical director, Morris W. Stoloff. 92 minutes. Cast: Ida Lupino, Louis Hayward, Evelyn Keyes, Elsa Lanchester, Edith Barrett, Isobel Elsom.

Moontide (1942)

Twentieth Century-Fox; producer, Mark Hellinger; director, Archie Mayo; assistant director, Saul I. Wurzel; screenplay, John O'Hara, from a novel by Willard Robertson; director of photography, Charles Clarke; film editor, William Reynolds; sound, Eugene Grossman, Roger Heman; art directors, James Basevi, Richard Day; set decorator, Thomas Little; music, Cyril J. Mockridge, David Buttolph; costumes, Gwen Wakeling; makeup, Guy Pearce. 95 minutes. Cast: Jean Gabin, Ida Lupino, Thomas Mitchell, Jerome Cowan.

The Hard Way (1942)

Warner Bros.-First National; producer, Jerry Wald; director, Vincent Sherman; screenplay, Daniel Fuchs, Peter Viertel; director of photography, James Wong Howe; film editor, Thomas Pratt; sound, Stanley Jones; art director, Max Parker; dialogue director, Harold Winston; special effects, Willard Van Enger; montages, Don Siegel; set decorator, Walter F. Tilford; dances, LeRoy Prinz; music, H. Roemheld; songs, M.K. Jerome, Jack Scholl; orchestral arrangements, Ray Heindorf; musical director, Leo F. Forbstein; gowns, Orry Kelly; makeup, Perc Westmore. 109 minutes. Cast: Ida Lupino, Dennis Morgan, Joan Leslie, Jack Carson.

Life Begins at 8:30 (1942)

Twentieth Century-Fox; executive producer, William Goetz; producer, Nunnally Johnson; director, Irving Pichel; assistant director, Tom Dudley; screenplay, Nunnally Johnson, from Emlyn Williams's play *Light of Heart*; director of photography, Edward Cronjage; film editor, Fred Allen; sound, George Leverett, Roger Heman; art directors, Richard Day, Boris Leven; set decorators, Al Orenbach, Thomas Little; music, Alfred Newman; costumes, Earl Luick;

makeup, Guy Pearce. 85. minutes. Cast: Monty Woolley, Ida Lupino, Cornel Wilde, Sara Allgood.

Forever and a Day (1943)
RKO; directors, Rene Clair, Edmund Goulding, Cedric Hardwicke, Frank Lloyd, Victor Saville, Robert Stevenson, Robert Wilcox; screenplay, Charles Bennett, C.S. Forrester, Lawrence Hazard, Michael Hogan, W.P. Lipscomb, Alan Campbell, Alice Duer Miller, John Van Druten, Peter Godfrey, S.M. Herzig, Christopher Isherwood, Gene Lockhart, R.C. Sherriff, Claudine West, Norman Corwin, Jack Hartfield, James Hilton, Emmett Lavery, Frederick Lonsdale, Donal Ogden Stewart, Keith Winter; directors of photography, Robert De Grasse, Lee Garmes, Russell Metty, Nicholas Musuraca; film editors, Elmo J. Williams, George Crone; art directors, Albert S. D'Agostino, Lawrence P. Williams, Al Herman; special effects, Vernon L. Walker; musical director, Anthony Collins; production coordinator, Lloyd Richards. 104 minutes. Cast: Ida Lupino, Charles Laughton, Merle Oberon, Brian Aherne, Ray Milland.

Thank Your Lucky Stars (1943)
Warner Bros.-First National; producer, Mark Hellinger; director, David Butler; assistant director, Phil Quinn; screenplay, Norman Panama, Melvin Frank, James V. Kern, from a story by Everett Freeman, Arthur Schwartz; director of photography, Arthur Edeson; film editor, Irene Morra; sound, Francis J. Scheid, Charles Forrest; art directors, Anton Grot, Leo E. Kuter; set decorator, Walter E. Tilford; dialogue director, Herbert Farjean; special effects, H.F. Koenekamp; music and lyrics, Arthur Schwartz, Frank Loesser; orchestral arrangements, Ray Heindorf; vocal arrangements, Dudley Chambers; musical director, Leo F. Forbstein; dances, staged and directed by LeRoy Prinz; makeup, Perc Westmore; gowns, Milo Anderson. 127 minutes. Cast: Ida Lupino, Olivia de Havilland, George Tobias, Eddie Cantor, Dinah Shore, Bette Davis, Joan Leslie, Dennis Morgan, Ann Sheridan, Humphrey Bogart, Errol Flynn, John Garfield, Alan Hale, Jack Carson, Hattie McDaniel.

Hollywood Canteen (1944)
Warner Bros.-First National; producer, Alex Gottlieb; director, Delmer Daves; assistant director, Art Lueker; screenplay, Delmer Daves; director of photography, Bert Glennon; film editor, Christian Nyby; sound, Oliver S. Garretson,

Charles Forrest; art director, Leo Kuter; set decorator, Casey Roberts; musical adaptor, Ray Heindorf; musical director, Leo F. Forbstein; dances, LeRoy Prinz; wardrobe, Milo Anderson; makeup, Perc Westmore. 127 minutes. Cast: Bette Davis, Joan Crawford, Jack Carson, Robert Hutton, Dane Clark, Ida Lupino, John Garfield, Peter Lorre, Sidney Greenstreet, Alexis Smith, Eleanor Parker, the Andrews Sisters, Barbara Stanwyck, Eddie Cantor, Jack Benny.

In Our Time (1944)

Warner Bros.-First National; producer, Jerry Wald; director, Vincent Sherman; assistant director, Bill Kissel; screenplay, Ellis St. Joseph, Howard Koch; director of photography, Carl Guthrie; film editor, Rudi Fehr; sound, Clare A. Riggs; art director, Hugh Reticker; set decorator, Casey Roberts; montages, James Leicester; technical advisor, Stephen Barasch; music, Franz Waxman; musical director, Leo F. Forbstein; gowns, Milo Anderson; makeup, Perc Westmore; unit manager, Frank Mattison. 110 minutes. Cast: Ida Lupino, Paul Henreid, Nancy Coleman, Alla Nazimova, Victor Francen, Mary Boland.

Pillow to Post (1945)

Warner Bros.-First National; producer, Alex Gottlieb; director, Vincent Sherman; assistant director, Jesse Hibbs; screenplay, Charles Hoffman, from the play by Rose Simon Kohn; director of photography, Wesley Anderson; film editor, Alan Crosland Jr.; sound Charles Land; art director, Leo Kuter; set decorator, Walter E. Tilford; special effects, Walter Lynch; montages, James Leicest; music, Frederick Hollander; orchestral arrangements, Jerome Moross; musical director, Leo F. Forbstein; costumes, Milo Anderson; makeup, Perc Westmore. 94 minutes. Cast: Ida Lupino, Sydney Greenstreet, William Prince, Dorothy Dandridge.

Devotion (1946)

Warner Bros.-First National; producer, Robert Buckner; director, Curtis Bernhardt; assistant director, Jesse Hibbs; screenplay, Keith Winter, based on a story by Theodore Reeves; director of photography, Ernest Haller; film editor, Rudy Fehr; sound, Stanley Jones; art director, Robert M. Haas; special effects, Jack Holden, Jack Oakie, Rex Wimpy; set decorator, Casey Roberts; dialogue director, James Vincent; music, Erich Wolfgang Korngold; musical director, Leo F. Forbstein; makeup, Perc Westmore; gowns, Milo Anderson. 104 minutes. Cast: Ida Lupino, Paul Henreid, Olivia de Havilland, Sydney Greenstreet.

The Man I Love (1946)
Warner Bros.-First National; producer, Arnold Albert; director, Raoul Walsh; assistant director, Reggie Callow; screenplay, Catherine Turney, adaptation, Catherine Turney, Jo Pagano, from a novel by Maritta Wolff; director of photography, Sid Hickox; film editor, Owen Marks; sound, Dolph Thomas, David Forrest; art director, Stanley Fleischer; dialogue director, John Maxwell; special effects, Harry Barndollar, Edwin Du Par; set decorator, Eddie Edwards; music adapted by Max Steiner; orchestral arrangements, Hugo Friedhofer; musical direction, Leo F. Forbstein; wardrobe, Milo Anderson; makeup, Perc Westmore. 96 minutes. Cast: Ida Lupino, Robert Alda, Andrea King, Martha Vickers.

Escape Me Never (1947)
Warner Bros.-First National; producer, Henry Blanke; director, Peter Godfrey; assistant director, Claude Archer; screenplay, Thames Williamson, from the play by Margaret Kennedy; director of photography, Sol Polito; film editor, Clarence Kolster; sound, Dolph Thomas; dialogue director, Robert Stevens; art director, Carl Weyl; set decorator, Fred M. MacLean; special effects, Harry Barndollar, Willard Van Enger; ballet sequences, LeRoy Prinz; music, Erich Wolfgang Korngold; orchestral arrangements, Hugo Friedhofer; musical director, Leo F. Forbstein; wardrobe, Bernard Newman; ballet costumes, Travilla; makeup, Perc Westmore; unit manager, Al Alleborn. 103 minutes. Cast: Errol Flynn, Ida Lupino, Eleanor Parker, Gig Young.

Deep Valley (1947)
Warner Bros.-First National; producer, Henry Blanke; director, Jean Negulesco; assistant director, Art Lueker; screeplay, Salka Viertel, Stephen Morehouse Avary, from the novel by Dan Totheroh; director of photography, Ted McCord; film editor, Owen Marks; sound, Clare A. Riggs; dialogue director, John Maxwell; art directors, Max Parker, Frank Durlauf; special effects, William McGann, H.F. Koenekamp; set decorator, Howard Winterbottom; music, Max Steiner; orchestral arrangements, Murray Cutter; musical director, Leo F. Forbstein; wardrobe, Bernard Newman; makeup, Perc Westmore; unit manager, Frank Mattison. 104 minutes. Cast: Ida Lupino, Dane Clark, Wayne Morris, Fay Bainter.

Road House (1948)
Twentieth Century-Fox; producer, Edward Chodorov; director, Jean Negulesco;

assistant director, Tom Dudley; screenplay, Edward Chodorov, based on a story by Margaret Gruen, Oscar Saul; director of photography, Joseph La Shelle; film editor, James B. Clark; sound, Alfred Bruzlin, Harry M. Leonard; special effects, Fred Sersen; art directors, Lyle Wheeler, Maurice Ransford; set decorator, Thomas Little; music, Cyril J. Mockridge; musical direction, Lionel Newman; costumes, Kay Nelson; wardrobe, Charles La Maire; makeup, Ben Nye. 95 minutes. Cast: Ida Lupino, Cornel Wilde, Celeste Holm, Richard Widmark.

Lust for Gold (1949)
Columbia; producer and director, S. Sylvan Simon; associate producer, Earl McEvoy; assistant director, James Nicholson; screenplay, Ted Sherdeman, Richard English, based on the book *Thunder God's Gold* by Barry Storm; director of photography, Archie Stout; film editor, Gene Havlick; sound, Ledge Cunningham; art director, Carl Anderson; set decorator, Sidney Clifford; music, George Duning; musical director, M.W. Stoloff; Lupino's wardrobe, Jean Louis; makeup, Clay Campbell. 90 minutes. Cast: Ida Lupino, Glenn Ford, Gig Young, William Prince.

Woman in Hiding (1949)
Universal; producer, Michael Kraike; director, Michael Gordon; assistant director, Frank Shaw; screenplay, Oscar Saul, adaptation, Roy Huggins, based on the story "Fugitive from Terror" by James R. Webb; director of photography, William Daniels; special photography, David S. Horsley; film editor, Milton Carruth; sound, Leslie I. Carey, Robert Pritchard; art directors, Bernard Herzbrun, Robert Clatworthy; set decorators, Russell A. Gausman, Ruby R. Levitt; music, Frank Skinner, musical direction, Milton Schwarzwald; gowns, Orry Kelly; makeup, Bud Westmore. 93 minutes. Cast: Ida Lupino, Stephen McNally, Howard Duff.

On Dangerous Ground (1951)
RKO; producer, John Houseman; director, Nicholas Ray; screenplay, A.I. Bezzerides, based on an adaptation by A.I. Bezzerides and Nicholas Ray of the novel *Mad with Much Heart* by Gerald Butler; director of photography, George E. Diskant; film editor, Roland Gross; sound, Phil Brigandi, Clem Portman; art directors, Albert S. D'Agostino, Ralph Berger; music, Bernard Herrmann; musical director, C. Bakaleinikoff. 82 minutes. Cast: Ida Lupino, Robert Ryan, Ward Bond, Charles Kemper.

Beware My Lovely (1952)

Filmakers (RKO release); producer, Collier Young; associate producer, Mel Dinelli; director, Harry Horner; screenplay, Mel Dinelli, based on his play *The Man;* director of photography, George E. Diskant; film editor, Paul Weatherwax; sound, John Cass, Clem Portman; art directors, Albert S. D'Agostino, Alfred Herman; music, Leith Stevens; musical director, C. Bakaleinikoff. 77 minutes. Cast: Ida Lupino, Robert Ryan, Taylor Holmes, Barbara Whiting.

Jennifer (1953)

Allied Artists; producer, Berman Swartz; director, Joel Newton; assistant director, Austin Jewell; screenplay, Bernard Girard, Richard Dorso, based on a story by Virginia Myers; director of photography, James Wong Howe; film editor, Everett Douglas; sound, Jean L. Speak; music, Ernest Gold; song "Angel Eyes" by Matt Dennis, Earl Brent; production manager, Lonnie D'Orsa; set decorator, George Sawley; makeup, Dan Greenway; wardrobe, Ruth Matthews. 73 minutes. Cast: Ida Lupino, Howard Duff, Robert Nichols, Mary Shipp.

The Bigamist (1953)

Filmakers; producer, Collier Young; associate producer, Robert Eggenweiler; director, Ida Lupino; screenplay, Collier Young, from a story by Larry Marcus, Lou Schor; director of photography, George Diskant; film editor, Stanford Tischler; sound, Dick Tyler, Howard Wilson; art director, James Sullivan; music, Leith Stevens. 79 minutes. Cast: Joan Fontaine, Edmond O'Brien, Ida Lupino, Edmund Gwenn, Jane Darwell.

Private Hell 36 (1954)

Filmakers; producer, Collier Young; associate producer, Robert Eggenweiler; director, Don Siegel; assistant directors, James Anderson, Leonard Kunody; screenplay, Collier Young, Ida Lupino; director of photography, Burnett Guffey; film editor, Stanford Tischler; sound, Thomas Carmen, Howard Wilson; art director, Walter Keller; set director, Edward Boyle; music, Leith Stevens; song, John Franco; makeup, David Newell. 81 minutes. Cast: Ida Lupino, Steve Cochran, Howard Duff, Dean Jagger.

Women's Prison (1955)

A Bryan Foy Production (Columbia release); producer, Bryan Foy; director, Lewis Seiler; assistant director, Carter DeHaven Jr.; screenplay, Crane Wilbur,

Jack DeWitt; director of photography, Lester H. White; film editor, Henry Batista; sound, George Cooper; art director, Cary Odell; set director, Louis Diage; music, Mischa Bakaleinikoff. 80 minutes. Cast: Ida Lupino, Jan Sterling, Cleo Moore, Audrey Totter.

The Big Knife (1955)
Associates and Aldrich Co. (UA release); producer and director, Robert Aldrich; screenplay, James Poe, based on the play by Clifford Odets; director of photography, Ernest Laszlo; film editor, Michael Luciano; sound, Jack Solomon; art director, William Glasgow; music, Frank De Vol; production supervisor, Jack R. Berne. 111 minutes. Cast: Jack Palance, Ida Lupino, Wendell Corey, Shelley Winters.

While the City Sleeps (1956)
RKO; producer, Bert E. Friedlob; director, Fritz Lang; assistant director, Ronnie Rondell; screenplay, Casey Robinson, based on the novel The Bloody Spur by Charles Einstein; director of photography, Ernest Laszlo; film editor, Gene Fowler Jr.; sound, Jack Solomon, Buddy Myers; sound editor, Verna Fields; art director, Carroll Clark; set decorator, Jack Mills; music, Herschel Burke Gilbert; costumes, Norma. 100 minutes. Cast: Dana Andrews, Rhonda Fleming, Sally Forrest, Thomas Mitchell, Vincent Price, Howard Duff, Ida Lupino.

Strange Intruder (1956)
A Lindsley Parsons Production (Allied Artists release); producer, Lindsley Parsons; associate producer, John H. Burrows; director, Irving Rapper; assistant directors, Ken Walters, Lindsley Parsons Jr.; screenplay, Cyril Hume, Warren Douglas, Lewis Arnold, based on the novel The Intruder by Helen Fowler; director of photography, Ernest Haller; film editor, Maurice Wright; sound, Tom Lambert; art director, Leslie Thomas; set decorator, Morris Hoffman; music, Paul Dunlap; production manager, Ken Walters; makeup, Willard Coles; casting, Fred Messenger. 82 minutes. Cast: Edmund Purdom, Ida Lupino, Ann Harding, Jacques Bergerac.

Backtrack (1969)
MCA-TV (Universal release); producer, David J. O'Connell; director, Earl Bellamy; assistant directors, Henry Kline, Carter de Haven, III; James M. Walters; screenplay, Borden Chase; directors of photography, Richard H. Kline,

John L. Russel, Andrew Jackson; film editor, Michael R. McAdam; sound, Waldon O. Watson, Frank H. Wilkinson, Earl Crain, Robert R. Bertrand; art directors, George Patrick, Howard E. Johnson; set decorators, John McCarthy, James M. Walters, Sr., Perry Murdock, Oliver Emert; music, Jack Marshall; makeup, Bud Westmore. 95 minutes. Cast: Neville Brand, James Drury, Doug McClure, Peter Brown, Ida Lupino.

Deadhead Miles (1972)
A Biplane Cinematograph Production (Paramount release); producers, Vernon Zimmerman, Tony Bill; associate producer, John Prizer; director, Vernon Zimmerman; assistant directors, Fred Brost, Russell Vreeland; screenplay, Terrence Malick; director of photography, Ralph Woolsey; film editors, Eve Newman, Dan Greene, George Hively; sound, Charles Knight; sets, Spencer Quinn; music, Tom T. Hall; songs, Dave Dudley; costumes, Richard Bruno; production manager, Jack Bohrer; technical advisor, Joe Madrid. 93 minutes. Cast: Alan Arkin, Paul Benedict, Ida Lupino, George Raft.

Women in Chains (1972)
Paramount TV for ABC-TV; producer, Edward K. Milkis; director, Bernard L. Kowalski; teleplay, Rita Lakin; director of photography, Howard Schwartz; film editor, Argyle Nelson; music, Charles Fox. 74 minutes. Cast: Ida Lupino, Lois Nettleton, Jessica Walter, Belinda Montgomery.

Junior Bonner (1972)
ABC Pictures Corp.-Joe Wizan-Booth Gardner Production-Solar Production (Cinerama release); producer, Joe Wizan; director, Sam Peckinpah; assistant director, Frank Baur; screenplay, Jeb Rosebrook; director of photography, Lucien Ballard; film editor, Robert Wolf; sound, Charles Wilborn, Larry Hooberry; art director, Edward S. Haworth; set designer, Angelo Graham; dialogue director, Frank Kowalski; costumer, Eddie Armand; makeup, Donald Roberson; production manager, James Pratt. 100 minutes. Cast: Steve McQueen, Robert Preston, Ida Lupino, Ben Johnson.

The Strangers in 7A (1972)
Carliner Productions for CBS-TV; producer, Mark Carliner; director, Paul Wendkos; assistant director, Kurt Neumann; teleplay, Eric Roth, based on the novel by Fielden Farrington; director of photography, Robert B. Hauser, Gil

Geller; film editor, Bud S. Isaacs; art director, Jim Hulsey; set decorator, Warren Welch; music, Morton Stevens; costumes, Stephen Lodge, Voulee Giokanis; makeup, George Lane. 73 minutes. Cast: Andy Griffith, Ida Lupino, Michael Brandon, James Watson.

Female Artillery (1973)
Universal TV for ABC-TV; producer, Winston Miller; director, Marvin Chomsky; assistant director, Thomas Blank; teleplay, Bud Freeman, story by Jack Sher, Bud Freeman; director of photography, Enzo A. Martinelli; film editors, John Elias, John Kaufman, Albert J. Zuniga; sound, John Kean; art director, Sydney Z. Litwack; set decorator, John M. Dwyer; special effects, Albert Whitlock; music, Frank De Vol; musical supervisor, Hal Mooney; unit manager, Les Berke. 73 minutes. Cast: Dennis Weaver, Ida Lupino, Sally Ann Howes, Linda Evans.

I Love a Mystery (1973)
NBC-TV; producer, Frank Price; director, Leslie Stevens; teleplay, Leslie Stevens, from the radio serial by Carlton E. Morse; director of photography, Ray Rennahan; film editor, Robert F. Shugrue; art director, John J. Lloyd; music, Oliver Nelson. 113 minutes. Cast: Ida Lupino, Les Crane, David Hartman, Jack Weston.

The Letters (1973)
Spelling-Goldberg Productions for ABC-TV; executive producers, Aaron Spelling, Leonard Goldberg; producer, Paul Junger Witt; associate producer, Tony Thomas. "The Andersons": director, Gene Nelson; teleplay, James G. Hirsch; director of photography, Tim Southcott; film editor, David Berlatsky. "The Parkingtons": director, Gene Nelson, teleplay, Ellis Marcus, Hal Sitowitz; director of photography, Tim Southcott; film editor, Carroll Sax. "The Forresters": director, Paul Krasny; teleplay, James G. Hirsch; director of photography, Leonard J. South; film editor, Robert L. Swanson. Also: art director, Tracy Bousman; set decorator, Frank Rafferty, Don Webb; sound, Jack Lilly, Don Rush; music supervisor, Rocky Moriana; makeup, Howard Smit, Bob Romero. 73 minutes. Cast: Pamela Franklin, Ida Lupino, Ben Murphy.

The Devil's Rain (1975)
A Sandy Howard Production (Bryanston release); exec. producer, Sandy Howard;

producers, James V. Cullen, Michael S. Glick; director, Robert Fuest; assistant director, Mario Cisneros; screenplay, Gabe Essoe, James Ashton, Gerald Hopman, based on a novel by Maud Willis; director of photography, Alex Phillips Jr.; film editor, Michael Kahn; sound, Manuel Topete; production designer, Nikita Knatz; art director, José Rodriguez Granada; music, Al De Lory; special effects, Cliff and Carol Wenger, Thomas Fisher, Frederico Farfan; makeup, Burman's Studio. 90 minutes. Cast: Ernest Borgnine, Eddie Albert, Ida Lupino, William Shatner.

Food of the Gods (1976)

American International; exec. producer, Samuel Z. Arkoff; producer-director, Bert I. Gordon; assistant director, Flora Gordon; screenplay, Bert I. Gordon, based on a portion of the novel by H.G. Wells; director of photography, Reginald Morris; film editor, Corky Ehlers; sound, George Mulholland; art director, Graeme Murray; set decorator, John Stark; miniatures, Erik von Buelow; music, Elliot Kaplan; unit manager, Flora Gordon. 88 minutes. Cast: Marjoe Gortner, Pamela Franklin, Ralph Meeker, Ida Lupino.

My Boys Are Good Boys (1978)

Lone Star Pictures; exec. producer, Ralph Meeker; producers, Colleen Meeker, Bethel Buckalew; director, Bethel Buckalew; assistant director, John Goff; screenplay, Fred F. Finklehoffe, Bethel Buckalew; director of photography, Don Jones; film editors, Dan Seeger, Graham Mahnin; sound, Dean Gilmore, Ross Howe; art director, Joe Saussaye; music, Doug Goodwin; production manager, Stewart Dell; makeup, Lynn Brooks, Craig Reardon; wardrobe, Craig Stearns. 90 minutes. Cast: Ralph Meeker, Ida Lupino, Lloyd Nolan, David F. Doyle.

FEATURE DIRECTORIAL CREDITS

Not Wanted (1949)

Emerald Productions (Film Classics release): production supervisor, Collier Young: producers, Ida Lupino, Anson Bond; director, Elmer Clifton; assistant director, Maurice Vaccarino; screenplay, Paul Jarrico, Ida Lupino, based on the original story by Paul Jarrico, Malvin Wald; director of photography, Henry Freulich; film edltor, Wllllam Ziegler; sound, Victor Appel, Arthur Smith; art director, Charles D. Hall; set decorator, Murray Walte; music, Leith Stevens; script supervisor, Sam Freedle; costumes, Jerry Bos; makeup, David Grayson. 94 minutes. Cast: Sally Forrest, Keefe Braselle, Leo Penn, Dorothy Adams.

Never Fear (1949)

Filmakers (Eagle Lion Films release); producer, Collier Young; associate producer, Norman Cook; director, Ida Lupino; assistant director, James Anderson; screenplay, Collier Young, Ida Lupino; director of photography, Archie Stout; film editors, Harvey Manger, William H. Ziegler; sound, William Randall; production design, Van Nest Polglase; set decorator, Joseph Kish; script supervisor, Don Wels; dialogue director, Leslie Urbach; technical advisor, O. Leonard Huddleston; music, Leith Stevens; songs, John Franco; makeup, James Barker; costumes, Reta Dawson, Margaret Greenway, John E. Dowsing. 81 minutes. Cast: Sally Forrest, Keefe Braselle, Hugh O'Brian, Eve Miller.

Outrage (1950)

Filmakers-RKO; producer, Collier Young; associate producer, Malvin Wald; director, Ida Lupino; assistant director, James Anderson; screenplay, Collier Young, Malvin Wald, Ida Lupino; director of photography, Archie Stout; film editor, Harvey Manger; sound, John Cass, Clem Portman; production designer, Harry Horner; set decorators, Darrell Silvera, Harley Miller; music, Paul Sawtell; musical director, C. Bakaleinikoff; song, "Didn't You Know," by John Franco; production supervisor, Norman Cook; script supervisor, Don Wise; makeup, William Phllllps. 74 minutes. Cast: Mala Powers, Tod Andrews, Robert Clarke, Raymond Bond.

Hard, Fast and Beautiful (1951)

Filmakers (RKO release); producer, Collier Young; associate producer, Norman Cook; director, Ida Lupino; assistant director, James Anderson; screenplay, Martha Wilkerson, based on the novel *Mother of a Champion* by John R. Tunis; director of photography, Archie Stout; film editors, George S. Shrader, William Ziegler; sound, Philip Brigandi, Clem Portman; art directors, Albert S. D'Agostino; Jack Oakie; set decorators, Darrell Silvera, Harley Miller; music, Roy Webb; musical direction, C. Bakaleinikoff; assistant to the producer, Robert Eggenweiler; technical advisor, Eleanor Tennant. 76 minutes. Cast: Claire Trevor, Sally Forrest, Carleton G. Young, Robert Clarke.

The Hitch-Hiker (1953)

Filmakers (RKO release); producer, Collier Young; associate producer, Christian Nyby; director, Ida Lupino; assistant director, William Dorfman; screenplay, Collier Young, Ida Lupino, adaptation, Robert Joseph; director of photography,

Nicholas Musuraca; film editor, Douglas Stewart; sound, Roy Meadows, Clem Portman; art directors, Albert S. D'Agostlno, Walter E. Keller; set decorators, Darrell Silvera, Harley Miller; special effects, Harold E. Wellman; music, Leith Stevens; musical director, Constantin Bakalemikoff; makeup, Mel Berns; assistants to producer, James Anderson, Robert Eggenweller. 71 minutes. Cast: Edmond O'Brien, Frank Lovejoy, William Talman, José Torvay.

The Bigamist (See Filmography)

The Trouble With Angels (1966)
Columbia; producer, William Frye; director, Ida Lupino; assistant director, Terry Nelson; screenplay, Blanche Hanalls, based on the novel by Jane Trahey; director of photography, Lionel Lindon; film editor, Robert C. Jones; sound, Josh Westmoreland; set decorator, Victor Gangelin; art director, John Beckman; music, Jerry Goldsmith; orchestration, Arthur Morton; nun's habits and Hayley Mills's wardrobe designed by Sybil Connolly; makeup, Ben Lane; assistant to the producer, James Wharton. 111 minutes. Cast: Rosalind Russell, Hayley Mills, June Harding, Binnie Barnes.

TELEVISION DIRECTORIAL CREDITS
(Compiled with assistance from Jack Edmund Nolan, Vincent Terrace
and Larry James Gianakos.)

Screen Director's Playhouse
    "No. 5 Checked Out," Jan. 18, 1956
On Trial (after Mar. 1957, *The Joseph Cotten Show*)
    "The Trial of Mary Surratt," Nov. 23, 1956
The Donna Reed Show
    Dec. 10, 1956
Tate
    "The Mary Hardin Story," Sept. 21, 1960
Have Gun Will Travel
    "Lady with a Gun," Apr. 9, 1960
    "The Trial," June 11, 1960
    "The Gold Bar," Mar. 18, 1961
Hotel de Paree
    "Sundance and the Boat Soldier," Feb. 5, 1960
The Untouchables
    "A Fist of Five," Dec. 4, 1962

"The Man in the Cooler," Mar. 5, 1963
"The Torpedo," May 7, 1963.

Thriller

"Dialogs with Death," 1961
"Trio for Terror," Mar. 14, 1961
"Mr. George," May 9, 1961
"What Beckoning Ghost," Sept. 18. 1961
"Guillotine," Sept. 25, 1961
"The Last of the Sommervilles," Nov. 6, 1961
"La Strega," Jan. 15, 1962
"The Bride Died Twice," Mar. 19, 1962
"The Lethal Ladies," Apr. 16, 1962

The Fugitive

"Fatso," Nov. 19, 1963
"The Glass Tightrope," Dec. 3, 1963
"The Garden House," Jan. 14, 1964

Bewitched

"A Is for Aardvark," Jan. 10, 1965

The Rogues

"Hugger-Mugger by the Sea," Dec. 10, 1964
"Bow to a Master," Feb. 7, 1965

The Twilight Zone

"The Masks," Mar. 20, 1964

Dundee and the Culhane

"The Deadman's Brief," Oct. 4, 1967

The Virginian

"Deadeye Dick," Nov. 9, 1966

Bob Hope Presents the Chrysler Theatre

"Holloway's Daughters," May 11, 1966

Daniel Boone

"The King's Shilling," Oct. 19. 1967

The Ghost and Mrs. Muir

"Madeira, My Dear?" 1968

Alfred Hitchcock Presents

"Sybilla," Dec. 6, 1960
"A Crime for Mothers," Jan. 24, 1961

Mr. Novak

"Day in the Year," Mar. 24, 1964

"May Day, May Day," Mar. 2, 1965
"Love in the Wrong Season," Dec. 3, 1965
Breaking Point
    "Heart of Marble, Body of Stone," Feb. 23, 1963
Dr. Kildare
    "To Walk in Grace," Feb. 13, 1964
Kraft Suspense Theatre
    "The Threatening Eye," Mar. 12, 1964
Gilligan's Island
    "Wrongway Feldman," Oct. 17, 1964
    "The Return of Wrongway Feldman," Oct. 24, 1964
    Episode 19, co-directed with G.M. Cahan, Oct. 3, 1966

Ida Lupino also directed episodes of the following series.
G.E. Theatre
Hong Kong
The Road West
The Big Valley
Gunsmoke
Honey West
Nanny and the Professor
Sam Benedict
77 Sunset Strip
The Bill Cosby Show

TELEVISION APPEARANCES

Four Star Playhouse
    EPISODE
    34   "House for Sale," Dec. 31, 1953
    38   "Indian Taker," Jan. 28, 1954
    48   "Masquerade," Apr. 15, 1954
    55   "Adolescent," Dec. 28, 1954
    59   "Marked Down," Nov. 25, 1954
    65   "Bag of Oranges," Jan. 6, 1955
    74   "Eddie's Place," Mar. 10, 1955
    80   "With all My Heart," Apr. 21, 1955

88 "Award," June 30, 1955
90 "Face of Danger," Oct. 13, 1955
99 "One Way Out," Dec. 15, 1955
100 "Dark Meeting," Jan. 5, 1956
104 "The Listeners," Feb. 2, 1956
112 "The Case of Emily Cameron," Mar. 29, 1956
118 "That Woman," May 10, 1956
121 "Beneath the Surface," May 3, 1956
124 "Woman Afraid," June 21, 1956
128 "The Stand-In," July 19, 1956

Ford Theatre
"Marriageable Male," Feb. 25, 1954
"A Season to Love," May 6, 1954

Zane Grey Theatre
"The Fearful Courage," Oct. 12, 1956

Mr. Adams and Eve
sixty-six episodes

Lux Playhouse
"Various Temptations," Feb. 20, 1959

I Love Lucy
"Lucy's Summer Vacation," June 6, 1959

The Twilight Zone
"The 16 mm Shrine," Oct. 23, 1959

Bonanza
"The Saga of Annie O'Toole," Oct. 24, 1959

G.E. Theatre
"Image of a Doctor," Feb. 26, 1961

Frontier Justice
"The Fearful Courage," Aug. 31, 1961

The Investigators
"Something for Charity," Dec. 21, 1961

Sam Benedict
"Not Even the Sea Gulls Shall Weep," Jan. 5, 1962

Death Valley Days
"Pamela's Oxen," 1962

The Virginian
"A Distant Fury," Mar. 20, 1963

Kraft Suspense Theatre
"One Step Down," Nov. 14, 1963
Burke's Law
"Who Killed Lenore Wingfield?" Nov. 4, 1964
The Rogues
"Two of a Kind," Nov. 8, 1964
The Virginian
"We've Lost a Train," Apr. 21, 1965
The Wild, Wild West
"Night of the Big Blast," Oct. 7, 1966
Judd for the Defense
"Kingdom of the Blind," Feb. 9, 1968
Batman
"The Entrancing Dr. Cassandra," Mar. 7, 1968
It Takes a Thief
"Turnabout," Apr. 2, 1968
The Outcasts
"The Thin Edge," Feb. 17, 1969
Mod Squad
Mar. 18, 1969
The Name of the Game
"The Perfect Image," Nov. 7, 1969
Family Affair
"Maudie," Dec. 18, 1969
Bracken's World
"The Anonymous Star," Nov. 13, 1970
Nanny and the Professor
"The Balloon Ladies," Feb. 12, 1971
Columbo
"Short Fuse," Jan. 19, 1972
Alias Smith and Jones
Feb. 24, 1972
Medical Center
"Conflict," Mar. 1, 1972
The Strangers in 7A, Oct. 14, 1972
The Bold Ones
"A Terminal Career," Dec. 26, 1972

APPENDIX

Female Artillery, Jan. 2, 1973
I Love a Mystery, Feb. 27, 1973
The Letters, Mar. 6, 1973
Barnaby Jones
    "The Deadly Jinx," Aug. 31, 1974
The Streets of San Francisco
    "Blockade," Jan. 24, 1974
Columbo
    "Swan Song," Mar. 3, 1974
Manhunter
    "The Ma Gantry Gang," May 11, 1974
Ellery Queen
    Sept. 18, 1975
Switch
    Sept. 30, 1975
Police Woman
    "The Chasers," Oct. 10, 1975
Charlie's Angels
    "I Will Be Remembered," Mar. 9, 1977

NOTES

Prologue
xiii "Mr. Donati ..." Ida Lupino (hereafter cited as IL) to William Donati (hereafter cited as WD), Apr. 30, 1981.
xiv "It is fascinating ..." IL to WD, Oct. 23, 1983.

1. Drama in Her Veins
1 "Death by misadventure ..." *London Times,* Feb. 1, 1918.
2 "They didn't expect ..." *Film Pictorial,* Apr. 8, 1933.
3 "Could make you cry ..." *Stardom,* Nov. 1943.
3 "He never stopped ..." *Cosmopolitan,* Jan. 1943.
3 "My father once ..." IL to WD, Oct. 23, 1983.
5 "Uneasy lies ..." S. Lupino, *Stocks to Stars.*
5 "You are truly ..." ibid.
7 "He was the big ..." Connie Miles to WD, Nov. 27, 1985.
7 "I should have a little ..." Diana Volz Meredith to WD, Apr. 14, 1990.
8 "If he didn't ..." *Colliers,* June 26, 1937.
9 "An awful phobia ..." *Silver Screen,* Nov. 1940.
9 "The little people ..." *Cosmopolitan,* Feb. 1943.
9 "It was looking ..." S. Lupino, *Stocks to Stars.*
10 "I saw her. *This Is Your Life.*
10 "Suddenly, there ..." *Silver Screen,* Nov. 1940.
11 "We're going to ..." Sol Saks to WD, Apr. 23, 1986.
11 "But you will ..." S. Lupino, *Stocks to Stars.*
11 "Were a piece ..." ibid.
12 "Mr. Lupino keeps ..." *New York Times,* Sept. 14, 1926.
13 "And now ..." S. Lupino, *Stocks to Stars.*
14 "No more scathing ..." *Movie Show,* May 1943.
15 "Try counting ..." S. Lupino, *Stocks to Stars.*

2. Like a Little Queen

18 "The girl who was ..." S. Lupino, *Stocks to Stars.*
19 "Loops." *Movie Mirror,* July 1936.
20 "Dear Mr. Haines ..." Shaw correspondence, May 24, 1948. Profiles In History catalog.
20 "Lupino ... obviously ..." *Hollywood Citizen-News,* Feb. 2, 1949.
21 "She is the only ..." *Liberty,* Oct. 5, 1940.
21 "Too young ..." *Film Weekly,* Nov. 24, 1933.
22 "I'll make a level ..." ibid.
22 "I was a very bad ..." *Family Circle,* June 4, 1943.
22 "Those were pitifully ..." *Hollywood,* Feb. 1936.
23 "Oh, my Gawd ..." *Interview Magazine,* Feb. 1976.
24 "They cannot ..." *Film Weekly,* Nov. 24, 1933.
25 "So you don't ..." *New York Times,* Sept. 3, 1933.
25 "By the time ..." *Film Weekly,* Oct. 13, 1933.
26 "Potential Jean ..." ibid.
27 "Fine possibilities." *Variety,* Mar. 27, 1934.
27 "You cannot play naive ..." *Los Angeles Times,* Mar. 18, 1934.
28 "Your family ..." Paula Stone to WD, July 1, 1986.
28 "A lot of my ..." *Movie Show,* July 1946.
29 "Suppose I can ..." *Photoplay,* May 1946.
31 "Tell Loops ..." *Movie Mirror,* July 1936.
31 "A psychic feeling ..." IL to WD, Oct. 23, 1983.
32 "You may call Ida ..." *Film Weekly,* Oct. 26, 1934.

3. Louis

34 "A personable ..." *Variety,* Aug. 21, 1935.
34 "Don't look ..." *Movie Mirror,* July 1936.
34 "Excellent ..." *New York Times,* Nov. 8, 1935.
35 "The No. 2 ..." *Variety,* Jan. 12, 1936.
36 "She is rarely ..." *Film Weekly,* Sept. 5, 1936.
36 "Once ..." *Picture Play,* May 1936.
36 "I'm mad ..." *Motion Picture,* Oct. 1936.
39 "Well, Ida ..." *Los Angeles Times,* Dec. 24, 1935.
40 "The most glamorous ..." *Los Angeles Examiner,* Jan. 3, 1936.
41 "I will tell ..." *Los Angeles Examiner,* Jan. 8, 1936.
42 "An artist ..." *Liberty,* Oct. 5, 1940.
43 "He bored me ..." *Photoplay,* Oct. 1936.
43 "Just another dizzy ..." *Liberty,* Oct. 5, 1940.
43 "I saw him at ..." *Photoplay,* Oct. 1936.

43 "Binoculars." *Ladies Home Journal,* Apr. 1972.

44 "I haven't ..." *Photoplay,* Oct. 1936.

44 "My eyes ..." *Movie Mirror,* Dec. 1940.

45 "I have worked ..." *Motion Picture,* Oct. 1936.

46 "Practically ..." *Hollywood Citizen-News,* Dec. 21, 1935.

47 "It hurts ..." *Motion Picture,* Oct. 1936.

47 "I never ..." ibid.

48 "Ida, you'll never ..." *Movies,* Nov. 1944.

48 "She burst ..." Harry Mines to WD, Mar. 24, 1986.

50 "I ripped ..." *Movie Mirror,* Dec. 1940.

50 "Nobody wants ..." *Cosmopolitan,* Feb. 1943.

50 "About Ida ..." *Picturegoer,* July 19, 1941.

51 "It is a grave ..." *New York Times,* July 25, 1943.

51 "It's Ida ..." *Cosmopolitan,* Feb. 1943.

51 "You are not ..." *Movie Mirror,* Dec. 1940.

52 "We'll give you ..." *Illustrated Daily News,* Nov. 26, 1938.

53 "An Ida ..." *Picturegoer,* July 19, 1941.

53 "On the way ..." Mines to WD, Mar. 24, 1986.

54 "Who in the hell ..." ibid.

55 "Twice a ..." *Movie Mirror,* Dec. 1940.

57 "You're doing ..." Thompson, Wellman.

57 "If you aren't ..." *Boston Globe,* Nov. 10, 1974.

58 "The size ..." *Daily News,* Feb. 12, 1982.

59 "You panned me ..." Mines to WD, July 9, 1986.

59 "A little ingenue ..." *New York Times,* Dec. 25, 1939.

4. The Years of Glory

61 "Let's sign her up ..." *Liberty,* Oct. 5, 1940.

63 "When I was ..." *Silver Screen,* Nov. 1940.

63 "Raft and Bogart ..." *Newsweek,* July 29, 1940.

64 "Miss Lupino goes ..." *New York Times,* July 27, 1940.

64 "And the result ..." *World Telegram,* July 27, 1940.

64 "Ida, go crazy." *Silver Screen,* Nov. 1940.

64 "Dear Hal ..." telegram, Warner Archives.

65 "He was just a heavy ..." Vincent Sherman to WD, June 8, 1994.

65 "Punk ..." MPA review, Academy Library.

66 "I have ..." *Screenland,* Nov. 1945.

66 "Mayo was very ..." Irving Rapper to WD, May 18, 1987.

66 "Let's be ready ..." ibid.

66 "Listen ..." Bogart documentary.

67 "Yeah …" Buster Wiles to WD, Dec. 4, 1983.

68 "Lupino …" memo, Warner Archives.

68 "This type …" Warner MacEwen, Warner Archives.

69 "He was the most …" Bogart documentary.

69 "Dearest Connie …" *Life Magazine,* Nov. 11, 1940.

70 "His real name …" IL to WD, Oct. 23, 1983.

72 "This rotten …" ibid.

72 "Excellent …" *New York Telegram,* Mar. 22, 1941.

72 "Give Miss …" *Night and Day,* Feb. 18, 1941.

73 "The man is …" *Silver Screen,* Nov. 1940.

74 "I'd rather work …" ibid.

74 "Terrible temper …" *Family Circle,* June 4, 1943.

74 "A woman in …" ibid.

75 "We don't deal …" Stine, *Stars and Star Handlers.*

75 "She was so vivacious …" Rena Lundigan to WD, Apr. 8, 1990.

75 "She seemed to look …" Diane Meredith Volz to WD, Apr. 14, 1990.

77 "Unacceptable …" MPA review, Nov. 26, 1940.

78 "It is not …" Lyons, memo, Feb. 14, 1941.

80 "It is ridiculous …" memo, Warner Archives.

80 "When she goes …" John Qualen to WD, Sept. 15, 1986.

80 "A moving …" *Variety,* June 6, 1941.

5. The Hard Way

82 "You are out …" *Movie Digest,* Nov. 1972.

82 "I'll do …" ibid.

82 "I take …" *New York Herald Tribune,* Nov. 2, 1941.

84 "Having my …" Lupino, telegram, Warner Archives.

85 "So as to …" Oct. 2, 1941, Warner Archives.

85 "To reject …" ibid.

90 "I started …" *Hollywood,* June 1942.

90 "Ida Lupino is the …" ibid.

92 "I see this picture …" Vincent Sherman to WD, June 8, 1994.

92 "Oh, I'm such …" ibid.

94 "I explained …" Alleborn memo, May 5, 1942, Warner Archives.

94 "Ida is in one …" Daily Production Report, May 9, 1942, Warner Archives.

95 "You'll have to …" *Cosmopolitan,* Feb. 1943.

96 "She always …" Geraldine Fitzgerald to WD, Oct. 11, 1986.

96 "This picture stinks …" Vincent Sherman to WD, July 14, 1984.

96 "Poor little ..." *Cosmopolitan,* Feb. 1943.

97 "It would ..." *The Hard Way* pressbook.

97 "Holy God ..." Vincent Sherman to WD, June 8, 1994.

98 "I'm going ..." *Silver Screen,* Feb. 1945.

6. Devotion

100 "She shot ..." *Cosmopolitan,* Jan. 1943.

101 "This girl is ..." Diane Meredith Volz to WD, Apr. 14, 1990.

102 "The De Havilland-Lupino ..." memo, Warner Archives, Dec. 11, 1942.

102 "When Ida and Reggie ..." Nadia Gardiner to WD, July 12, 1986.

103 "Getting Ida ..." *Cosmopolitan,* February 1943.

105 "Runners up ..." *Variety,* Jan. 20, 1943.

107 "His death ..." *The Hard Way* pressbook.

107 "When Lupino gets ..." *Movieland,* Nov. 1943.

109 "Works up ..." ibid.

109 "Cinderella Plots ..." *PM,* Feb. 13, 1944.

7. The Breakup

110 "I know all ..." Wheeler, *A Special Valor.*

113 "I wish you ..." *Screenland,* May 1944.

114 "Introspective ..." *Philadelphia Record,* Mar. 21, 1943.

115 "Miss Lupino, please ..." *Silver Screen,* June 1949.

115 "It's a ..." Harry Mines, July 29, 1986.

116 "Ida has been ..." *Los Angeles Examiner,* July 21, 1944.

116 "He's done ..." ibid.

119 "I didn't know ..." Rena Lundigan to WD, Apr. 8, 1990.

119 "It was all ..." *Los Angeles Examiner,* Jan. 3, 1945.

120 "He's full ..." *Silver Screen,* Nov. 1945.

120 "Definitely," ibid.

121 "A strong one." Wheeler, *A Special Valor.*

121 "My husband ..." *Los Angeles Examiner,* May 11, 1945.

121 "Louis had a ..." *Interview Magazine,* Feb. 1976.

8. Deep Valley

123 "Socrates had become ..." Mines to WD, Feb. 13, 1987.

123 "The low moral ..." MPA review, Jan. 28, 1943.

124 "Cut!" Andrea King to WD, May 31, 1986.

124 "Sorry I am ..." telegram, Warner Archives.

125 "You know ..." Catherine Turney to WD, Mar. 25, 1990.

125 "Well, it's …" Publicity release.
126 "William Threely." *Silver Screen,* Nov. 1945.
127 "Did you have …" IL to WD, Oct. 23, 1983.
128 "Ida was very …" Mines to WD, Apr. 30, 1987.
128 "Elephants …" David Niven Jr., letter to WD, Feb. 13, 1987.
128 "Nearly …" Mines to WD, Apr. 30, 1987.
128 "To Ida …" *Chicago Tribune,* Mar. 17, 1948.
128 "Lots …" ibid.
129 "As we got …" Mines to WD, Feb. 13, 1987.
131 "The postman …" *Silver Screen,* June 1949.
134 "We can have …" *Daily News,* Feb. 12, 1982.

9. Collie

135 "Poor, bewildered …" *Chicago Tribune,* Mar. 17, 1948.
136 "The security …" *Deep Valley* pressbook.
136 "Old scrub …" Harry Mines, July 29, 1986.
137 "Tremendously …" *Screen Guide,* May 1949.
139 "George Gershwin …" *Los Angeles Times,* Jan. 4, 1981.
139 "The most wonderful …" *Photoplay,* Nov. 1948.
140 "I'm in love …" *Los Angeles Herald Express,* Nov. 21, 1947.
140 "Fire the …" Negulesco, *Things I Did.*
141 "She was …" Cornel Wilde, May 18, 1987.
142 "Her voice …" Lionel Newman to WD, Sept. 23, 1986.
142 "No voice …" Negulesco, *Things I Did.*
142 "Frankenstein …" *Variety,* Sept. 22, 1948.
142 "She likes …" John Franco to WD, Oct. 4, 1986.
143 "I do!" Harry Mines to WD, July 29, 1986.
145 "Nine wives." *Screen Guide,* May 1949.
146 "In Hollywood …" *San Diego Tribune,* Feb. 2, 1949.

10. Filmmakers

147 "I was approached …" Paul Jarrico to WD, Apr. 6, 1987.
148 "Front office …" *New York Times,* Apr. 30, 1950.
149 "We pointed out …" MPA review, Feb. 14, 1949.
149 "I found them …" *San Diego Tribune,* Feb. 2, 1949.
149 "You may …" Maurice Vaccarino to WD, June 4, 1994.
150 "Heavens …" *Los Angeles Daily News,* Mar. 1, 1949.
150 "Sally …" ibid.
151 "The race angle." *Negro Digest,* Aug. 5, 1950.
152 "We're in …" ibid.

152 "Oh, Miss Arzner . . ." IL to WD, Oct. 23, 1983.
153 "The interior . . ." Harry Mines to WD, July 29, 1986.
153 "She was . . ." Sally Forrest, Directors Guild Tribute, Jan. 17, 1988.
154 "It was . . ." transcript, Feb. 18, 1949, Academy library.
155 "Done with taste . . ." *Hollywood Reporter*, June 20, 1949.
155 "Breach of good . . ." *New York Times*, July 25, 1949.
156 "We are trying . . ." *New York Herald Tribune*, July 9, 1950.
156 "Documentary movies." *New York Times*, Aug. 7, 1949.
156 "We're working . . ." *Chicago Tribune*, Sept. 4, 1949.
157 "I've never . . ." ibid.
158 "I know all . . ." Malvin Wald to WD, Apr. 1, 1986.
159 "It was the only . . ." *Modern Screen*, Apr. 1948.
160 "I can't afford . . ." *New York Times*, Aug. 7, 1949.

11. Howard

161 "She scared me . . ." *Screenland*, Feb. 1952.
161 "We couldn't stand . . ." *Photoplay*, Oct. 1967.
162 "No, but I . . ." ibid.
162 "Gave her . . ." Michael Gordon to WD, July 21, 1986.
163 "It's pretty hard . . ." *Colliers*, May 12, 1951.
163 "If Ida feels . . ." ibid.
164 "Study it . . ." Hugh O'Brian to WD, May 23, 1987.
164 "Ida has more . . ." *Colliers*, May 12, 1951.
165 "She told . . ." Malvin Wald to WD, Apr. 1, 1986.
166 "Howard Hughes had . . ." Wald to WD, Mar. 27, 1986.
167 "The diplomat." *Colliers*, May 12, 1951.
167 "We discovered . . ." Wald to WD, Apr. 1, 1986.
167 "The Howard Hughes thing . . ." John Franco to WD, Dec. 15, 1986.
168 "Collie would . . ." ibid.
168 "Do you know . . ." Wald to WD, Mar. 18, 1986.
168 "As written . . ." *Variety*, Jan. 4, 1950.
168 "She lost . . ." Wald to WD, Mar. 18, 1986.
169 "The torch . . ." *Modern Screen*, Oct. 1950.
170 "Personality . . ." *Motion Picture*, Oct. 1952.
170 "Actually added . . ." *New York Times*, Apr. 30, 1950.
171 "I had written . . ." Wald to WD, Apr. 1, 1989.
171 "Today the producer . . ." *Los Angeles Daily News*, June 5, 1950.
172 "Connie was a . . ." Wald to WD, Apr. 1, 1989.
172 "This is one topic . . ." *Variety*, Aug. 23, 1950.

173 "With courage . . ." *Los Angeles Examiner*, Nov. 11, 1951.
173 "More experimentation . . ." *Hollywood Citizen-News*, Mar. 24, 1952.
173 "Hughes rejected . . ." Wald to WD, Apr. 1, 1989.
173 "We are deep . . ." *Variety*, Feb. 20, 1950.
174 "Communing . . ." Wald to WD, Apr. 1, 1989.
175 "Paint it." Harbin and Jewell, *The RKO Story*.
175 "Very finicky . . ." George Shrader to WD, Sept. 15, 1986.
175 "Hughes thought . . ." Wald to WD, Mar. 4, 1986.
176 "Children . . ." *Los Angeles Daily News*, May 24, 1951.
176 "Poured on . . ." ibid.
176 "We were fleeced . . ." Wald to WD, Mar. 27, 1989.

12. The Turning Point

178 "Miss Lupino is . . ." *New York Compass*, June 19, 1950.
178 "To the woman . . ." *Holiday Magazine*, Jan. 1951.
179 "I know I can . . ." *Motion Picture*, Apr. 1951.
179 "We're all crazy . . ." *Modern Screen*, Oct. 1950.
179 "Howard's a real . . ." Malvin Wald to WD, Apr. 1, 1986.
181 "Cultural workers . . ." Supreme Court brief, Oct. 1949.
182 "Communist conspirators . . ." Bentley, *Thirty Years of Treason*.
183 "He was blacklisted . . ." *Hollywood Studio Magazine*, Feb. 1983.
183 "Julie . . ." IL to WD, Oct. 23, 1983.
183 "Howard Duff, radio . . ." Bentley, *Thirty Years of Treason*.
184 "It was crazy . . ." *TV Guide*, Sept. 5, 1981.
184 "Buddies . . ." IL to WD, May 3, 1981.
184 "Hi, doll . . ." IL to WD, Oct. 23, 1983.
186 "My wife was . . ." Harry Horner to WD, Apr. 22, 1987.
186 "Things aren't . . ." *Colliers*, May 12, 1951.
188 "A marvelous . . ." Diane Volz Meredith to WD, Apr. 14, 1990.
188 "Darling . . ." Harry Mines to WD, Feb. 13, 1987.
189 "Always befriended . . ." *Photoplay*, Nov. 1951.
193 "Love, honor . . ." *Los Angeles Examiner*, Oct. 22, 1951.
194 "Underhanded trick." Bennett letter, Mar. 31, 1952, Academy library.
194 "Valid and legal . . ." ibid.
194 "No picture shall . . ." MPA review, Apr. 18, 1952.
195 "It would have . . ." *Colliers*, May 12, 1951.
196 "After trying . . ." *Hollywood Yearbook*, 1953.
197 "A crisp . . ." *Time*, Apr. 6, 1953.
198 "I simply . . ." *Photoplay*, Jan. 1973.

13. *The Long Goodbye*

199 "There is something . . ." *Los Angeles Examiner*, Mar. 1, 1953.
199 "The strangest . . ." ibid., Jan. 10, 1953.
200 "Sunset Strip . . ." ibid., Mar. 1, 1953.
201 "We want to . . ." *Hollywood Citizen-News*, July 3, 1953.
202 "I'd always sworn . . ." *The Bigamist* pressbook.
202 "She wasn't . . ." Stanford Tischler to WD, Aug. 20, 1986.
203 "This fragile . . ." *New York Times*, Oct. 16, 1953.
203 "A very unhappy Ida." *Los Angeles Examiner*, July 20, 1953.
204 "Television . . ." *Action*, May 1967.
205 "She can . . ." *TV Guide*, June 1, 1957.
205 "Darling . . ." Ted Post to WD, Aug. 29, 1986.
206 "He was Sam . . ." John Franco to WD, Oct. 4, 1986.
206 "There was too much . . ." Kaminsky, *Don Siegel*.
207 "We made one . . ." *Action*, May 1967.
207 "It was Ida's . . ." Audrey Totter to WD, May 29, 1986.
208 "I did not . . ." *Movieland*, Nov. 1953.
209 "Ida, I'm going to . . ." IL to WD, Oct. 23, 1983.
209 "The picture is not . . ." *New York Times*, Nov. 6, 1955.
209 "My God . . ." IL to WD, Oct. 23, 1983.

14. *Mr. Adams and Eve*

211 "We are getting . . ." *Los Angeles Examiner*, Mar. 3, 1957.
211 "She is . . ." *TV Guide*, Dec. 3, 1955.
212 "A weapon . . ." press release, Aug. 14, 1956.
213 "I worked with . . ." Ronnie Rondell to WD, Aug. 27, 1986.
213 "The nicest smelling . . ." *Variety*, Apr. 2, 1956.
213 "It was a quickie." Irving Rapper to WD, May 18, 1987.
214 "Always feuding." Sol Saks to WD, Apr. 23, 1986.
215 "I guess he just . . ." *TV Guide*, June 1, 1957.
215 "Sixty percent . . ." ibid., June 1, 1957.
216 "When I directed . . ." *Los Angeles Examiner*, Mar. 5, 1957.
216 "Mr. Adams and Eve . . ." Richard Kinon to WD, May 22, 1986.
217 "This is like . . ." Jerry Hausner to WD, Mar. 24, 1987.
219 "All America . . ." *This Is Your Life*, Jan. 15, 1958.
221 "Did you hear it?" Harry Mines to WD, Sept. 27, 1986.
222 "He was one . . ." *Mirror News*, Oct. 15, 1959.
223 "She told me . . ." Harry Mines to WD, Mar. 24, 1986.

15. Mother

225 "Directing is much . . ." *TV Guide*, Dec. 3, 1955.

225 "Terrified." *Los Angeles Herald Examiner*, Nov. 9, 1972.

225 "I don't care . . ." *TV Guide*, Oct. 8, 1966.

226 "Darling . . ." *Evening Outlook*, Nov. 13, 1975.

226 "Not that she . . ." *Los Angeles Examiner*, Oct. 3, 1960.

226 "The things . . ." John Franco to WD, Oct. 4, 1986.

227 "We're a fine . . ." *Hollywood Studio Magazine*, Feb. 1983.

228 "Bridget goes to . . ." *Modern Screen*, July 1956.

229 "The female . . ." *Time*, Feb. 1963.

229 "I love being called . . ." *Action*, Mar. 1967.

230 "Peter . . ." *Time*, Feb. 8, 1963.

230 "Ida, darling . . ." IL to WD, Oct. 23, 1983.

231 "I sometimes . . ." *TV Guide*, Oct. 8, 1966.

231 "I have my old . . ." *Action*, May 1967.

231 "It was Gilligan's Island . . ." Sol Saks to WD, Apr. 23, 1986.

231 "Dream project." *Los Angeles Times*, May 6, 1973.

232 "A feminine approach . . ." *Long Island Press*, Dec. 5, 1965.

232 "I'll go enjoy . . ." *Action*, May 1967.

233 "The most wonderful . . ." *Motion Picture Herald*, Mar. 31, 1965.

233 "The sex of a . . ." *Hollywood Citizen-News*, Sept. 16, 1965.

234 "People are still . . ." *Photoplay*, Oct. 1967.

236 "Frightfully nervous." *TV Guide*, May 25, 1968.

236 "I was . . ." *New York Times*, Aug. 24, 1969.

16. Alone

240 "I don't know why . . ." *New York Times*, Oct. 10, 1972.

242 "You'd better be . . ." *Radio Talk*, Feb. 1974.

242 "You've had . . ." Sol Saks to WD, Apr. 23, 1986.

243 "He's making no . . ." Rena Lundigan to WD, Apr. 8, 1990.

243 "My personal life . . ." *Los Angeles Herald Examiner*, Mar. 6, 1975.

243 "Lupi . . ." Marvin Paige to WD, Feb. 27, 1987.

244 "If someone would . . ." *Los Angeles Herald Examiner*, Mar. 6, 1975.

244 "I didn't want to leave . . ." *Box Office*, Sept. 29, 1975.

246 "She was fired . . ." Paula Stone to WD, July 1, 1986.

247 "She was very unhappy . . ." Nat Holt to WD, Apr. 3, 1987.

248 "See this?" Harry Mines to WD, July 29, 1986.

248 "Taylor is no . . ." Jerry Hausner to WD, Mar. 24, 1987.

17. Madame Director

250 "Yours is the . . ." Nadia Gardiner to WD, July 12, 1986.

251 "I complained . . ." *Los Angeles Times*, Mar. 10, 1974.

251 "For Hayden . . ." Hayden Rorke to WD, July 21, 1986.

253 "Was I tough . . ." IL to WD, Oct. 23, 1983.

256 "I am informed . . ." Lupino affidavit, conservatorship file, May 3, 1984.

258 "Changing mental . . ." Mary Ann Anderson, conservatorship file, Mar. 14, 1987.

258 "Of seventeen years." *Los Angeles Times*, July 10, 1990.

260 "Ida never had . . ." S. Lupino, *Stocks to Stars*.

260 "She never saw . . ." ibid.

260 "Spectator and actor . . ." ibid.

260 "Asleep on the floor . . ." ibid.

260 "But you will . . ." ibid.

260 "I'll tell you what . . ." *Motion Picture*, Oct. 1936

262 "You're a strange one . . ." IL to WD, Oct. 23, 1983.

18. A Critical Appraisal

268 "The range of . . ." Barbara Scharres to WD, July 20, 1994.

268 "You name . . ." *Hollywood Reporter*, Nov. 16, 1972.

268 "What Ida . . ." Directors Guild Tribute, Jan. 17, 1986.

SOURCES

Bentley, Eric. *Thirty Years of Treason*. New York: Viking, 1971.

Bishop, Jim. *The Mark Hellinger Story*. New York: Appleton, 1952.

Bogart. Film documentary. Flaum-Grinberg Productions, 1967.

Enciclopedia Dello Spettacolo. Firenze: Sansoni, 1954.

Fontaine, Joan. *No Bed of Roses*. New York: Morrow, 1978.

Freeland, Michael. *The Two Lives of Errol Flynn*. New York: Morrow, 1979.

Harbin, Vernon, and Richard Jewell. *The RKO Story*. New York: Arlington, 1982.

Henreid, Paul. *Paul Henreid*. New York: St. Martin's, 1984.

Hirschhorn, Clive. *The Warner Bros. Story*. New York: Crown, 1979.

Kaminsky, Stuart M. *Don Siegel, Director*. New York: Curtis, 1974.

Kiersch, Mary. *Curtis Bernhardt*. Metuchen, N.J.: Scarecrow, 1986.

Kobal, John. *People Will Talk*. New York: Knopf, 1989.

Lupino, Stanley. *From the Stocks to the Stars*. London: Hutchinson, 1934.

"My Awful Past." Film Pictorial. London. Mar. 1933 through May 1933.

Negulesco, Jean. *Things I Did*. New York: Simon and Schuster, 1984.

Niven, David. *Bring on the Empty Horses*. New York: Putnam, 1975.

Robinson, Edward G. *All My Yesterdays*. New York: Hawthorne, 1973.

Scharres, Barbara. "Ida Lupino in a New Light." *Film Center Gazette*. February, 1987.

Schickel, Richard. *The Men Who Made the Movies*. New York: Athenaeum, 1975.

Silke, James R. *Here's Looking at You, Kid*. New York: Little, Brown, 1976.

Stine, Whitney. *Stars and Star Handlers*. Santa Monica: Roundtable, 1985.

This Is Your Life. "Ida Lupino." Ralph Edwards Productions. Jan. 15, 1958.

Thompson, Frank T. *William A. Wellman*. Metuchen, N.J.: Scarecrow, 1983.

Tornabene, Lyn. *Long Live the King*. New York: Simon and Schuster, 1976.

Vermilye, Jerry. *Ida Lupino*. New York: Pyramid, 1977.

Wheeler, Richard A. *A Special Valor*. New York: Harper and Row, 1983.

White, James Dillon. *Born to Star*. London: Heinemann, 1957.

Who Was Who in the Theatre. Detroit: Gale Research, 1961.

Wiles, Buster, and William Donati. *My Days With Errol Flynn*. Santa Monica: Roundtable, 1988.

INDEX